JIHAD
and the
WEST

JIHAD
and the
WEST

BLACK FLAG
OVER BABYLON

.

Mark Silinsky

INDIANA UNIVERSITY PRESS

Bloomington and Indianapolis

This book is a publication of

Indiana University Press
Office of Scholarly Publishing
Herman B Wells Library 350
1320 East 10th Street
Bloomington, Indiana 47405 USA

iupress.indiana.edu

The paper used in this publication meets the minimum requirements of
the American National Standard for Information Sciences—Permanence
of Paper for Printed Library Materials, ANSI Z39.48–1992.

Manufactured in the United States of America

Cataloging information is available from the Library of Congress.

ISBN 978-0-253-02701-6 (cloth)
ISBN 978-0-253-02720-7 (ebook)
ISBN 978-0-253-02712-2 (paperback)

1 2 3 4 5   21 20 19 18 17 16

To all those murdered by the Caliphate.
May you rest in peace.

CONTENTS

■
FOREWORD

SEBASTIAN GORKA

THE WORD "JIHAD" IS MISUNDERSTOOD AND MISREPRESENTED. It is a human concept (rather than a heavenly mandate) and has a historic and political as well as religious context, and has been applied in different ways by different users over the centuries.

Today its most important application is by the members of the Global Jihadist Movement, most specifically Al Qaeda and the Islamic State which grew out of Al Qaeda. For Abu Bakr al Baghdadi and the tens of thousands of young men who have joined his cause, "jihad" refers to the last Holy War against the Infidel, a war to be waged in the eschatologically highly significant territory of Syria and Iraq as well as on the soil of infidel lands, be it a nightclub in Orlando, a concert hall in Paris, or on the streets of Boston.

Many clichés are founded on a modicum of truth, and the wisdom inherited from Sun Tsu that one must "know the enemy" to defeat them is just such a fact-based cliché. (For the record, the ancient strategist actually advised that we must know ourselves *and* the enemy if we wish to be victorious, but that apparently was too long a phrase for general consumption!) Dr. Silinsky has done the Western world a great service by writing *Jihad and the West: Black Flag over Babylon*. In fact his contribution must be read by as many national security professionals, policy-makers, and leaders as possible if we are to truly understand the threat we face and soon vanquish the new totalitarianism that is Global Jihadism.

The facts about the religiously bounded ideology and strategy our foe follows is available for all to unearth without even having to learn Arabic. Al Qaeda has its English-language internet magazine *Inspire*, and the Islamic State, as I write these words, is already on the fifteenth issue of its End-Times-suffused Jihadi magazine *Dabiq*. These publications are the "field manuals" of modern Jihad. But the story of where these ideas came from and how they evolved over time is a far richer one than can be gleaned from solely reading today's internet propaganda. The information is available but it is dispersed, scattered around the globe. What Dr. Silinsky has done is bring all the disparate threads together in one tome, backed up by the latest news reports and on-the-ground information, which allows us to do the most important thing any nation can do in a war: understand the enemy as they understand themselves.

More importantly, the author does so not to fulfill some abstruse academic requirement but to support the war-fighter and the policy-maker. With decades of practical experience inside the "machine" that is the US Intelligence community, Dr. Silinsky only writes of that which is relevant. This is best exemplified by the numerous case studies and three dozen profiles his book is built around. If the fact is not relevant to the war, it is not important. This is how such works should be written and is an exemplar for others.

Dr. Silinsky must also be commended for braving the political correctness that has so infected and distorted Western threat-assessment in recent years. Denying that Jihadism is but "Fascism with an Islamic face" will not secure our nations or help undermine our enemy. In fact such distortions of reality will strengthen groups like the Islamic State and weaken our Muslim allies who know full well just how adroitly the Jihadis leverage and exploit religious themes to recruit fighters and justify their atrocities. The willful blindness on behalf of our leaders has led in part to the abysmal reality that 2015 saw the highest number of Jihadi plots on American soil since 2001, and the highest number of terrorist attacks on the European continent since the EU started recording terrorist attacks. (It is no accident that halfway through the Orlando massacre, the largest US Jihadi attack since 9/11, the perpetrator stopped to call 911 and pledge his allegiance to Abu Bakr and the Islamic State).

Lastly, I have a personal thank you to make. As someone who makes his life by reading and utilizing such works, I am indebted to the author for making *Jihad and the West: Black Flag over Babylon* just so enjoyable a text. As Dr. Silinsky subtly injects quotes from fine literature and stage plays to get his points across, he achieves that which I thought was nigh impossible: making a book on the horrors of Jihad eminently readable.

May as many people as possible learn what they need to know about our enemy from this book, and may the city of Palmyra rise again.

GLOSSARY

Caliphate In this this book, the Caliphate is also referred to as the Islamic State, the State, the Islamic State in the Levant (ISIL), and the Islamic State in Syria (ISIS). All these terms refer to the same organization.

Eurabia A term coined by Switzerland-based scholar Bat Ye'or to refer to a set of agreements, contracts, treaties, and unspoken assumptions between European government, leaders in civil society, corporations, universities, and media outlets that promote the positive image and general interests of Islam and Islamic, particularly petrol-exporting, states. More recently, the term has been used to refer to the growth of the Muslim demographic and political influence in Europe.

foreign fighters As used in this book, foreign fighters are persons who serve the Caliphate in the Middle East who were not residents or citizens of Syria or Iraq before 2014.

Islamism Refers to political Islam, as defined by Sharia, which is Islamic law. Its principles conflict with democracy. The conflict with Western norms and laws includes the requirement that non-Muslims must assume a subordinate religious, political, and social status when they are ruled by Muslims; the inferior status of women; the prohibition on homosexuality; the death penalty for apostasy; and many other laws. The term was popularized by Daniel Pipes, a Middle East scholar.

Islamic mandates Requirements made of Muslims that are often non-negotiable. They are driven by Sharia and articulated through judicial pronouncements, called fatwas.

Islamic World Muslims would consider this the land in which there is a majority of Muslims and lands in which Sharia is practiced. The term sometimes refers to areas of Western states in which there are majority Muslim populations. Some Muslims argue that any territory that had been under Muslim rule will, forever, be part of the Muslim world. These countries include Israel, Spain, vast parts of India and the Balkans, and other parts of the world.

Islamofascism A term popularized, but not coined, by the late Christopher Hitchens. It refers to the fusion of Western fascistic principles with Islamism. The two political philosophies share a totalitarian view of society, intolerance of dissent, anti-Semitism and anti-Western sentiment, a homicidal hatred of their perceived enemies, and utopic aspirations.

Islamophobia Refers to a perceived irrational fear of Islam and Muslims. Critics of this term claim that the neologism was crafted to prevent a full-throated debate on Islam, particularly the conflict between Muslim and Western values.

Islamic State attack An attack that is verified as having at least two out of three of the following elements: the perpetrator or the leader of the perpetrators claims to be associated with the State; the State's leadership, often through its information operations, claims that the perpetrator is part of the State; security and political leaders in the country in which the attack occurred verify linkages between the perpetrator(s) and the State.[1]

Jihad There are two "Jihads." The "Greater Jihad" is a determination to become a better, generally more pious, Muslim. The "Lesser Jihad" is armed conflict to protect Muslims or expand the land of the Muslims. The word "Jihad," as used by leaders in Muslim communities around the world, generally means the "Lesser Jihad." The call to Jihad is generally a call to violence.

Jihadist or Jihadi A militant Muslim who uses violence, among other tools, to defend Muslims or to expand the frontiers of Islam.

red-green alliance An informal partnership of Muslim and leftist intellectuals, activists, policy makers, and leaders in civil society who are united by their contempt for Western values and policies.

Salafist These are people who want to re-create societies to resemble the world in which, they imagine, the first generation of Muslims lived. This was the time of Muhammad and those who knew him. Salafists are often identified by distinct dress. Men often have beards and wear baggy clothing. Women are heavily covered in clothing.

the West Historically, the term referred to all land west of Persia, but by the nineteenth century it meant the more industrialized countries in Europe, the United States, Canada, and other states with high levels of science, education, medical practices, and military capabilities. Since the twentieth century, Japan and several other states, such as Australia and New Zealand, have been considered part of the West.

Notes

1. This is not a scientific formula. But if, for example, a person detonates a bomb in Switzerland and claims he is part of the Caliphate, leaders in the Caliphate verify his association, and Swiss leaders confirm the connection, that attack, for the purposes of this book, is considered a Caliphate attack.

JIHAD
and the
WEST

INTRODUCTION

*I pledge my alliance to [ISIS leader] Abu Bakr al-Baghdadi.
May Allah accept me.*

—Omar Mateer, Florida, June 2016[1]

THE WORLD BEGAN AS DREAMS, ACCORDING TO BABYLONIAN myth.[2] Then the god Marduk, with serpents as allies, made war against rival gods. Marduk threw hurricanes into the mouths of the enemies. He won the battle and became king of the gods. After his victory, he wove reeds into loose soil and built a platform on the sea, where the sweet water and the salt water blend. Then he created man, using the blood of a conquered god.[3] Men and women now stood on firm land, which was known as Mesopotamia.

Many civilizations have risen and fallen since this story was first told. Dreams have come and gone with the generations. But the land, built of Marduk's reeds, still stands in what is today Iraq and Syria. And something else remains, perhaps as a gift of Marduk. This is the bequest of war.

The explosive birth of the Islamic State, also referred to as the Caliphate, the Islamic State in the Levant (ISIL), or the Islamic State in Syria (ISIS), has shaken the greater Middle East. As of 2016, the Caliphate has murdered over 19,000 people, including women and children.[4] The Caliphate has withstood thousands of airstrikes but still stands and still kills.

The force that was once sniffed away as "junior varsity" and bombastic puffery has metastasized to command legions of adherents. The killing in the Caliphate's zone of operations reverberates throughout the world. The Caliphate's penumbra covers lands far beyond the Middle East. Its black flag looms over the West. In summer 2016, FBI Director James Comey said that the State is "the top threat America is facing."[5] It recruits abroad and in the United States.[6] In Europe, the fear of the State has changed the Continent. Sports events and concerts are canceled, vacation plans are scrapped, and tourist facilities look like armed camps. Some observers have speculated that this is the "new normal."[7]

Perhaps the State will soon be a spent force and an author will offer its autopsy—its rise, decline, and fall. But, as of this writing, the Caliphate is very much alive, and this book is a vivisection of how it functions and, more specifically, how it draws, fields, and holds Western recruits. This is also a story of the Islamic State's battle with Western states, civilizations, values, and agencies. This is a dark and, in many ways, an ugly book.

THREE WARS

The Caliphate is engaged in three wars. It is a *revolutionary war* because combatants intend to eradicate the existing, largely secular governments in Syria and Iraq and reconstitute vast tracks of the Middle East as a single Sharia state. Stephen Walt called it a small and "under-resourced revolutionary movement, too weak to pose a significant security threat" to its neighbors.[8] Others disagree and find the Caliphate ever threatening, to its neighbors and to the world.

It is a *civil war* because ancient and enduring Shia–Sunni rivalries have pitted sects against each other in battle. The civil feuds and ill will, effectively suppressed under Ba'athist rule in Iraq and Syria, have hatched out into war. The shrine of Muhammad's granddaughter Zeinab, in Damascus, is revered by the Shia. They make pilgrimages from all over the region to pay tribute to her there. And this makes it a target for Sunnis who hate the Shia. In one day alone, in January 2016, forty-five people were killed near the shrine.[9]

Like the civil war in Spain of the 1930s, the fighting in Syria and Iraq lures Westerners to the roar of its cannons. Some are drawn by political and religious conviction, others are adventurers or dead-enders, and many others feel the pull of a religious war, or jihad. Likening the two wars, Spanish novelist Juan Goytisolo assesses, "History is repeating itself, and brute force is overwhelming ethics."[10]

Despite the vast slaughter, great art rose from the shattered cities and broken lives in Spain. Hemingway, Orwell, Picasso, Dali, and Miro captured the wages of war on paper and canvas. Great novels and one of the most famous paintings of the twentieth century endure to inform our world of the nature of war, perhaps as a cautionary tale. Will the current war in the Middle East produce artistic masterpieces, such as Picasso's *Guernica*? Let history judge.

But it is certain that many of the current fighters in Mesopotamia will apply lessons they learn today to tomorrow's wars. This happened in the Spanish Civil War, which groomed future world war leaders. The commander of the German Condor Legion used similar tactics to obliterate Warsaw several years after he destroyed Guernica. Will those fighting in the Middle East today fight elsewhere tomorrow? Perhaps.

In addition to a revolutionary and a civil war, it is *world war*, given the intervention of world and regional powers. There is a head-spinning confusion of alliances, bearing some resemblance to the Cold War–style proxy wars.[11, 12] A scholar of the Middle East, William McCants, observed that the Caliphate's black flag is so common that "in the public's mind, any Muslim militant who waves a 'black flag' is ISIS."[13] As of late summer 2016, there were over 30,000 foreign fighters from eighty-six countries with the Caliphate.[14] There are many Westerners, particularly Europeans. Of the 5,000 to leave Europe for Syria, 3,695 are from four countries—Britain, Germany, France, and Belgium.

The Caliphate has not been recognized as an independent state by the United Nations or by prominent international organizations, but Muslims are drawn from all over the world to its flag. In 2014, it replaced al Qaeda as the most attractive brand of Islamic extremism. Some of the recruits were born in America, Europe, or Australia, and many were raised as Muslims. Others were converts to the faith. The "blue-eyed" Jihad is the legion of Westerners who have left their homes in the West to fight for the Caliphate. Some have died; some have returned to their Western homes; some are hiding in Syria, Iraq, or Turkey; and some have vanished. Their whereabouts are, if temporarily, unknown to Western authorities. But others thrive in their new home, the "Black Heaven," and work to build a new Caliphate. Each foreign fighter has his or her story.

PLANET CALIPHATE

In a darkly literary sense, the Caliphate exists as a distant and cold planet. The Polish resistance fighter and novelist Marian Pankowski wrote the book *Planet Auschwitz*, depicting a surreal world of infamous brutality and dark emotion. Tapping memories of his life in Nazi concentration camps, Pankowski described the Nazis' inverted moral code, in which sadism was encouraged and compassion scorned.

This is a world uncannily similar to today's Islamic State, which is a place of dreamlike violence and where its leaders celebrate a pageantry of slaughter. Men die slowly on crucifixes; homosexuals are tossed to their deaths from tall buildings; men and women are publicly and energetically whipped. The Caliphate cut off the ears of forty-two citizens of Mosul because a few of them were suspected of insulting its leader.[15] There are an estimated 3,500 slaves, mostly Yazidi women and girls, in the Caliphate.[16] Women and girls are given as sex-slave prizes in Koran-reciting competitions. Some are traded as human cargo and raped five or more times a day. A twelve-year-old girl recounted how a State fighter first prostrated himself in prayer and then said, "by raping me, he is drawing [himself] closer to God."[17] The Caliphate's leaders declared that if a girl or woman is raped ten times by Muslims, she becomes a Muslim.[18] If she tries to leave Islam, she will be killed for apostasy.[19] Bereft of hope, many prisoners beg for death, and some achieve it.

Children try to make sense of their new world and its free-floating brutality. They cry when they see rows of headless bodies along the roadside and writhing men pinioned to wooden crosses. Their dreams are haunted. Christians are enduring some of the worst torments of their 2,000-year history, as their houses of worship and personal homes are set ablaze. There are few concerns for the Jews of Syria or Iraq; almost none are left.

Even the most hardened and courageous humanitarians can be emotionally devastated. The British "Indiana Jones of surgery," Dr. David Nott, volunteered with Médecins Sans Frontières and treated children in Iraq, some of whom had been tortured and mutilated by the State.[20] He wrote about the suffering of children in Mesopotamia and his need for therapy after witnessing the pain. His bravery and torment and fame earned him an audience with the queen of England.

"A Research Laboratory for World Destruction"

Karl Kraus, the Austrian satirist and café critic, referred to the last days of the Hapsburg Empire as "a research laboratory for world destruction."[21] He probed the 1914–1918 war, which destroyed the world he knew, in his avant-garde play *The Last Days of Mankind*. Its satirical profiles burlesqued the militarism of the European charnel house. It was a pastiche on then current, historical, and imaginary characters who were a part of the slaughter. One of his characters bellowed, "Lord forgive them for they *do* know what they do."[22] In 1938, his fellow Austrians publicly burned his literature in Vienna, his beloved home. Had he not died two years earlier, they might have burned him, too.

But *Last Days* is, in a sense, as alive today as when the author penned it exactly one hundred years ago. Then, "his ink flowed like blood."[23] The play's ranting militarists, jingoistic journalists, and composites such as the "Optimist" and the "Grumbler," shout universal themes. The love of war, demonized enemies, consuming tribalism, wild optimism, and grumbled cynicism are all part of the current tragedy called the "Islamic State." I have borrowed Kraus's style by offering readers personal and social profiles to present the Caliphate in a still-unexplored light.

This book puts the Caliphate at the center of the Western–Muslim contest for world power. For this reason, I have developed a cultural context. What drives the Caliphate's extensive and international support base? Unlike Karl Kraus, I use only real characters, and I let them speak for themselves. There is no need to embellish dialogue or stray from any historical facts.

WHAT'S IN A NAME?

Names are important. A journalist wrote, "The first thing you learn about a person is his name. It is also something you remember."[24] This applies to groups, too. There is much debate about the name of the entity at the center of this book. I generally call it the Islamic State or the Caliphate because that is what it calls itself. Nazi Germany called itself the Third Reich and called its political philosophy National Socialism. The communist regime in Russia called itself the Soviet Union, and that is how it was referred to by international diplomats and writers on the subject.

Others in academia or the media often use different terms. One American general rebranded the Jihadists as Daesh, though most of the Pentagon brass call it the Islamic State in Syria and the Levant (ISIL). One British journalist is particularly allergic to the word "Daesh" because, in his words, it is used only by "those who wish to kid themselves that the Islamic State is a rogue singularity, entirely outside the normal Islamic mindset."[25] The director general of the BBC refused the demand of a hundred parliamentarians to use the term "Daesh" because that would, in his view, corrupt BBC's impartiality.[26]

The British newspaper *the Independent* calls it the Islamic State in Iraq and Syria (ISIS) because that title confers less legitimacy than "Caliphate" and because "people know where Syria is."[27] A veteran British journalist snickered that "journos" use "ISIS" because it is the name of Lord Grantham's dog on the popular TV show *Downton Abbey* and because it is the name of Oxford's river.[28]

But others dodge the acronym "ISIS" for precisely that reason. A high school in Oxford, England, the Isis Academy, was named after a branch of the Thames near the famed university. In February 2016, it announced that it was changing its name.[29] The university itself has felt some heat, and a presumed Oxford graduate opined, "So please . . . let us not allow some bad abbreviation to tarnish a name that we Oxonians are so proud of, and celebrate it again for all it is worth."[30] Oxford's reserve rowing boat is named *Isis*. The university has refused to change the boat's name or "pander to the hype" of the name's detractors.[31] As a graduate of that university, I am pleased.

Turning to the slaughter in the Caliphate, some snuff killings are so monstrous that I found them, initially, unbelievable. Not since the Nazis and the Mongols before them has there been such gratuitous and ostentatious sadism. The cruelty beggars the imagination, as bands of the Caliphate's killers compete against each other to produce macabre phantasmagoria. The killings are filmed and placed on social media. Weekly new methods of killing are tested and filmed. In May 2016, social media showed an executioner testing a new tactic—plunging a knife directly into the heart of a victim.[32] Killing en masse comes from lowering twenty-five prisoners into a tub of nitric acid and keeping them there "till their organs dissolved."[33] I have offered examples of grotesque sadism because I would have been derelict if I had failed to do so. But I have been sparing.

Many killings are verified by international security and diplomatic services. Nongovernmental organizations (NGOs) have witnessed and compiled records of some of the crimes. Journalists, often at great risk, have investigated atrocities and conditions close to the lines of combat, and several particularly brave reporters have gone undercover there. Newspapers of varying credibility and levels of objectivity have established sources in the West and in the State.

If some observers are quick, perhaps too quick, to connect the Caliphate to terrorist attacks, others speedily rule out any Caliphate link. For example, a student at the University of California's Merced campus, Faisal Mohammad, went on a stabbing spree in November 2015 after being tossed out of a study group. Within a day of the attack, the county sheriff said the stabbings were unrelated to terrorism. This is inconsistent with Mohammad's background and behavior. Mohammad wrote that he wanted to cut heads off, and he smiled while he slashed his victims.[34] He praised Allah in a manifesto the day before his stabbing fling. Paraphernalia of the State was found in his backpack, and his laptop contained pro-Caliphate propaganda. I am not convinced that his motives for attack were unrelated to Islam and do not know why the sheriff was so quick to sniff away the connection.[35]

The rhetorical spine of the book is built, largely, on current events covered in the media. Some of the material I have used came from academic sources, but much of the book is supported by Western daily newspapers and journals of opinion that cite authorities and events. This is for several reasons. British magazines labeled as tabloids have, in my opinion, provided valuable insights into the human dimension of the foreign fighters. Their reporters interview neighbors, teachers, associates, and friends of the Western Jihadis. They then reveal their detective work in their newspapers. The tabloids compete against each other for readership and have a business incentive to be sensational, because sex and violence sell, but also to be accurate, lest they lose credibility.

This book has used articles from newspapers, weekly magazines, and journals of opinion, as well as commentary from known experts in the field of political Islam and the Middle East. Particularly useful were several think tanks. Raqqa Is Being Slaughtered Silently, a loose confederation of Syrians who began four years ago in peaceful protest of Syrian dictator Bashar al-Assad, but were trapped in the city when the State took control, have documented the horrors of life under the State.

The image on the book's cover is of Palmyra, a town of Roman origin (which makes it Western) that was excavated largely by the British and later destroyed by the Caliphate, which is at war with the West. There are already plans by Western powers to rebuild it as best they can.

I wrote this book as an independent scholar during a period when I was an adjunct, distance professor at the US Army War College and an affiliate professor at Haifa University. This monograph represents the judgment of the author and not necessarily of any element of the US Army, the Department of Defense, or Haifa University. Any errors are mine and mine alone.

Mark Silinsky,
Kensington, Maryland, 2016

NOTES

1. Malia Zimmerman, "Orlando Terrorist's Chilling Facebook Posts from Inside Club Revealed," *Fox News*, June 15, 2016.

2. Tor Eigeland, *When All the Lands Were Sea* (Northampton, MA: Interlink Books, 2015), 9.

3. Various, "Eastern Mythology: Babylonian Mythology," *Monarch Notes*, January 1, 1963.

4. Nick Cumming-Bruce, "In 22 Months, Civilian Toll in Iraq Approaches 19,000," *International New York Times*, January 20, 2016.

5. Associated Press, FBI Director: Islamic State Is Still the Number One Threat Facing the U.S. Homeland," The Blaze, June 7, 2016, http://www.theblaze .com/stories/2016/06/07/fbi-director-islamic-state-is-still-the-number-one -threat-facing-the-u-s-homeland/.

6. "FBI Director: ISIS Is Top Threat to US," *The Clarion Project*, June 9, 2016.

7. Andrew Sullivan, "Orlando's Gay Victims Died in the Place They Could Feel Fully Alive," *Sunday Times*, June 19, 2016.

8. Stephen Walt, "ISIS as Revolutionary State: New Twist on an Old Story," *Foreign Affairs*, November–December 2015.

9. "Syria Conflict: Deadly Blasts Near Sayyida Zeinab Shrine," *BBC*, January 31, 2016.

10. Hisham Aidi, "Spanish Leftists Join Fight Against ISIL," *Al Jazeera Online in English*, April 17, 2015.

11. "Syria Sparks Cold War Deja Vu (Op-Ed), Moscow," *The Moscow Times Online*, October 19, 2015.

12. Gregory Katz, "Syria's Civil War Now Europe's War after Paris Attacks," *AP Online*, November 16, 2015.

13. The writing on the flag is the shahada—the Muslim profession of faith: "There is no god but God." In the center of the flag is the prophet's seal in white containing three words in black: "Allah, Rasul [prophet], Muhammad." Muhammad is the messenger of God.

14. Petaling Jaya, "Malaysia: Nearly 30,000 'Foreign Terrorists' in Syria, Iraq: UN," *Sundaily Online*, July 5, 2016.

15. "ISIS Cuts Off Ears of Citizens of Mosul for Cursing Islamic State," *Clarion Project*, October 11, 2015.

16. "About 3,500 Isis Slaves Held in Iraq, Says UN," *The Irish Times*, January 19, 2016.

17. Robert Spencer, "Islamic Texts Justify Sex Slavery," *Jihad Watch*, August 14, 2015.

18. "ISIS Cuts Off Ears."

19. Delivering the death penalty for apostasy is supported by large segments of the Islamic world. In 2010, Pew Research found that 84 percent of Egyptian Muslims, 86 percent of Jordanian Muslims, 30 percent of Indonesian Muslims, 76 percent of Pakistanis, and 51 percent of Nigerian Muslims support the death penalty for leaving Islam. "Muslim Publics Divided on Hamas and Hezbollah Most Embrace a Role for Islam in Politics," *Pew Research Center*, December 2, 2010.

20. Camilla Tominey, "How the Wonderful Queen and Her Corgis Helped Top Surgeon Cope with Horrors of Aleppo," *Express (Online)*, June 5, 2016.

21. "Syria—the Laboratory of World Destruction," *New Statesman* 144, no. 5291 (December 4, 2015): 3–5.

22. Karl Kraus, *The Last Days of Mankind*, translated by Michael Russell, accessed on December 24, 2015, thelastdaysofmankind.com. Emphasis in the original.

23. Richard J. Evans, "Ink Flowed Like Blood," *The Wall Street Journal*, November 25, 2015.

24. Margena A. Christian, "The Importance of a Name," *Jet*, August 7, 2006.

25. Rod Liddle, "Anybody Who Uses the Phrase 'Daesh' Is Terminally Deluded," *The Spectator*, December 2, 2015.

26. Soren Kern, "The Islamization of Britain in 2015, Sex Crimes, Jihadimania and 'Protection Tax,'" *The Islamization of Britain in 2015*, December 31, 2015.

27. Will Gore, "The Jihadist Will Peddle Their Perverted Fantasies, Wherever We Call Them ISIS or Daesh," *The Independent*, June 29, 2015.

28. Robert Fisk, "ISIS? Islamic State? Daesh? Who Exactly Is the Greatest Threat to Civilization?" *The Belfast Telegraph*, December 7, 2014.

29. "School Ditches Isis Name after Terrorist Jibes," *Daily Mail* (London), February 9, 2016.

30. Jennifer Waller, "Let Us Celebrate This Historic Oxford Name," *Oxford Mail*, September 5, 2014.

31. Victoria Ward, "Oxford Rowing Club Will Not Change Isis Name," *The Telegraph*, November 6, 2014.

32. Patrick Christs, "Blood-thirsty ISIS Jihadis Stab Prisoner Through the Heart in Savage New Execution Method," *Express*, May 10, 2016.

33. "Spies Thrown into Acid Vat," *The Times*, May 20, 2016, http://search.proquest.com/docview/1789950433?accountid=4444.

34. Matthew Gonzales, "Were Law Enforcement Leaders and UC Chancellor Aware of Threat by Terrorsits [sic]/Extremists to Attack UC Merced?" *Merced TV News*, November 7, 2015.

35. Tim Walker, "Campus Attacker Inspired by ISIS but 'Self-Radicalised,'" *The Independent*, March 19, 2016.

Map of Syria and the Two Rivers

1. BLACK FLAG OVER BABLYON

I say to America that the Islamic Caliphate has been established.
Instead send your soldiers, the ones we humiliated in Iraq.

—Abu Mosa, a spokesperson for the Islamic State,
throwing down the gauntlet to the United States, August 2014[1]

We're going to degrade and ultimately defeat ISIL the same way
we've gone after al-Qaeda

—President Barack Obama, October 2014[2]

INTRODUCTION

Chapter 1 will offer a brief historical context for the fight. It begins in the Garden of Eden and concludes with the declaration of the Caliphate.

On the Banks of the Garden of Eden

The Western world is rooted firmly in Mesopotamia, which is civilization's cradle. Prophets of all three Abrahamic faiths—Judaism, Christianity, and Islam—trod its soil. The Tigris River is mentioned twice in the Bible; once in Genesis, with a reference to its flow in the Garden of Eden, and again in Daniel.[3] In the Talmud, the waters of the Tigris were celebrated as healthy for the body and the mind.[4] But the river's image had changed by summer 2015, as its environs became strewn with corpses. On the banks of the serpentine river, Islamic State cadets as young as twelve years old blasted bullets into the heads of kneeling Shia captives.[5]

On one side of the Tigris lay the ruins of Nineveh, once a thriving metropolis. According to the Bible, Nineveh was built by Nimrod, and God sent Jonah to preach to the people of the "Great City" to repent for their sins. But a storm thrashed the ship and tossed Jonah into the sea, where he was consumed by a "great fish."[6] Jonah thought better of his defiance of God and apologized.[7] Jonah preached in Nineveh, and Jesus used that humility as an exemplar for men of his day.[8] The Islamic State would destroy the monument Christians and Jews left for Jonah.

Iraq was very important in the rise of Islam and shone during the religion's golden age. Under the Abbasid rule, starting in the eighth century, Baghdad became the center of science and philosophy. According to some accounts, in the twelfth century there were thirty independent schools, an engineering school, and three medical schools, as well as many libraries.[9]

In the nineteenth century, Nineveh became a European sensation. Western scholars, particularly amateurs, plowed carefully through the mounds of soil to resurrect, as best they could, the vestiges of Babylon and Assyria. In 1845, Austen Henry Layard, a young English adventurer, published his accounts of the great dig. Henry Rawlinson, the British diplomat in Baghdad, caught the fever to unearth Nineveh's past. Christians were thrilled about Assyrian accounts referring to a great flood that had engulfed Mesopotamia. Could this have been the biblical flood?[10]

In 2000, 35,000 Christians lived in the city, but this dwindled to 3,000 on the eve of the Caliphate's conquest. By 2015, the State's destruction spree had begun, erasing millennia of religious artifacts. They devastated large parts of the ancient wall of Nineveh, an important landmark, as well as other ancient buildings.[11] The tomb of Seth, Adam and Eve's third son, was blasted into dust. Then they tormented and killed many of the Christian survivors. In August 2015, the Caliphate posted pictures of disheveled and saucer-eyed Christian women waiting to be auctioned as slaves.[12]

Michael Finch, a contemporary poet, set the generalized slaughter to verse in 2016. He wrote of the ancient city:

> On the plains of Nineveh comes a plague,
> Sura-sent and Satan's hell fury,
> Swept wide, over, through, and pillaged complete,
> An ancient world's ringing bells no more.[13]

On the other side of the river stands Mosul, a city of a million inhabitants. It, too, has a storied history. In mid-nineteenth century, an American preacher and his wife erected a mission there.[14] They remarked on the many Christian churches and denominations, Orthodox

A Western Artist's Imagined Nineveh

and Catholic, among them Chaldeans, Assyrians, and Armenians, who lived side by side with the region's other religious and ethnic groups. Jews and Yazidis were there, too.[15] Today, this is only a memory, but a Western influence, of sorts, has returned to the biblical city. In July 2016, al-Baghdadi announced the appointment of a new military commander for the province; he is a German.[16]

The Euphrates is the other great river in Iraq. According to Genesis 2:14, the Euphrates, "the River" or "the Great River," flowed to the Garden of Eden. The river is mentioned in Jeremiah.[17] Its 1,730-mile flow mingles with Tigris before emptying into the Persian Gulf. It was the source of life for the Marsh Arabs. Saddam Hussein drained these marshes to destroy the livelihood of the Shiite in southern Iraq. Today, the Great River is dying, exacerbated by a multiyear drought. The Caliphate has attacked the river's dam's power stations, reducing its flow by over half.[18] Some Western scientists attribute the environmental calamity to man-produced global warming. Many locals attribute this misfortune to the wrath of God.

"Holocaust on Horseback": The Return of the Mongols

If today's Islamic State had role models for the savagery of their tactics, it would likely be the Mongols, who swept like a storm from the Asian steppes to the gates of Baghdad in the thirteenth century. In 1258, Hulagu and his army sacked the city in an orgy of bloodletting. Described as a "holocaust on horseback," the brutality of the Mongols was unsurpassed in the Middle East. Baghdad had been one of the most sophisticated cities in the world, with soft living for the privileged, elegant architecture, and tiled fountains, its lyric beauty was the scene of many stories of *One Thousand and One Nights*.[19] In Syria and Baghdad, Timur the Lame, or Tamerlane, created "pyramids of skulls" and buried families alive to terrorize those whom he conquered, both Muslim and Christian.

Life in Iraq and Syria today more approximates the era of Mongols than the halcyon days that brought Ali Baba, Aladdin, and Sinbad to the Middle Eastern imagination. Like the Mongols, the Caliphate uses primitive "shock and awe."[20] Like the world of the Mongols, daily living is unforgiving for the conquered and privileged for the conquerors. Everyone in the Islamic State must show signs of his or her devotion to Islam. This is particularly the case in the Caliphate's unofficial capital, Raqqa.

Raqqa was the first important Syrian city the Caliphate seized and, along with Mosul in Iraq, is one of the Caliphate's two pillars. The city has a long history. Founded around 244 BCE, Raqqa, then named Kallinikos, was conquered by the Byzantines, destroyed by the Persian Sassanids in 542 CE, and later rebuilt by the Byzantine emperor Justinian I. In the sixth century, Raqqa was a center for Syriac Christianity. Between 796 and 809 CE, the town was the capital of the Abbasid Caliphate. Today, it is the heartland of the Caliphate.

War on Christianity

Land in the Caliphate's clutch today was once part of Christendom. The Middle East was largely Christian before Islam. In approximately 400 CE, John Cassian, a European monk, legged his way to Egypt. He heard the "sounds of prayers and hymns of the monks, scattered in the desert, from the monasteries and from the caves."[21] One house of worship was the Elian monastery, in Homs province, Syria. It was named after St. Elian, a native of Homs, who refused to renounce his Christian faith and was killed by his Roman father. After the Caliphate conquered Homs, they bulldozed the monastery.[22]

The Caliphate hates symbols of Christianity. In 2014, its soldiers celebrated Christmas by blowing up a church. Long a symbol of Christian Mosul, the Clock Church was built in the late 1870s. The wife of French emperor Napoleon III paid for the tower, which rose over the city's rooftops. The Caliphate blew it up.[23] In fall 2014, the State destroyed the oldest monastery in Iraq. For 1,400 years it had stood in Mosul, and the Greek chi-rho carved into the stone of the gatepost represented the name "Christ."[24] It had withstood earthquakes and Mongols and Ba'athism, but it did not survive the Caliphate.[25]

The Caliphate continues to eliminate the memory of Christianity in Mosul. Its fighters have torn down crosses from domes of Mosul churches and searched homes of Christians suspected of hiding crosses.[26] All but a few Christians have been driven from the ancient city, and signs of the faith—crosses and Bibles—have been ferreted out and discarded as trash. In neighboring Turkey, near the Syrian border, the Islamic State destroys churches, too. Parts of one of the most ancient churches in the world were demolished by a Caliphate suicide bomber. According to legend, the three wise men visited the site after they had given their presents of gold, frankincense, and myrrh to the baby Jesus in Bethlehem, under a star.[27] In a perverse twist on history, a Muslim suicide bomber, disguised as a Christian priest, attempted to enter a commemoration for the Muslim murder of Assyrian Christians in Syria. The bomber detonated his bomb outside the hall, killing himself and three Christians.[28]

From the Crusades—The West and Mesopotamia

Mahound is in his paradise above the evening star,
Don John of Austria is going to the war.
He moves a mighty turban on the timeless houri's knees,
His turban that is woven of the sunset and the seas.

—G. K. Chesterton, "Lepanto," 1915

Westerners have long trekked to the Middle East for combat, exploration, and adventure. Medieval and modern conflicts have pitted Europeans against Arabs in the Middle East. Though an all-but-forgotten historical footnote for many Europeans, the Crusades endure in the sulfurous rhetoric and imagination of many of today's Muslims. Islamic intellectuals, theologians, and firebrands promote images of Christian armies at the gates of Jerusalem. The Crusades are a recruiting meme of the Islamic State.

The Knights Templar and the Knights Hospitaller came with the First Crusade in 1099. Sometimes referred to as the world's first non-governmental organizations, they supplied Crusaders with provisions, finance, medicine, and military assistance. Some of the Crusaders were young. In 1212, French and German children gathered to trek to the Holy Land. Called the "wandering poor," they were inspired and led by Stephan, a charismatic fifteen-year-old French shepherd.[29] This was the ill-fated "Children's Crusade," few of whose child soldiers survived to reach the Holy Land.[30]

To the Holy Land! The Image of the Crusaders Endures in the Muslim Mind

Europeans were ultimately defeated in the Crusades, but men from the West would return as conquerors centuries later. If one battle signified the turning point in the Christian–Islamic struggle, it was Lepanto in 1571. Cervantes fought in the battle, with the Catholic Holy League. The magnitude of Christianity's victory secured a place for the story of Lepanto in Western literature. Chesterton wrote, "Cervantes on his galley sets the sword back in the sheath . . . Don John of Austria rides homeward with a wreath." The Romantic and prolific Lord Byron was a Western foreign fighter of sorts. In the early nineteenth century, he traveled to Greece to fight against the Ottoman Empire. He died young and his heart was buried there. Later, triumphant Europeans would dissolve the Ottoman Empire and build their own empires in Muslim lands.[31]

America went to war against North African Muslim potentates; they were the Barbary pirates of Morocco in Tunis, Algiers, and Tripoli. The Muslim rulers demanded tribute, or *jizya*, because the Koran required it of infidels. Instead, in 1815, James Madison used the navy to defeat the Barbary sheikhs at sea and on "the shores of Tripoli."[32] Later, Americans would come as missionaries and merchants.

In the middle of the nineteenth century, an American Protestant missionary described Mosul as a prosperous trading town known for its diverse mix of religious and ethnic communities.[33] He described Orthodox and Catholic Christians living next to Sunni Muslims, Jews, Kurds, Turkmen, and Yazidis. According to the missionary, "You will scarcely find a lad in his teens who does not use at least two tongues; and to travel a hundred miles from Mosul, four are necessary."[34]

In the twentieth century, Muslims and Christians would be, at different times, both enemies and allies. The British–Arabian partnership against the Ottomans was made world famous through the exploits of Lawrence of Arabia. British general Allenby would conquer Jerusalem in 1917, which would mark the first time since the Crusades that a Western force dictated terms of surrender to an Islamic force in that holy city.

In the wake of the Great War, Colonial Secretary Winston Churchill assembled a band of politicians and scholars, whom he called the "Forty Thieves."[35] The only woman "thief" of this 1921 conference was Gertrude Bell—diplomat, scholar, and spy—who is cited as the midwife for the birth of the Iraqi state. She loved Iraq, and many Iraqis returned that affection. Some tended to her gravesite for years.[36] A California professor ventured, in mid-2016, "Bell would be dismayed to see the museum she founded sacked and looted . . . or the damage ISIL inflicted upon the ancient site of Hatra in Iraq, which she visited in 1911."[37] But she would be even more distraught to see the devastation it wrought on "Iraq's human heritage," particularly the Yazidis.[38]

There are disputed accounts of political maneuvering of the post–World War I Middle East. Lawrence, calling himself "the chief crook of our gang," wept at what he saw as the British betrayal of agreements, particularly those made to the Arabian King Hussein. Today, leaders of the Caliphate rail against the postwar division of Mesopotamia, but objective scholarship is more sympathetic toward the West. Historians note that the Ottomans had ruled Syria, Baghdad, Basra, Mosul, and other cities as distinct political units.[39] Further, the Western presence did promote sustained human development in the area.

Some Westerners wanted to grab the region's oil wealth, but others loved it for its civilization. Driven by "desert lust" and a passion for history, British scholars subsidized by wealthy patrons rebuilt some of the vanished greatness of Mesopotamia's past. The home of the Sumerian, Akkadian, Assyrian, Babylonian, and Arab civilizations and the birthplace of writing, Baghdad had a substantial library in 1921, funded and supervised by the British. But this symbol of modern Iraq, which housed ancient books and codices, was set aflame by the Caliphate in December 2014.[40] Days after the Central Library's ransacking, militants broke into the University of Mosul's library and made a bonfire out of 900 years of Arab science, philosophy, and literature. Students cried while staring at the flames.[41]

Many Middle Eastern Muslims did not appreciate European gifts of scholarship, law, and technology to the Arab world. The European colonization transformed law in the Middle East in the eighteenth, nineteenth, and early twentieth centuries. In areas under European colonization, many elements of Western law supplanted Sharia, or Islamic law. Western rule abolished many capital crimes, such as converting to Christianity, and it offered greater protections to women and girls.[42] Other elements of Sharia were modified to eliminate amputations, crucifixions, and other practices considered excessively cruel.[43]

Western-imposed modification of Sharia created a backlash among the more conservative elements of both Sunni and Shia sects and spurred nascent Islamic revivalism.[44] This boosted Islamic resurgence in Iran and the surge of the Islamic Brotherhood in Egypt in the twenty-first century.[45]

Between 1920 and 1932, Britain tried to build a modern democratic state in Iraq from three former provinces of the Ottoman Empire, which it had conquered and occupied during the First World War.[46] Democracy did not take hold; Britain intervened in 1941 to remove the pro-Nazi Rashid Ali government.[47] Iraq became very important during the Second World War.[48] Rashid Ali would have availed the country's oil assets to the Axis.[49]

In the Second World War, Allied and Axis powers clashed over vital oil supplies in North Africa and the Middle East. They fought for control of territory and sea lanes and vied for the allegiance of Muslims in their areas of operations. Germany's Thirteenth Mountain Division of the Waffen SS, the Handschar, recruited Balkan Muslims, and the

Mufti of Jerusalem, then living in Berlin, called them to Jihad.[50] These Muslims fought for Hitler.[51]

Ba'athism, Zarqawi, Baghdadi

After the Second World War, Britain and France reduced their colonial holdings in the Middle East. The United States and the Soviet Union vied for regional influence. The Ba'ath Party, which espoused Pan-Arabism, socialism, and elements of Islam, was founded by three French-educated Syrian intellectuals. Michel Aflaq, the party's philosopher, like Abu Bakr al-Baghdadi, wanted to abolish Arab nation-states and forge a single state.[52]

Ba'athist parties held power in Iraq and Syria in the 1960s. Membership in the parties became a path to influence in the civil services. The autocratic regimes of Saddam Hussein in Iraq and the Assad clan in Syria made the Ba'athist philosophy and parties irrelevant in both states.[53] But some of those who served as young men with the Ba'athists are fighting for the Caliphate today.

In Syria, the Assad family held dictatorial power and destroyed political rivals. It is ruled today by a dictator, Bashar al-Assad. In Iraq, Saddam Hussein could not bequeath his country to either of his sons because both had been killed in battle, while he was hanged by his compatriots. This left a power vacuum and opportunities for political bullies. Among the more ruthless contenders was Abu Musab al-Zarqawi, described by then US secretary of state Colin Powell as a collaborator of Osama bin Laden. Zarqawi was killed in 2006, and there was a temporary void in power.[54] After a hiatus, an Islamic scholar now known as Abu Bakr al-Baghdadi proclaimed a new Caliphate on June 29, 2014.[55] He announced a grand strategy to build a complete society for Muslims.[56] *Time* magazine would later give him the moniker "the brooding muezzin of death."[57]

The borders associated with European treaties were, literally, bulldozed by the Islamic State. In 2014, the State released a video in which bulldozers leveled the Iraqi–Syrian border points. The clip was called "The End of the Sykes-Picot Agreement" and was posted to social media to symbolize the end of Western influence and the dawn of a new era— the reign of the Caliphate.[58]

A Caliphate Is Born

There are different explanations for the Caliphate's creation. One view sees Western intervention in the Middle East, particularly that of the United States, as the key driver for the State's existence. Former British prime minister Tony Blair submitted that the Anglo-American invasion of Iraq in 2003 "helped give rise to the Islamic State."[59] In the presidential-election year of 2015–2016, politicians blamed each other. Some isolationist Republicans blamed the more interventionist Republicans, whom they called "neoconservatives." Democrats accused Republicans for invading Iraq, and Republicans countered that Iraq was largely stable when President Bush left office. They argued that the chaos and blood swamps came on President Obama's watch. A PBS documentary titled *The Secret History of ISIS* faults both Democrats and Republicans.[60] The Arab media, as well as left-of-center journals of opinion, blame generalized American meddling.[61]

Another view holds that Islam, and not the West, is largely responsible for the birth of the State. The Caliphate's leaders claim that divine providence guided them to build an Islamic state. The State's propagandists underscore this theme in all of their publications. There are other unconventional explanations for the State's creation, including climate change and Zionism.[62] Secretary of State John Kerry linked the Caliphate's success to Israeli policy toward the Palestinians.[63] Others who scold the United States include long-standing enemies of successive presidential administrations. For example, Cuban ex-president Fidel Castro placed Israel's Mossad intelligence agency behind the radical Islamic State.[64] In Holland, a Ministry of Justice and Security official declared that the Islamic Caliphate is a "preconceived idea from Zionists deliberately to make Islam look bad."[65]

Blood Antiques and Killing Pits

The origins of the Caliphate continue to be debated, but few observers can deny the State's commitment to erasing the region's non-Islamic past and present. Mesopotamian history is for sale as "blood antiques."[66] The plunder includes ancient coins, gold chains, figurines, and other Byzantine treasures that are sold to European vendors. The State hires diggers to scour the earth for archeological items and sells them via a network of brokers and other intermediaries. Looters receive from 20 to 50 percent of the profit from anything they sell.[67]

Prospectors in the State's soil sometimes find gold and jewelry. Sometimes they find statuary. But sometimes diggers find decomposing victims of the Caliphate. This is what happened when a mass grave was unearthed in October 2015. The al-Sheitaat tribe had rebelled against the Caliphate in late summer 2015. In response, nearly 1,000 were killed and tossed into mass graves. Animals unearth the corpses to feed on the decaying flesh.

Today, the Caliphate destroys gems of decayed empires simply because they exist.[68] A critic moaned, "They even ruin the ruins." Nobel

Zenobia—Warrior Queen and National Hero of Syria

laureate V. S. Naipaul wrote of this in *Among the Believers*: "The time before Islam is a time of blackness; that is part of Muslim theology. History has to serve theology." A leading scholar at Johns Hopkins University cited the Caliphate's destruction as the worst since that of the Byzantine Iconoclasts in the eighth and ninth centuries.[69] Today, there is no room for aesthetic beauty that is unconnected to Islam.[70] The Caliphate made no room for Palmyra, which is the subject of the profile below.

PROFILE ONE: THE LION, THE POET, AND THE SCHOLAR

Once prospering at the crossroads of Roman and Parthian empires, the ancient city of Palmyra is now gone. The city was once a cultural potpourri of architectural styles, mostly Roman, and a stopping place for caravans traveling from Rome to the Euphrates. It sprang to life as a trading hub in the first and second centuries CE and flourished with cultural dynamism. The many languages—Greek, Roman, Parthian—and religions, food dishes, and musical instruments fused to give Palmyra, in the words of the Roman Pliny the Elder, "its own fate."[71]

After the fifth century, Palmyra became home to many Christians.[72] It was rich in houses of worship, some lost to the earth over the centuries, but some resurrected by Western archeologists. Thousands of archeology amateurs traveled to the once-thriving desert outpost, which was once called the "Bride of the Desert." Emperor Hadrian visited the town around 129 CE. And a queen warrior, Zenobia, held Palmyra in her grip in the mid-third century CE.

Palmyra's austere beauty was fêted in verse by Percy Bysshe Shelley's good friend, Thomas Love Peacock.[73] In "Palmyra" (1806), he wrote of its "spirit of the days of yore! What countless charms around her rise! What dazzling splendor sparkles in her eyes! On her radiant brow enshrin'd."[74] Britain's youngest-ever prime minister visited the city in 1813. Later, Jane Elizabeth Digby, Lady Ellenborough, trekked to Palmyra from Damascus in 1853 to visit the home of an ancient fellow aristocrat—the strong-willed Queen Zenobia, who had ruled from the city 1,700 years ago.[75] Lady Jane's tombstone was carved from stone quarried from Palmyra.

There is also Islamic heritage in Palmyra, which was once adorned with shrines to Islamic heroes. But the Caliphate does not like shrines. In 2015, its soldiers destroyed the tomb of Sheikh Mohammed Ali, near Palmyra, condemning it as a "landmark of polytheism."[76]

The Lion—Al-Lata

Palmyra's temples, some of which would become churches, theaters, and beautifully designed graves, decayed over the centuries.[77] One temple was renovated and enlarged by the Roman emperor Hadrian in about 130 CE.[78] In the twentieth century, Western archeologists unearthed lost civilizations in the area. A Syrian–Polish archaeological mission uncovered statues of mythical animals and winged goats and lions. Particularly treasured was the four-meter tall Lion of al-Lat sculpture.[79] This pre-Christian lion dates from the first century CE and was dedicated to the pre-Islamic Arabian goddess al-Lata.

But the Caliphate had no use for the lion or anything else deemed un-Islamic. The State blew the statue to pieces and crushed the remnants; it is unlikely that it can ever be restored. A Palmyra resident recalled, "'I heard a loud noise, so I went up to the roof to see what is going on . . . I saw Daash crushing the 'god lion' statue with construction machines."[80] Throughout the day, they plowed into dust the fragments of the wealthy caravan oasis that had once teemed with entrepreneurship and shone with architectural pride.[81] There was more to come.

The killing started in the afternoon. In the Roman amphitheater, in which long-lost plays of countless themes were performed in many languages, spectators sat on the stone seats and watched an entirely new performance.[82] Twenty-five captured soldiers were shot on stage in front of an audience of several hundred.

The Poet

Palmyra has produced celebrated men of letters, one of whom was Omar al-Farra. Born in 1949, he started writing about village life in Syria at age thirteen. His poems sang his love for his country, and his breakout poem was titled "Hamda." It was about a young Bedouin woman who killed herself rather than submit to an arranged marriage.[83] Other poems shone with optimism, particularly on themes of personal and national independence. His upbeat prose turned to laments as he saw his people suffer, particularly under the Caliphate. His son explained, "The destruction of Syria wore him down."[84]

Omar al-Farra died in June 2015, in the same week, perhaps the same day, that the Caliphate rigged Palmyra's architectural treasures with explosives and obliterated them. The poet's death came unexpectedly, and his surprised son remarked that he had looked to be in good shape. Palmyra's poet was mourned by his compatriots.

The Scholar

In the whole history of Syria we haven't witnessed anything like this. They are like wolves after blood.

—Walid al-Asaad, son of Khaled al-Asaad[85]

Khaled al-Asaad, "Mr. Palmyra," a beloved eighty-two-year-old antiquities scholar, devoted his life to exploring, saving, and studying the town's treasures. Holding degrees from Damascus University, he named his daughter Zenobia, after the warrior-queen of Palmyra's folklore.[86] He directed the Antiquities and Museums Department archaeological site for forty years and then retired to read, write, dig, and educate the world on Palmyra.[87] The Caliphate knew about him, and they beat and tortured the old man. Held for twenty-five days, he could not speak to or see his family, but there is no evidence that he betrayed a single artifact.[88] The vandals demanded gold, but there was no bullion he could offer. As his son Mohammed said, "There was nothing to tell them; the gold in Palmyra is in the statues and the architecture."[89]

The scholar could have escaped earlier, even after the Caliphate had conquered Palmyra. With his celebrity and prestige, he could have taken refuge in the West and lived near a prestigious university. But he told a fellow scholar, "I am from Palmyra, and I will stay here even if they kill me."[90] And they did.

Trundled into a van, he was tossed into the town's main square. He was not dressed in an orange jumpsuit; he wore his ordinary clothes.

Caliphate leaders read charges against him, and the town's greatest antiquities scholar was branded a "director of idols." Further, he represented Syrian scholars at international "infidel conferences." Finding him guilty, they beheaded him.[91] After that, they strung what remained of his corpse to an ancient Roman column.[92] Palmyra mourned.

Palmyra Tomorrow

There is still life in Palmyra. Its territory is contested and jockeys between pro-government and Caliphate forces. In March 2016, the Caliphate was expelled. One month later, Russia's Mariinsky Theatre Orchestra traveled to Palmyra and played works by Bach and Prokofiev in the amphitheater that the State had used to kill its enemies.[93] The conductor declared that it was a concert against barbarism, and a Russian visitor paid tribute to the life of Khaled al-Assad.[94] Nonetheless, an Islamic State spokesperson reveled in the devastation they had left: "We captured a whole town and houses from them, and they recaptured sand and destruction."[95] He was partially correct.

But today Palmyra is more than sand and ruin. Omar Al-Farra's warm poems and elegiac verse will likely be recited for years, albeit in hushed tones. They will remind Palmyra's future generations of a sweeter, if bygone, life in Syria. The books of Palmyra's bard, Khaled al-Asaad, will be read by lovers of history and art and Syria. True, the proud Lion of Palmyra has been turned to dust. But it is not entirely lost. Its bold visage endures in photographs, and it will live in memory.

In the World of Islam

In the Islamic world, some nationalities support the Caliphate—its agenda, philosophy, and tactics—and others do not. In Pakistan, less than one-third of the population hold negative views of the Caliphate. This is particularly alarming to some observers given the ever-growing nuclear arsenal of the South Asian country. Other states that have sizable support for the Islamic State are Nigeria, in which 20 percent of its Muslim population support it, and Malaysia, in which 12 percent of Muslims support the State. Though the proportion of Muslim populations is often small, the combined number of Muslims who support the Caliphate is troubling. A Pew poll in 2015 revealed that for eleven nation-states with significant Muslim populations, there are between 63 and 287 million persons who either support the Caliphate or are ambivalent.[96]

The Lion of Palmyra

A home of empires and a host to religious monuments, Mesopotamia has enduring ties to the West. A succession of empires has risen and fallen there, and one Islamic civilization became world renowned for science as well as piety. Europeans have engaged Muslims as both enemies and allies at different times and in different places. The balance of power in that part of the Middle East has shifted several times and in many ways. But today's Caliphate is a unique challenge to Western interests, power, and prestige.

In 2003, Saddam Hussein threatened that the West would "open the gates of hell" if he was removed.[97] He *was* removed and the gates flung wide open for the Islamic State. The Caliphate devastates the treasures of ancient civilizations in Iraq and Syria that had survived for millennia. In summer 2016, it dynamited the 2,500-year-old temple of Nabu in Iraq. One week later it boasted that soon it will destroy the pyramids of Egypt. As for today, the State is struggling to hold its Mesopotamian ground while infiltrating its cadre to Europe and throughout the West. This and more is the subject of chapter 2.

JIHAD and the WEST

Notes

1. Robert Spencer, "ISIS Threatens America: 'We Will Raise the Flag of Allah in the White House,'" Jihad Watch, August 8, 2014.

2. "Obama: We Will Defeat ISIS Like We Did al-Qaeda," *AFP*, September 5, 2014.

3. Isadore Singer, Schulim Ochser, "Tigris," *Encyclopedia Judaica*, 2007. Accessed on September 1, 2016. http://jewishencyclopedia.com/search?utf8 =%E2%9C%93&keywords=tigris&commit=search.

4. Ibid.

5. The bodies were then rolled into the Tigris and were videoed as they floated downstream. In the background, someone waves the black flag of the Caliphate. Mary Chastain, "ISIS Video: 12-Year-Old Boy Tosses Bodies into Bloody Tigris River," *Daily Mail*, July 15, 2015.

6. Irfan Al-Alawi, "Extreme Wahhabism on Display in Shrine Destruction in Mosul," Gatestone Institute, August 4, 2014.

7. Ibid.

8. L. A. Bushinski, "Nineveh," *New Catholic Encyclopedia*, 2003.

9. Mehdi Noorbaksh, "Shiism and Ethnic Politics in Iraq," *Middle East Policy Council*, Summer, 2008. http://www.mepc.org/journal/middle-east-policy -archives/shiism-and-ethnic-politics-iraq.

10. Reade Julian, "Layard's Nineveh and Its Remains," *Antiquity*, December 1, 1998.

11. "Daash Blows Up Nineveh's Wall," *National Iraqi News Agency*, June 25, 2015.

12. Jay Akbar, "ISIS Post Pictures of 'Christian Women Kidnapped in Syria Threatening That They Will Become Sex Slaves If Ransom Is Not Paid,'" *Mailonline*, August 15, 2015.

13. Michael Finch, "The Plains of Nineveh Gone," *Frontpage Magazine*, January 25, 2016.

14. Kate Seelye, "Mosul from a 19th Century Perspective," *Middle East Institute*, August 16, 2014.

15. Shortly after arriving in Mosul in 1851, Frederic Williams described in a report to the American Board a breakfast with six villagers who used nine dialects of five languages every day. "You will scarcely find a lad in his teens that does not use at least two tongues; and to travel a hundred miles from Mosul, four are necessary," he wrote in a later report. Diaries of Frederic Williams, 1851, Personal Diary, Amherst College.

16. "Iraq: ISIL Appoints German National as Military Commander for Nineveh," *Asia News Monitor*, July 4, 2016.

17. "Euphrates," *Encyclopedia Judaica*, accessed on September 1, 2016, http://jewishencyclopedia.com/search?utf8=%E2%9C%93&keywords=tigris&commit=search.

18. "Daesh Shuts Down Ramadi Dam in Iraq," *Anadolu Agency*, February 6, 2015.

19. Dan Murphy, "ISIS Leader Baghdadi Cementing Reputation as the New Hulagu Khan," *Christian Science Monitor*, February 5, 2015.

20. "ISIL Turns 'Shock and Awe' Doctrine Against Islam," *Doha Al Jazeera*, July 5, 2016.

21. Abba Anthony, "Coptic Orthodox Patriarchate, Saint Anthony Monastery," *Front Page Magazine*, August 31, 2015, http://www.frontpagemag.com/fpm/259965/how-islamic-world-was-forged-exercise-common-sense-raymond-ibrahim.

22. "ISIS Destroys Ancient Monastery in Homs," *MEMRI*, August 20, 2015.

23. "ISIS Blows Up Mosul's Iconic Clock Church," *Fox News*, April 26, 2016.

24. Adam Withnall, "ISIS Razes to Ground the Oldest Christian Monastery in Iraq, Satellite Images Show," *Independent*, January 20, 2016.

25. "Reports: In Mosul, IS Kills Iraqis Whose Wives Didn't Wear Proper Hijab," *States News Service*, January 13, 2015.

26. "The Cross Is ISIS' Main Enemy; Today No Trace of a Cross Can Be Seen in Mosul,' *Pravoslavie*, September 26, 2015.

27. Katie Mansfield, "'We Three Kings' Church—Oldest in Christianity—Blown-Up by Muslim Suicide Bomber," *Express (Online)*, June 8, 2016.

28. "Suicide Bomber Targets Assyrian Event in Syria, 3 Killed," *AINA*, June 19, 2016.

29. "Church History: The Children's Crusade," *Christian History Institute*, accessed November 8, 2014. https://www.christianhistoryinstitute.org/magazine/article/childrens-crusade/.

30. Ibid. Details of the Crusade's end are somewhat confused. Many of the children died of hunger and disease before ever reaching Marseilles.

31. Churchill fought in the Sudan and was open about his general contempt of Islam. In his 1899 book *The River War*, Churchill described what he witnessed in

countries where Islam ruled: "Individual Moslems may show splendid qualities, but the influence of the religion paralyzes the social development of those who follow it. No stronger retrograde force exists in the world. Far from being moribund, Mohammedanism is a militant and proselytizing faith." "Revisiting Churchill's Thoughts about Islamic Radicals," *The Gazette* (Colorado Springs, CO), May 28, 2013, 8.

32. A. J. Caschetta, "Dhimmi Nation," *PJ Media*, June 3, 2016.

33. Kate Seelye, "Mosul from a 19th Century Perspective," *Middle East Institute*, August 16, 2014.

34. Diaries of Frederic Williams, 1851, Private Diary, Amherst College.

35. David Thomas, *Christians at the Heart of Islamic Rule: Church Life and Scholarship in Abbasid Iraq* (Boston: Brill, 2003), vii.

36. Tim Arango, "For British Spy, a Fragile Legacy in Iraq; Affection Remains Strong for the Shaper of a Nation Still Struggling to Survive," *International New York Times*, June 16, 2014.

37. Ibrahim al-Marashi, "The Women Behind Sykes-Picot," *Al Jazeera*, May 22, 2016.

38. Ibid.

39. Akil N. Awan and A. Warren Dockter, "ISIS and the Abuse of History," *Today's History*, January 2016, 19–21.

40. On the same day the library was destroyed, ISIS abolished another old church in Mosul: the church of Mary the Virgin. The Mosul University Theater was burned as well, according to eyewitnesses. In al-Anbar province, Western Iraq, the ISIS campaign of burning books has managed to destroy 100,000 titles, according to local officials. Riyadh Mohammed, "ISIS Burns 8000 Rare Books and Manuscripts in Mosul," *The Fiscal Times*, February 25, 2015.

41. Ibid.

42. Wael B. Hallaq, *A History of Islamic Legal Theories: An Introduction to Sunni Usul al-fiqh* (Cambridge, UK: Cambridge University Press, 1997).

43. Ibid.

44. Gilles Kepel, *The War for Muslim Minds: Islam and the West* (Cambridge, MA: Harvard University Press, 2004).

45. Charles Hirschkind, "What Is Political Islam," in *Political Islam: A Critical Reader*, ed. Frederic Volpi (London: Routledge, 2011), 13–15.

46. Fred Rhodes, "Inventing Iraq: The Failure of Nation Building and a History Denied. (Book Review)." *The Middle East*, June 22, 2004.

47. From 1941 to 1958 the Iraqi regime was dominated by Nuri al-Sa'id, who brought the exercise of coercion and patronage to new heights of manipulation. Stephen Blackwell, "A History of Iraq. (Review)," *Middle Eastern Studies*, April 1, 2001.

48. Trevor Royle, "'Remarkable Example of Military Daring,'" *VFW Magazine*, April 3, 2003.

49. Ibid.

50. They were deployed to Hungary and Bosnia. The units were heavily, though not exclusively, Muslim. There were some Croatian Catholics who fought in Handschar. "Grow Your Own Diesel," *Daily Mail* (London), April 5, 2006.

51. After the Axis was defeated, nearly 4,000 made their way to Syria to fight with the Arab Liberation Army against Palestinian Jews. Seth J. Frantzman, "Strange Bedfellows," *Jerusalem Post*, May 9, 2008.

52. Lain McLean, ed., *The Concise Oxford Dictionary of Politics* (Oxford, UK: Oxford University Press, 1996), 29.

53. "Nasserism, Ba'athism and Political Islam, "Gulf Art Guide," accessed January 11, 2016. http://gulfartguide.com/essay/nasserism-baathism-and -political-islam/.

54. Daniel Benjamin and Steven Simon, "Zarqawi's Life after Death Iraq," *International Herald Tribune*, 2006.

55. "Islamic State, the Offspring of Saddam," *The World Today* 71, no. 1 (February/March 2015): 53.

56. Ian R Pelletier, Lief Lundmark, and Rachel Gina Gardner, "Why ISIS' Message Resonates: Leveraging Islam, Socio-Political Catalysts and Adaptive Messaging," *Studies in Conflict Studies and Terrorism* 39 (2016): 10.

57. Massimo Calabreski, "Person of the Year Shortlist," *Time* magazine, accessed July 23, 2016, http://time.com/time-person-of-the-year-2015-runner-up -abu-bakr-al-baghdadi/.

58. "ISIS and the Abuse of History," *History Today* 66, no. 1 (January 2016): 19–20.

59. Kimiko De Freytas-Tamura, "Blair Suggests That Iraq Invasion Helped Give Rise to ISIS," *International New York Times*, 2015.

60. Peter Keough, "Redemption and Remembrance," *Boston Globe*, May 15, 2016.

61. "Egyptian TV Host Al-Ghiety to Clinton: Old Bag, You Are the Cause for What Happened in Syria, Iraq, and Libya," *Al-Tahrir TV* (Egypt), March 7, 2016.

62. The "root cause," according to former Maryland governor Martin O'Malley, was climate change and a "mega-drought": "This created . . . the poverty that has led now to the rise of ISIL." Michael Barone, "O'Malley Says Climate Change and Poverty Produced ISIS," *Examiner* (Washington, DC), July 23, 2015.

63. "Kerry Links ISIS Recruiting Success to Israel," *IPT News*, October 17, 2014.

64. "Fidel Castro Says Mossad behind Islamic State," *AFP*, September 2, 2014.

65. Its leader, Abu Bakr al-Baghdadi, is not a Muslim. He's an agent of Mossad. Abigail R. Esman, "ISIS a Jewish Plot? Propaganda and Islamic Jihad," The Investigative Project, August 22, 2014.

66. R. Abigail Esman, "How ISIS Makes Money from the Art Market," *The Investigative Project*, July 27, 2015.

67. Ibid.

68. Verse 3:137 in the Koran reads, "Many were the Ways of Life that have passed away before you: travel through the earth, and see what was the end of those who rejected Truth." As interpreted by some Islamic scholars, this gives a mandate to obliterate pre-Islamic civilization remnants because they represent *jahliyya*, the pre-Islamic era of darkness.

69. James Harkin, "Murdering History," *Smithsonian* 46, no. 10 (2016): 39–51.

70. "The sites have included ancient ruins like Nineveh, Nimrud and Jonah's Tomb in Iraq, and Palmyra in Syria, as well as medieval Islamic sites like the tombs of Yahya ibn al-Qasim and Ibn Hassan Aoun al-Din in Mosul." Steven Lee Myers "ISIS Razed Ancient Christian Site in Iraq," *International New York Times*, January 20, 2016.

71. Empress Zenobila: Palmyra's Rebel Queen, Times Higher Education, April 16, 2009, https://www.timeshighereducation.com/books/empress-zenobia -palmyras-rebel-queen/406208.article.

72. "Archaeologists Unearth Mosaic Board under 5th Century Building," *AP Worldstream*, May 29, 2002.

73. Stuart Manning, "Why ISIS Wants to Erase Palmyra's history," *CNN*, September 1, 2015.

74. Thomas Love Peacock, *Palmyra*, 2nd ed., accessed September 3, 2015. http://www.thomaslovepeacock.net/palmyra1.html.

75. Daily Garnett, "The Chic of Araby," *The New York Times*, August 18, 2002.

76. UNESCO called it a landmark of "outstanding universal value." Jack Moore, "ISIS Destroys Palmyra Shrine as Group Vows to 'Remove Polytheism,'" *Newsweek*, June 23, 2015.

77. Judith Weingarten, "Roman Palmyra: Identity, Community, and State Formation," *The Times Higher Education Supplement*, June 13, 2013.

78. "ISIS Blows Up Ancient Baal Shamin Temple in Palmyra," *Firat News Agency*, August 24, 2015.

79. "Syrian-Polish Expedition Begins Work in Churches Quarter in Palmyra," *Syrian Arab News Agency*, October 3, 2009.

80. John Hall, "ISIS 'Destroys' Famous Lion God Statue in Captured Syrian City of Palmyra . . . Just Days after Promising Locals They Would Not Obliterate Ancient Monuments," *MailOnline*, May 28, 2015.

81. Morris Loveday, "Islamic State Militants Seize Syrian City of Palmyra, Threatening Ancient Ruins," *Washington Post*, May 20, 2015.

82. "Islamic State Murders 25 Men in Palmyra," *BBC News*, July 4, 2015.

83. "Syrian Poet Omar Al Farra Dies," *Gulf News Report*, June 22, 2015.

84. "Syria's Famous Poet Omar Al-Farra Dies," *Amman Ammun News*, June 1, 2015.

85. "UK Source Talks to Son of Murdered Palmyra Archaeologist about ISIL's Destruction of Historic Sites," *London Sunday Times Online*, September 6, 2015. Report by Christina Lamb "'Like Wolves After Blood, ISIS Is Smashing All.'"

86. "Late Archeologist Khaled al-Asaad Honored in Ceremony at Damascus National Museum," *SANA Online*, August 23, 2014.

87. "Islamic State 'Beheads' Archaeologist in Palmyra," *Daily News Egypt*, August 19, 2015.

88. Ben Hubbard, "A Protector of Palmyra Falls Victim to ISIS' Hands: In Ancient Syrian City, Ex-Director of Antiquities, 83, Is Beheaded in Public," *International New York Times*, November 1, 2015.

89. "UK Source Talks to Son of Murdered Palmyra Archaeologist about ISIL's Destruction of Historic Sites," *London Sunday Times Online*, September 6, 2015. Report by Christina Lamb, "'Like Wolves After Blood, ISIS Is Smashing All.'"

90. "Great Man Pays after Refusing to Flee IS," *Morning Bulletin* (The Rock-hampton, AU), August 21, 2015.

91. Albert Aji and Mroue Bassem, "Islamic State Group Beheads Aging Syrian Antiquities Scholar," *The Seattle Times*, August 20, 2015.

92. Bassem Mroue, "Activists: Islamic State Destroys Temple at Syria's Palmyra," *AP Online*, August 23, 2015.

93. "Syria: Russian Orchestra Holds Concert in Palmyra Ruins," SyndiGate Media (Lyon), May 6, 2016.

94. Ibid.

95. Bryan Denton, "A Syrian Jewel, Where 'Ruins Have Been Ruined,'" *New York Times*, April 5, 2016, Late Edition (East Coast).

96. Sierra Rayne, "Pew Poll: Between 63 Million and 287 Million ISIS Supporters in Just 11 Countries," *American Thinker*, November 18, 2015.

97. "US General: Now We Understand What Saddam Intended in Saying 'You Will Open the Gates of Hell,'" *Shafaq News*, June 30, 2016.

2. EURABIA AND BEYOND: THE CALIPHATE'S BREEDING GROUND

We will conquer your Rome, break your crosses,
and enslave your women, by the permission of Allah.

—Shaykh Abu Muhammad al-'Adnani ash-Shami, of the Islamic State[1]

More than half of the territory that once made up Christendom—
including Egypt, Syria, Turkey, North Africa—converted to Islam
due to bouts of extreme violence and ongoing financial bleeding.

—Raymond Ibrahim[2]

INTRODUCTION

Chapter 1 traced the Western experience in the Middle East, from the Garden of Eden through the rise of the State. Chapter 2 pivots toward the West. It examines the suburbs, slums, towns, and villages of Europe to probe Muslim–non-Muslim relations. Today's Caliphate is a potpourri of nationalities and ethnicities bonded by anger, passion, and professions of Islam. Many recruits are from Europe, the United States, Australia, and the former Soviet Union. Tens of thousands more come from all Islamic corners of the Third World. Some have returned to Europe to fight for the Islamic State.

The Caliphate Declares War on the West

Soon after al-Baghdadi declared a Caliphate, he called upon Muslims to travel to Raqqa and join their brothers and sisters in arms. If that was not possible, they were to murder non-Muslims in the West. The State declared, "If you are not able to find an IED [improvised explosive device] or a bullet, then single out the disbelieving American, Frenchman, or any of their allies. Smash his head with a rock or slaughter him with a knife or run him over with your car or throw him down from a high place or choke him or poison him."[3] Muslims in Europe were listening.

An eclectic cavalcade of Muslims, including schoolteachers, rapists, converts from Christianity, university dropouts, doctors, clerics, and others filtered to the Middle East.[4] Some were multicultural, like abu Khaled al-Cambodi, an Australian citizen of Cambodian and Fijian heritage.[5] Others were converts to Islam, and yet others were born and raised as Muslims.

By August 2014, only several months after a Caliphate was declared, more than 1,000 Westerners had gone to Raqqa to fight for the State.[6] Many more thousands of supporters stayed in the West and engaged in fund-raising. In July 2015, a poll showed that 1.5 million Britons supported the Caliphate's goals.[7] Similar surveys in other European states, particularly France, Germany, and Belgium, showed alarming rates of solidarity.[8]

The Caliphate took its war to the West, too. The first of the Caliphate's killings struck "nations of the cross" abruptly, and Europeans braced for more. Did these attacks herald the future? The Caliphate promised that they did, declaring, "The French must die by the thousands."[9] For the Archbishop of Canterbury, the terror attacks on Paris in November 2015 made him "doubt the presence of God."[10]

The face of Europe had changed. The continent's more senior citizens remarked that it felt like the European fortress of the Second World War. The optics and the rhetoric harkened back to very dark days in which Britain had pondered its survival. In summer 2016, a "ring of steel" was deployed around British airports. Layered security systems, long familiar in Israel, were becoming common in Europe.[11] In England, Wembly, the venue of the popular entertainment show *Britain's Got Talent*, became known as "Fortress Wembly."[12]

The 2016 Tour de France required 23,000 security personnel to keep things safe. Europeans were warned not to say or wear things that might antagonize Muslims. The BBC warned English soccer fans not to dress as crusaders while attending the European 2016 soccer tournament in France because it might inflame Islamic passions.[13] The event was well patrolled, with 5,000 French police officers deployed at key venues. But even before the tournament began, French officials said that there would not be a victory parade on the Champs Élysées should France win, citing security concerns.[14] In the end, the event went off without any Caliphate-driven attacks. That would come weeks later on the Riviera in Nice.

Having heard the shrill call for killing and having seen images of Muslims killing Christians in Europe and elsewhere, Westerners, expecting a tsunami of blood, asked, "Why do they hate us?" Would there be "Ramadan Bombathons" in 2016 and 2017? There were no easy answers, but there was some history to review, as traced below.

"Nations of the Cross"

In the early and mid-twentieth century, European states had significant colonial holdings in the Islamic world. Algeria was governed, in many ways, as a part of France. In colonies, European tastes, culture, fashion, and political philosophies were au courant. But succeeding generations of Muslims were more reluctant to embrace and mimic the West. Many Muslims whose parents migrated to the West are torn between two worlds.

Today, Europe is home to teeming, if sometimes seething, communities of Muslims. In 2011, the Pew Forum predicted that Europe's Muslim population will swell to nearly fifty-seven million by 2030, from just under thirty million in 1990.[15] Since the 1960s, millions of Muslims have immigrated to and been born in a largely secular Europe. This infusion has not been seamless, and despite large-scale efforts of integration, many Muslims remain socially cocooned.

In Germany, the Turks, who came to work temporarily as "guest workers," never left. Many moved into subsidized apartments near factories. In response, many Germans bolted from those areas, creating a parallel and insular society of unassimilated Muslims. In Britain and France, Muslims from foreign colonies came to Europe to stay. Other European states, too, needed unskilled labor, and the Muslim world supplied the human capital. Islamic populations clustered themselves in cities, and radical networks, some of which support the Islamic State, began to mushroom.

Much of this went largely unnoticed in elite opinion. Until the twentieth century, Muslims were not seen as a political challenge to the West. Western diplomats and intellectuals who warned of the growing social division were branded as alarmists or as smash-mouthed extremists. It was not the key concern on the international stage in the postwar West. Islam was seen as one of many benign religions in the West. With the collapse of the Soviet Union, some political scientists wrote of "the end of history," referring to an apparent triumph of a liberal global order.

But history had not ended; neither were liberal values embraced by the entire Third World. Many Muslims, with new lives in the West, held

Culture Clash

fast to their faith and regional customs. Further, multiculturalism had replaced a centuries-old conviction that Western norms, values, and religions were superior to others. Multiculturalism holds that cultures are different from one another but are not superior or inferior. In January 2015, then British home secretary Theresa May explained, "Without its Jews, Britain would not be Britain, just as without its Muslims, Britain would not be Britain—without its Sikhs, Hindus, Christians and people of other faiths, Britain would not be Britain."[16] The European Union's Federica Mogherini echoed this: "Islam belongs in Europe ... I am not afraid to say that political Islam should be part of the picture."[17]

But some politicians have warned against this "Islamization" of Europe for years. Geert Wilders, a Dutch politician, has argued that multiculturalism has been a Continental cancer. Lambasted for insensitivity, tried for hate speech, and threatened with death, Wilders has long been seen as a "one-man crusade against Islam."[18] For years, he has decried European collective efforts to integrate Muslims as a masterwork of self-delusion.[19] Speaking for many in 2011, he looked to the future and lamented, "The lights are going out all over Europe."[20]

Eurabia

Many Europeans were, initially, nonchalant about the cultural shift, but some later regretted this indifference. Many of today's late-middle-aged and elderly intellectuals miss the artistic and cultural freedoms of their youth in the 1950s and 1960s. Today's Continental literati reminisce on a long-faded, culturally confident, and economically prosperous Europe. For years after the Second World War, Europe was exciting and liberal, and it arts scene burst with creative energies. But the freedoms then turned to restraint, which turned to self-censorship driven by fear of angering Muslims. European journalists have been threatened with death for unfavorable commentary on the Caliphate.[21] Often, journalists cannot ask man-in-the-street questions in heavily Muslim areas because they are attacked.[22] Some have been killed.

British moderate Muslims also face challenges. In 2009, Baroness Warsi from Dewsbury literally had egg on her face after pleading to her coreligionists that they embrace women's rights. A convert to Islam pelted her with the produce while he and others chanted in Urdu and English for more Sharia in Britain. More cynical public intellectuals foresee a European future, sometime later this century, in which churches are replaced by mosques, civil law by Sharia, and the liberal values of the Enlightenment by a strict Islamic code of conduct.[23]

A prominent man of letters, Bernard Lewis warned that Europe was becoming "part of the Arab West, the Maghreb."[24] And some Muslims gloat at the prospect. An example can be seen on a YouTube video by a man who crows that the march of Islam in Germany is inevitable: "Islam is coming to take over Germany whether you want it or not."[25] The tool of conquest, he says, is not war but reproduction because "Muslims have seven or eight children each." He said, "What does the German man have? One child and maybe a little pet dog!"[26] And for the future? "Your daughters will wear the hijab."[27]

The surge of migrants entering Europe in 2015 and 2016 brought shocks to the continent. In several countries, young women, some of whom had welcomed Middle Eastern and Eurasian migrants, were molested.[28] Local police advised fair-skinned and blonde women, particularly in Northern Europe, to change their lifestyles and appearances. Police counseled to dress modestly and dye their hair dark.[29] Local municipalities instituted separate times for males and females to use public swimming pools. For the first time in modern memory, train station waiting rooms had separate waiting areas for males and females.[30] Many Continentals no longer have faith in their local police or government. In 2015 and 2016, applications for firearm permits and membership in European shooting clubs increased perceptibly.

All this terrifies vulnerable minorities. The Islamic State is just one of many outlets that churns out anti-Semitic, misogynistic, and anti-homosexual literature. Jews in traditional religious clothing and identifiable homosexuals can no longer stroll some of Europe's streets without fear of being spat on, beaten, or slashed.[31] This increasingly dark world has become untenable for some Europeans, who feel there are few safety zones left. Many are emigrating to escape what they see as the unremitting buzz saw of Muslim immigration. Michel Houellebecq (pronounced "Wellbeck") writes about this with a very sharp pen, as shown below.

PROFILE TWO: FRENCH "BAD BOY" MICHEL HOUELLEBECQ— NO SUBMISSION!

Some see him as a poseur; some see him as a literary prophet. Editors of the satirical magazine *Charlie Hebdo* placed him on the cover with the words "The predictions of the Great Houellebecq."[32] The famous novelist was dressed as a magician and said, "In 2015, I will lose my teeth. In 2022, I will celebrate Ramadan."[33] Others see him as an alarmist Islamophobe, and others call him the bad boy of French letters.[34] But most of the French intelligentsia are simply fascinated with his maverick novels and poetry. *Le Figaro* and *Le Monde* printed a series on his life, views, ambitions, and the impact his work has had on France. Some wondered if this late-middle-aged, mild-mannered intellectual was determined to have a fatwa placed on his head.[35]

For years, Michel Houellebecq had been the enfant terrible of France's salon culture. He takes his literary inspiration from Albert Camus, and one American literary critic compares his style to that of Martin Amis, "at heart a deeply braised moralist, an unflinching observer of ugly human nature."[36] One literary highbrow described his style as a fusion of Gore Vidal, Kurt Vonnegut, and Dennis Miller.[37]

If French antihate laws muzzle his open criticism of Muslims, Houellebecq gives fictional characters unfettered freedom. A character in his novel *Platform* relished the death of Palestinian terrorists or children because "it meant one less Muslim."[38] The same character continued, "Islam could only have been born in a stupid desert among filthy Bedouins who had nothing better to do than—excuse my language— shag their camels."[39] In physiological metaphor, he describes Muslims as "clots" in Europe's "blood vessels."[40]

His sixth novel, *Submission*, vaulted him to international literary fame. Readers are asked to imagine France in 2022, when ruling French Socialists partner with Islamists to govern the country. The Sorbonne is now an Islamic university. France has absorbed Francophonic North Africa to become a Muslim superstate. France itself is governed by Muslims, collaborators, and unctuous civil servants. The narrator of *Submission*, François, is a middle-aged professor of literature. He is underpaid, jaded, pathetic, and lonely.

Within days of the book's publication, Prime Minister Manuel Valls assured the nation that "France is not *Submission*, it's not Michel

Houellebecq, it's not intolerance, hate, or fear."[41] France would not sell the Sorbonne to Saudi Arabia, period! And the French left erupted with *outragé*! But the timing of the publication did much for sales. The book was first available for sale on January 7, 2015—the same day that Islamists slaughtered *Charlie Hebdo* cartoonists.

Contested Zones in the West—
Breeding Grounds for the Caliphate

It does not take people long to discover that the Global Village
is in reality the dark incarnation of Gotham City without Batman.

—Geert Wilders, Dutch parliamentarian, 2016[42]

Some Europeans have left the cities for the non-Muslim suburbs, and others have emigrated to the United States or Israel. But others do not have the resources or inclination to escape what they see as pools of social pathologies stagnating at the outskirts of their own cities. They call these places "no-go zones," and some members of the Caliphate have grown up there.[43] This hotly debated expression refers to the Muslim-dominated, chaotic neighborhoods that saturate Western Europe. London, Paris, Stockholm, and Berlin are home to over 900 areas where authorities have little control.[44]

In France, areas of high-immigrant density are called *banlieues* or *quartiers*, which were originally built to house immigrants from former French colonies.[45] European leaders do not like the term "no-go zone" and neither do many journalists and scholars. Some refer to them as "cultural islands." Daniel Pipes sees the "no-go" term as gratuitously derogatory and prefers the official French nomenclature: "sensitive urban zones."[46]

When in January 2015 American journalist Steven Emerson claimed "there are actual cities like Birmingham that are totally Muslim, where non-Muslims just simply don't go in," he was roundly censured.[47] Some are gritty metropolitan areas hidden from tourists. An example is Nice, France. Dozens of its Muslim residents have traveled to Syria to fight for the State.[48] In Germany, the Berlin Wall that separated the East from the West has long crumbled, but there is a new civilizational divide, according to local Germans; they call it the "Arab Street."[49] A play on words, "Arab streets" are geographic locations where Muslims outnumber non-Muslims in Europe. It is also a synonym for Arab public opinion.

But whether called "no-go zones" or "sensitive urban zones," or occasional armed camps, these Muslim-only areas serve as recruiting

Out for a Walk

pools for criminal syndicates.⁵⁰ These areas are ideal grooming places for foot soldiers for the Caliphate, and the Caliphate's leaders have
promised to use Muslims from those zones to attack Western targets.⁵¹
They provide sanctuary for the Caliphate's cells, some of which fester in
Dewsbury, as discussed below.

PROFILE THREE: PORTRAIT OF AN ENGLISH VILLAGE—
"EVEN THE ICE CREAM LADY WEARS A BURKA"

In many ways, the West Yorkshire town of Dewsbury is unremarkable.
Along its terraced streets are a few pubs, snooker clubs, and tea shops.
The elderly tend their English gardens. Jean Wood, looking back on her
seventy-five years in Dewsbury, reflects on its transformation: "The
change happened so quickly. One day it seemed it was all whites, and
then it was all Asians."⁵² The first Asians in Dewsbury were novelties.
"We peered at them, and they peered back."⁵³ Slowly, the churches were
shuttered, as were the garment-producing industries. The town crick-
et pavilion was torn down. A journalist noted that almost everyone
seemed to be Muslim. "Even the woman serving ice cream . . . wearing
a burka."⁵⁴ Girls waiting in line to buy the ice cream were also swathed
in Islamic garb. And, today, Dewsbury boasts a disquieting status; it has
produced more Islamic suicide bombers per capita than any other town
in England.

The leader of the pack of suicide bombers responsible for the attack in London on July 7, 2005, came from this town. The blasts killed
fifty-two people. One of Britain's youngest convicted terrorists, then
sixteen years old, was arrested carrying bags of ball bearings. His broth-

er, along with a friend, had traveled to Syria to fight for the Caliphate. There were other Islamic extremists linked to the town's mosques.[55]

The town's Muslims publicly condemn the suicide bombing. A journalist asking man-in-the-street questions heard, "He is not a martyr . . . is a statistic," "He was . . . brainwashed," and similar comments disassociating Dewsbury's Muslims from violence.[56] They denounced the Caliphate. Former Tory minister Baroness Warsi is from Dewsbury and hopes to unmask the "drivers of radicalization" in her hometown.[57]

Nonetheless, many of the remaining non-Muslims are not pleased with the demographics. Jean Wood is unhappy about the increase in crime and the white flight. Once, some Asians threw stones at her church's bus, which alarmed her. Most of her friends are gone. Jean Wood misses the long-lost Dewsbury of her youth. England was very different then.

Islamophobia—The Muslim Side of the Story

Many Muslims are unhappy with their status in the West, particularly in Europe. Tensions are high between Muslims and non-Muslims in Europe. Restive and alienated second- and third-generation Muslims feel themselves to be victims in a secular Europe. They see a continent beset by "Islamophobia," a neologism meaning an irrational fear or hatred of Muslims. Outside of their immediate Islamic neighborhoods, many do not feel at home. This has prompted some to leave for the Caliphate.

Many young Muslims share a fatalism about their social status in Europe.[58] This cohort is a recruiting pool for Islamists.[59] Many Western Muslims who have joined the State claim that they did so because they could not live according to their faith in Europe. One wedge issue centers on Muslim apparel. In 2004, the hijab, the Islamic headscarf, was banned from French public schools and government office buildings.[60] Women who left for Syria have cited what they claim as unwanted and hostile glares by non-Muslims in Europe when they wear their hijab in public.[61]

Europe's Daunting Demographics

There are twenty million refugees waiting at the doorstep of Europe.

—Johannes Hahn, European Union Commissioner for European Neighbourhood Policy and Enlargement Negotiations, summer 2015[62]

Whatever the current state of relations, Europe's future is likely to become notably more Islamic because of the high fertility rate of Muslim Europeans, patterns of immigration, and conversion to Islam.[63] Domestic and foreign-funded efforts to convert Europeans to Islam have been steady, dynamic, and successful. In 2016, a former Archbishop of Canterbury warned that the Church of England is "one generation away from extinction."[64]

A void of faith in the West provides opportunities for Muslims proselytizing and recruiting for the Islamic State.[65] Islam offers an extended community of religious adherents who share religious, social, and, usually, political values. Some converts to Islam have become enthusiastic soldiers in the ranks of the Caliphate. Other European Muslims give rhetorical, financial, and logistical support to the State. In many European cities, the Islamic State has its champions, who are usually young and are called "fanboys."

Finally, there is a net emigration of native-born Europeans. For example, more Swedes chose to emigrate in 2015 than at any other time since the famine 160 years earlier. The most popular destination was the United States.[66] If many young secular or Christian Europeans are trying to leave for the United States, many Muslim Europeans are content to live on the continent without becoming part of its dominant culture. Others loathe the non-Muslim West, and Asghar Bukhari is one of them. He is profiled below.

PROFILE FOUR: THE EVER-ANGRY MR. BUKHARI
WANTS HIS SHOE BACK

Asghar Bukhari is a leading voice for angry Muslims in Britain. A founder of Muslim Public Affairs Committee UK, he speaks about world events on European television and radio. He has spoken about the Islamic State on *Sky News*, on *Russia Today*, on the BBC, on the VIP, on the *James O'Brien Show*, and on many other media venues. He has a supportive audience. Some viewers see his analysis of Islamic–Western relations as conspiratorial and incoherent; others see it as insightful. When he speaks on television talk shows, bearded men and hijab-clad women in the audience clap, smile, and nod in agreement.[67]

He defined the Caliphate as a "Sunni uprising." Its members are not terrorists, and according to Bukhari, they do not represent a significant threat to Britain. "ISIS is not the problem." Rather, Western elites are intent on forging a new "Sykes-Picot" version of the Middle East.[68] "Muslims are the most oppressed people on earth, we have been denied our freedom, we have been denied our equality, we have been denied any justice, we have even been denied the right to tell the world our own story."[69] The public intellectual Douglas Murray accused him of living in "intellectual fever swamps."[70]

Whatever the case, Bukhari is convinced he is being stalked by Zionist agents. He cites as an example a recent break-in of his home by Zionists. A Jew stole one of his shoes. The goal was, according to Bukhari, not financial gain but intimidation. "They left one shoe behind, to let me know someone had been there."[71] He concedes that this sounds implausible but adds, "Why are you so shocked that a Zionist would try to intimidate or steal something from me? Man, they stole Palestine! Are you crazy?"[72] Some bloggers clowned back. On the blog *Israellycool*, Aussie Dave wrote, "If Zionists harvest organs, will he next claim we stole his brain? Who stole his meds?"[73] Another blogger, Bullfrogger, snickered, "I believe that I have been targeted by Muslim spies. I awoke this morning and my goat and her two favorite outfits are missing."[74]

But not everybody is chuckling, and some fear that the likes of the snarling Bukhari may portend Britain's future. In 2006, Bukhari bemoaned the failing leadership of British Muslims, whom he described as "well intentioned . . . but out of touch."[75] They were a crusty old lot. He demanded that Britain's Muslims "hand over the reins to a new generation of leaders more in tune with today's young Muslims."[76] One decade later, Bukhari may be part of that new leadership.

SUMMARY

Muslims and non-Muslims in the West wrestle to accommodate each other while holding on to their traditions and values. At the same time, burbling just below society's surface is a widespread mutual distrust. Muslims decry Islamophobia in the West, but many Westerners feel besieged by Muslim immigrants. When Sadiq Khan was elected mayor of London, some people tweeted their fear and fatalism under the hashtag "Londonhasfallen."[77]

By mid-2016, the head of Britain's Equalities and Human Rights Commission, who had popularized the term "Islamophobia," regretted ever using this word. In self-effacing candor uncommon among senior public officials, Trevor Phillips publicly admitted that he had been well intentioned but naïve about the blistering Muslim integration into British society: "I thought Muslims would blend into Britain . . . I should have known better."[78]

Other Westerners have gone further, claiming to suffer from "Islamonausea," which is queasiness and fatigue at insatiable Muslim demands on democratic values and a growing fatalism that the conquering tide of Islam is now irreversible. They do not want to live in a "global village" or share in its burdens. Many are fatigued by what they see as empty gestures by preening politicians and of Sharia elbowing itself into common culture and law. One pundit wrote, "Je suis sick of it."[79] This and more is the subject of chapter 3.

1. Robert Spencer, "We Will Conquer Your Rome, Break Your Crosses, and Enslave Your Women, by the Permission of Allah," *Jihad Watch*, September 21, 2014, https://www.jihadwatch.org/2014/09/islamic-state-we-will-conquer-your-rome-break-your-crosses-and-enslave-your-women-by-the-permission-of-allah.

2. Raymond Ibrahim, "How the Islamic World Was Forged: An Exercise in Common Sense," *Islam Translated*, August 31, 2015.

3. Shaykh Abu Muhammad al-'Adnani ash-Shami, "In the Name of Allah the Beneficent the Merciful Indeed Your Lord Is Ever Watchful," from Robert Spencer, *Jihad Watch*, September 21, 2014.

4. Abul Taher, "Toasting His A-levels, Boy Who Signed Up for His Dream Job as a Suicide Bomber: British Teenager Named in Islamic State Files Handed to MoS," *Daily Mail*, March 14, 2016.

5. Alexandra Sims, "Australia's Top ISIS Recruiter 'Killed in Iraq Air Strike,'" *The Independent*, May 6, 2016.

6. "ISIS Fast Facts," CNN Library, accessed August 31, 2016, http://www.cnn.com/2014/08/08/world/isis-fast-facts/.

7. Tom Parfitt, "More Than 42 Million Muslims 'Support ISIS'—As Experts Warn the Figure Will Grow," *Express*, July 1, 2015.

8. "ISIS: French Suicide Attackers 'Ready to Strike' France," *ANSAmed*, June 18, 2015, http://pamelageller.com/2015/06/isis-french-suicide-attackers-ready-to-strike-france.html/.

9. Julian Robinson, "'The French Must Die by the Thousands': ISIS Cell in France Threatens Rocket Attacks on Passenger Jets and New Charlie Hebdo-Style Massacre in Chilling Undercover Video Filmed by Journalist Who Infiltrated Them," *MailOnline*, May 2, 2016.

10. "Paris Attacks Caused Archbishop to 'Doubt' Presence of God," *BBC*, November 22, 2015.

11. "'Ring of Steel' Security for UK Airports," *The Daily Mirror*, May 23, 2016.

12. Ed Gleave, "ISIS Threatens Live Britain's Got Talent Shows," *Express*, May 22, 2016.

13. Donna Rachel Edmunds, "BBC Warns Football Fans Dressing as Crusaders 'Offensive' to Muslims," *Breitbart*, June 4, 2016.

14. "Euro 2016: France Beefs Up Security Ahead of Final Match," *BBC*, July 10, 2016.

15. John Nelson, "America Alone: The End of the World as We Know It," *Military Review*, May 1, 2009.

16. Ben Tufft, "Theresa May Says 'Without Its Jews Britain Would Not Be Britain,'" *The Independent*, January 18, 2015.

17. Daniel Greenfield, "Integration Is Not the Answer to Muslim Terrorism," *Frontpage Magazine*, April 1, 2016.

18. Juliane von Mittelstaedt, "Geert Wilders' One-Man Crusade against Islam," *The Netherlands' Fearmonger* (Der Spiegel), November 12, 2009.

19. Citing his "Islamophobia," US congressmen Keith Elison and Andre Carson tried to have Wilders banned from the United States in 2015, when he was

scheduled to speak at a Muhammad Art Exhibit in Texas, at which Caliphate-supporting Islamists were killed in a shootout.

20. Mike Corder, "Anti-Islam Dutch Lawmaker Gains Support Amid Migrant Crisis," *Associated Press*, January 23, 2016.

21. Oliver JJ Lane, "Death Threats for Editor of Local Newspaper Who Published Story of Mosque Linked to Islamic State," *Brietbart News*, April 1, 2016.

22. Selina Sykes, "Female Journalist Attacked by Angry Teen Live on Air in Belgian Terror Town Molenbeek," *Express*, April 5, 2016.

23. Calev Ben-David, "While Europe Wakes," *Jerusalem Post*, January 19, 2007.

24. "Wise Words from Bernard Lewis," *New Criterion*, April 1, 2007. http://www.highbeam.com/doc/1G1–162620526.html

25. Robert Spencer, "Islam Is Coming to Take Over Germany Whether You Want It or Not," *Jihad Watch*, November 1, 2016.

26. Ibid.

27. Ibid.

28. Chris Tomlinson, "Report: Christians, Gays, Women Fleeing Asylum Centres Due to Persecution by Muslim Men," *Breitbart*, February 11, 2016.

29. "Attack Victim Claims Police Told Her to Dye Hair," *The Local*, May 6, 2016.

30. Oliver Lane, "Locals Fled Pool after Migrants Masturbated into Jacuzzi, Defecated into Kid's Pool, Invaded Girls Changing Rooms," *Breitbart*, January 22, 2016.

31. "There are many documented accounts and the frequency of occurrence is increasing. One attack is the thirteen-year-old boy identified by Jewish headwear being beaten." Joseph Byron, "13-Year-Old Jewish Boy Wearing Kippah Attacked in Paris," *European Jewish Press*, July 7, 2015.

32. Michael Karwowski, "Michel Houellebecq: French Novelist for Our Times," *Contemporary Review*, July 1, 2003.

33. Rachel Donadio, "Before Paris Shooting, Authors Tapped into Mood of a France 'Homesick at Home,'" *New York Times*, January 8, 2015.

34. Greg Keller, "Paris Review Editor Says New Houellebecq Book Misunderstood," *AP Online*, October 18, 2015.

35. Juliette Garside, "Infamy, Infamy: They've All Got It in for Me; Some Call Him a Genius, Others a Bigot. A Literary Star in His Native France, Michel Houellebecq Is Also One of Today's Most Controversial Novelists. But Is This Mild-Mannered Man Really 'Seeking a Fatwa'?" *The Sunday Herald*, September 8, 2002.

36. Sophie Masson, "The Strange Case of Michel Houellebecq. (Literature)," *Quadrant*, Winter 2003.

37. "Editor's Choice: Michel Houellebecq's 'Submission,'" *The Buffalo News*, November 1, 2015.

38. Garside, "Infamy, Infamy."

39. Ibid.

40. Lara Marlowe, "French Left Erupts in Outrage as Houellebecq Returns to Flaying Islam; Novelist's Return to French Obsession with Islam Already a Cause Celebre," *The Irish Times*, January 7, 2015.

41. Greg Keller, "Paris Review Editor Says New Houellebecq Book Misunderstood," *AP Online*, October 18, 2015.

42. Geert Wilders, "It Does Not Take People Long to Discover That the Global Village Is in Reality the Dark Incarnation of Gotham City without Batman," *Brietbart News*, May 27, 2016.

43. "Tower Hamlets in East London had the highest percentage of Muslims with 45.6 percent and neighbouring Newham wasn't far behind at 40.8 per cent. Outside the capital Blackburn in Lancashire was highest with 29.1 per cent of the city made up of followers of Islam." "Muslims in UK Top 3 Million for First Time," *The Sun*, February 1, 2016.

44. Larisa Brown and Corey Charlton, "Migration 'Has Created 900 No-Go Areas in EU': Devastating Report Shows Order Breaking Down—Including in London," *Daily Mail*, April 1, 2016.

45. In August 2014, an article in French magazine *Valeurs Actuelles* (Contemporary Values) mentioned 750 lawless areas where police officers might be met with serious assault, including mortar fire.

46. David Graham, "Why the Muslim 'No-Go Zone' Myth Won't Die," *The Atlantic*, January 20, 2015.

47. Prime Minister David Cameron called him "a complete idiot." "PM Hits Back over Brum 'No-Go' Zone," *Coventry Evening Telegraph* (England), March 1, 2015.

48. "Paradise Lost Has Been Terror Target 'for Years,'" *Daily Record*, July 16, 2016.

49. Donna Abu-Nasr, "The Berlin Walls Is Long Gone. Now a New Divide Threatens Europe," *Bloomberg*, May 20, 2016.

50. Soeren Kern, "Police Warn of No-Go Zones in Germany," *Gatestone Institute*, August 1, 2015.

51. "'You Will Not Live in Peace' Islamic State Warns France in New Video," *ZeeNews*, November 14, 2015.

52. Sue Reid, "The Breeding Ground for Jihadis Where Even the Ice Cream Lady Wears a Burka," *Mail Online*, June 15, 2015.

53. Sue Reid, "The Breeding Ground for Jihadis Where Even the Ice Cream Lady Wears a Burka," *Mail Online*, June 15, 2015.

54. Ibid.

55. Ollie Gillman, "How Former Mill Town Dewsbury in West Yorkshire Is Linked to More than a Dozen Islamist Extremists and Terrorists Including Britain's Youngest Suicide Bomber," *Daily Mail*, June 16, 2015.

56. "Beleaguered Town of Dewsbury Back in Spotlight," *BBC Online*, June 15, 2015.

57. "Lady Warsi: Ministers Fuelling Muslim Radicalization," *The Guardian*, June 16, 2015.

58. "Chilling' Posters in Cardiff Warn Muslims Not to Vote in the General Election Because 'It Violates the Right of Allah,'" *Daily Mail*, April 17, 2015.

59. Oliver Lane, "The Kensington Mosque at the Heart of Britain's ISIS Defectors," *Brietbart News*, October 17, 2014.

60. The ban on religious garb applied to the fashion of other faiths. But the hijab-restricting law provided fodder for Muslim firebrands who offered it as evidence of legally mandated and publicly supported discrimination against Muslims. Shaista Aziz, "Paris Muslims Struggle to Feel Accepted," *BBC News*, March 30, 2015.

61. An example of non-Muslims taunting Muslims is shown in a video in which a black woman in London hurls anti-Muslim invectives at two hijab-wearing women. The woman who made the religious slurs was subsequently arrested for "racist" speech. Mar Banham, "Police Arrest Willseden Green Woman over 'Isis Bitches' Racist Bus Rant," *IBT*, October 16, 2015.

62. Soeren Kern, "Germany's Muslim Demographic Revolution," Gatestone Institute, accessed August 31, 2015, https://www.gatestoneinstitute.org/6423/germany-muslim-demographic.

63. Pew Research Center's Forum on Religion and Public Life, "The Future of the Global Muslim Population," January 2011.

64. Thomas D. Williams, "Christianity Dying in Britain, Only Islam Growing," *Breitbart* (London), January 18, 2016.

65. Olga Stokke and Andreas Sletthold, "Increasing Number of Young People Are Turning to Literal Islam," *Oslo Aftenposten*, June 5, 2015.

66. Sweden and Migration, Sverige, accessed September 15, 2016. https://sweden.se/migration/.

67. "Prominent Poet Omar al-Farra Passes Away," *Damascus SANA Online*, June 21, 2015.

68. Asghar Bukhari, "The Beginning of the End: Why the West Can Never Beat ISIS," *Asghar Bukhari* (blog), accessed June 15, 2014, https://medium.com/@asgharbukhari/diary-of-asghar-bukhari-the-largest-picket-of-stores-in-british-muslim-history-war-the-bible-a-24487e45c20#.91h9or51b.

69. Paul Austin Murphy, "PACUK and 'Western Imperialism,'" *American Thinker*, June 12, 2014.

70. Douglas Murray, "If I Was Asghar Bukhari, I Would Hold onto Both of My Shoes Very Tightly," *The Spectator*, June 14, 2015.

71. Priya Josh, "Asghar Bukhari Warns 'Mossad Shoe-Stealer Is on the Loose," *IBT*, June 13, 2014.

72. Robert Spencer, "UK Muslim Leader Asghar Bukhari: Zionists Stole my Shoe," *Jihad Watch*, June 14, 2015.

73. Aussie Dave, "Comedy Gold: Asghar Bukhari's Shoe in Mouth Disease," *Israellycool*, accessed June 25, 2015, http://www.israellycool.com/2015/06/16/comedy-gold-asghar-bukharis-shoe-in-mouth-disease/.

74. Bullfrogger from Robert Spencer Video: "Asghar Bukhari Triples Down: This Is Your Brain on Islamic Supremacism," *Jihad Watch*, June 19, 2015, https://www.jihadwatch.org/2015/06/video-asghar-bukhari-triples-down-this-is-your-brain-on-islamic-supremacism.

75. "Voice of the Sunday Mirror: Our Young Muslims Must Have New Leaders," *Sunday Mirror* (London), August 13, 2006.

76. Ibid.

77. Mark Chandler, "Londoners Reject Racist 'London Has Fallen,' Tweets Messages of Unity after Sadiq Khan Victory," *Evening Standard*, May 7, 2016.

78. Raheem Kassam, "UK Equalities Chief Who Popularised the Term 'Islamophobia' Admits: I Thought Muslims Would Blend into Britain. I Should Have Known Better," *Breitbart*, April 10, 2016, http://www.breitbart.com/london/2016/04/10/thought-europes-muslims-gradually-blend-britains-diverse-landscape-known-better/.

79. Michelle Malkin, "Post-Jihad Gesture Theater: Je Suis Sick of It," *Townhall*, March 23, 2016.

3. THE CALIPHATE IN WESTERN CULTURE

Gaudeamus igitur,
Juvenes dum sumus,
Quis confluxus hodie Academicorum?
E longinquo convenerunt

Let us therefore rejoice,
While we are young;
Who has gathered now of the university?
They gather from long distances.

—Selected verses from a medieval European university drinking song[1]

INTRODUCTION

Western culture has tried to grapple with the Caliphate. Politicians, journalists, entertainers, and public intellectuals have coped with the Caliphate-inspired killings in the West. Some have disparaged it; others have joked about it; and others strain to understand it. Of all the perplexing questions, few are more frequently asked than "Is the Islamic State Islamic?"

THE ISLAMIC STATE THROUGH THREE PRISMS

Lest we get on our high horse and think this is unique to some other place,
remember that during the Crusades and the Inquisition,
people committed terrible deeds in the name of Christ.

—President Barack Obama, 2015[2]

How Islamic is the State? Some observers say it is not Islamic. Others, particularly the leaders and adherents of the State, declare that it is Islam distilled to its purist expression. Yet others see it as a hybrid Islam, crafted from the darker and more lurid passages of Islam's sacred scripts. Many others simply do not know what to make of it. It is helpful to examine the debate through these three prisms.

Prism One—The Islamic State Is Not Islamic

And they [the Islamic State] are also above all apostates, people who have hijacked a great religion and lie about its real meaning.

—John Kerry, US Secretary of State, 2016[3]

The very essence of the Islamic faith is peace.

—Jeh Johnson, US Secretary of Homeland Defense, 2016[4]

The first view is that the Islamic State is *not* Islamic. Proponents of this outlook are drawn from academic, political, and public intellectual circles. They do not agree on what the political philosophy or polity of the State should be called. Some call it a regime of thugs or miscreants. But they agree it is not Islamic. They compare it to al Qaeda and other militant groups who, in their view, warp texts of Islam to justify, recruit, and deploy fighters.[5]

This prism portrays the State as an autocratic regime with ethics similar to the Mafia and Mexican cartels. A Georgetown University professor claimed that the State "falsely boils down" the Islamic principles and cherry-picks the Koran and Hadith to "hijack" Islam.[6] This view is dominant in academia but may reflect the influence of oil-exporting benefactors to Middle East Studies departments.[7] Also, the "red-green axis"—or, as French prime minister Manuel Valls calls it, "Islamo-leftism"—the partnership between leftists and Islamists, is entrenched on campuses, as evidenced by myriad political resolutions passed by flagship organizations such as the Middle East Studies Association. Leftists and Islamists have developed an ideological front against what they see as a common enemy—Western values.[8] This alliance has also drawn in black activists to create a black-green alliance, as evidenced by the partnership of the Council on American Islamic Relations (CAIR) and Black Lives Matter.

In the political arena, many leaders, including President Obama, are quick to disassociate Islam from the Caliphate. In the wake of the terror attacks in Paris on November 13, 2015, presidential candidate Hillary Clinton commented, "Let's be clear: Islam is not our adversary.

Muslims are peaceful and tolerant people and have nothing whatsoever to do with terrorism."[9] David Cameron, prime minister of the United Kingdom at the time, called the State "woman-raping, Muslim-murdering, medieval monsters."[10] They are killers with "a twisted, perverted ideology."[11]

However, politicians may have career incentives to disconnect the Caliphate from Islam. London's 600,000 Muslims represent a decisive swing vote in any mayoral election, as was demonstrated in the 2016 election of London's first Muslim mayor. In Europe, left-wing parties have successfully courted the bourgeoning Islamic vote. Politicians, conservative and liberal alike, have built a rhetorical firewall between the Caliphate and mainstream Islam. Western leaders see partnering with moderate Muslims as key to strategic victory in the war against terrorism. After the bombings in Brussels on March 22, 2016, President Obama underscored that Muslims are "our [America's] most important partners" in the fight against terrorism.[12]

But, increasingly, Western commentators find it difficult to completely decouple Islam from the Islamic State. A Princeton scholar calls the first prism a "cotton-candy" analysis of Islam and the Caliphate.[13] It is sweet, fluffy, and attractive but lacks substance. As the media becomes increasingly saturated with the State's Koranic slogans and fatwas, it becomes less credible to deny any tie to Islam. The comedy show *Saturday Night Live* ribbed President Obama's perceived naïveté in one of its sketches. In the skit, "President Obama" muses, "Did you know that the first *I* in ISIS stands for *Islamic*? I mean, who knew?"[14]

Prism Two—The Islamic State Is Islamic

I hear so many people say ISIS has nothing to do with Islam—
of course it has. They are not preaching Judaism.

—Aaqil Ahmed[15]

Another view is that the Islamic State is very Islamic. The loudest boosters of this prism come from the ranks of the Caliphate itself. They are very clear about the Caliphate's political and religious essence.[16] Further, many Muslims around the world are giddy over the State, and tens of thousands have migrated there to fight.[17] Many other groups have pledged fealty on the basis of Islamic solidarity. Significantly, the Caliphate's laws are based on Sharia and Koranic verses. A strong argument that the Islamic State is, at least partially, Islamic comes from the Grand Imam of Al Azhar University, the foremost Islamic university in the Sunni world.

The world of the Caliphate is anchored on the Koran and other texts of the Islamic canon. Other Islamic literature, such as the Hadith, or tales of Muhammad, are also sacred and are used as exemplars of how Muslims should live. The prophet Muhammad is held by Muslims to be the perfect man. All men before him and all men after him are judged against his actions, judgments, opinions, and lifestyle. Many passages in Islam's holy text support the Caliphate's claim that it is Islamic. The Koran is filled with verses demanding war against nonbelievers. They include "Fight against those who disbelieve in Allah. Make a holy war"[18] and "Fight against such of those to whom the Scriptures were given as believe neither in Allah nor the Last Day" (Surah 9:29). The Koran links slaughter with taking captives in Surah 8:67. Slavery is encouraged in the Koran. Former congressman Alan West advised, "You need to get into the Qur'an . . . the Sira [biography of Muhammad] . . . the Hadith [traditions about Muhammad], and then you can really understand that this is not a perversion: they are doing exactly what this book says."[19] The Caliphate would agree.

This prism sees the greatest difference between the Islamic State and other Islamist organizations, such as the Islamic Brotherhood, as a tactical one. Many of the groups have the goal of converting the world to Islam or of subjugating other faiths to Islamic rule. The Islamic State is not the only group that practices beheading, crucifixion, stoning, and ritualized rape. Other groups, such as Boko Haram and al-Shabaab, also engage in these practices.[20] As with Boko Haram and other violent Islamist organizations, the Islamic State's cruelty is mandated in the religion's sacred texts.

Prism Three—The State Is an Extremist Form of Islam

> *ISIS maybe is a perversion of Islam, but Islamic it is.*
>
> —Peter Bergen[21]

The third view sees the Caliphate as Islamic but unconventional, primitive, harsh, and unforgiving. It is only one, proportionately very small, variety of Islam, and it expresses the worst and largely rejected elements of the faith.[22] Holders of this view argue that the Islamic State is Islam at its most vile.

Critics argue that instances of sickening sadism, although uncommon, occur in many parts of the Islamic world.[23] The Caliphate's soldiers have buried non-Muslims alive for the crime of being non-Muslim.[24] Women suspected of "sorcery" have been beheaded, along with their husbands.[25] Children as young as seven years old have been killed for showing disrespect to Islam. However, this behavior is not a defining characteristic of the way Islam is practiced.

Many of the Caliphate's fatwas would be considered comedic elsewhere in the Islamic world. For example, senior Caliphate clerics issued a fatwa banning pigeon breeding because the sight of the birds' genitals is un-Islamic.[26] The State executed three breeders. Goats have had their genitals covered for the same reason. Most of the world's Muslims would not be offended by goat testicles and would find these fatwas to be farcical were there not seas of blood associated with them.[27]

But one Islamic intellectual begrudgingly concedes that the State has foundational Islamic elements. A columnist for the Arabic news network Al Arabiya said, "The Islamic State is as much a part of Islam as Baghdad, Cairo, Córdoba, and Damascus were during their golden ages as centers of learning and high culture."[28] Another Islamic reformer agreed, adding that the Caliphate expresses all that is wrong with contemporary Islam. "Too many young Muslims are attracted to blood, spears, and flying heads. ISIS is a loyal and bona fide implementation of our Islamic heritage, which is taught by Al-Azhar."[29]

Politics and the Islamic State—"Fascism with an Islamic Face"?

Of all the unanswered questions of our time,
perhaps the most important is: "What is fascism?"

—George Orwell, 1944[30]

We have to talk of Islamofascism.
The Islamic State wants to destroy everything.

—Patrick Pelloux, journalist for *Charlie Hebdo*[31]

Many Westerners try to place the Caliphate's political philosophy into a framework they can understand. It is not an easy fit. By no standards is it a part of Western liberalism, which extols personal liberty; free, fair, and contested elections; small government with limited governance; and equality before the law.[32] The Caliphate does not advocate these principles. Neither does it connect with communism, which is hostile to all religions.

But some observers see strong elements of fascism in the Caliphate's thinking. Almost always used derogatorily, the label "fascism" is hurled by pundits on the left and the right of the political spectrum, sometimes with imprecision. The late Christopher Hitchens, who coined the phrase "fascism with an Islamic face," offered a defense for the idiom in 2007. It could be applied to the Islamic State nearly a decade later. To the question "Does bin Ladenism or Salafism or whatever we agree to call it have anything in common with fascism?" Hitchens answered, "Yes."

In Hitchens's view, Salafism and fascism converge in cults of death that celebrate violence, nostalgia for a largely invented past, anti-Semitism, worship of leaders, and a loathing and intolerance for free expression. He concludes, "Technically, no form of Islam preaches racial superiority. But in practice, Islamic fanatics operate a fascistic concept of the 'pure' and the 'exclusive' over the unclean and the 'kufar,' or profane."[33]

Not all observers agree with this gloomy assessment. One former high-level American policymaker sees trace elements of humanity in the Islamic State and believes it can be reformed through compassion. She makes her case in Profile Five.

PROFILE FIVE: ROSA BROOKS— GAYS, COLLABORATORS, AND HUMANITY

"Send a Message"

Rosa Brooks is highly educated and accomplished. She writes on social issues, world affairs, and the Caliphate and helped guide legal policy in the early Obama administration. From April 2009 to June 2011, she served as policy counselor to the undersecretary of defense at the US Department of Defense.[34] An outspoken woman, Brooks is also an adviser to George Soros's Open Society Foundations. In her *Los Angeles Times* column, she recommended the involuntary incarceration of "George W. Bush and Dick Cheney [who] should be treated like psychotics who need treatment."[35] In her view, they are responsible for the creation of the Caliphate.

As a policy, Brooks opposes sending troops to fight in the Middle East. She has said it isn't America's feud, that regional powers are better suited to fight it, and that a US footprint would prompt new waves of anti-Americanism. Further, she is not convinced that Westerners have been any more humane than fighters of the State.[36] She reasons, "Consider the Roman games, the public burnings of heretics in England, the ritual violence of the Spanish Inquisition or the more than 15,000 enemies of the revolution sent to the guillotine during the reign of terror following the French Revolution. In the American South, lynchings of African Americans drew rowdy crowds well into the 20th century."[37]

Nonetheless, Brooks is optimistic about the world and convinced that people are fundamentally good and that things will work out well in the end. She declares, "Brutality and fear can keep people down for only so long. The Nazis learned this; the Soviets learned it; the Ku Klux

Klan learned it; Pol Pot learned it; the Rwandan génocidaires learned it. One of these days, the Islamic State and al Qaeda will learn it too."[38]

How will this lesson be learned in the Middle East? Brooks draws inspiration from a June 2015 US Supreme Court ruling extending full rights to homosexuals throughout America. She relishes the "joy . . . laughing . . . embracing and uncontained jubilation at their now-irrevocable rights to marry their same-sex loves."[39] And this celebration of homosexual freedom is Brooks's weapon of choice against the world's bigotry. She recommends sending pictures of gay marriages to "those masked gunmen in Iraq and Syria and to everyone else who gains power by sowing violence and fear."[40]

But not everyone is sure that this message will be persuasive any time soon. The Caliphate distributed its own pictures of homosexuals. On the same day Brooks posted her article on her foreign policy blog, black-clad Jihadists heaved four gay men off the roof of a tall building, killing them.[41] This, claimed the mullahs, was Sharia. They then posted pictures of their victims' mangled corpses on the internet as a warning to other gays to stay in the closet or join the dead. This was a very clear message, courtesy of the Caliphate.[42]

The Caliphate and Popular Culture

The Costs of Criticizing Islam—"Don't Let's Be Beastly"[43]

Western discussion of the Caliphate is often bounded by implicit and explicit rules of speech and unspoken assumptions of religious sensitivities. In the United States, there are legal protections for free speech. Americans can satirize any religion. The Supreme Court ruled in *Brandenburg v. Ohio* (1969) that only words that have "intent and the likelihood of inciting imminent violence or lawbreaking" can be restricted.[44] Nothing like this exists in Europe, where there are no legal assurances of unconstrained political or social commentary. All this makes an unfettered discussion of the State difficult.

At the end of the wars of religion, Western states, particularly those of Europe, developed a rich and often-tested tradition of lampooning religion. European theaters and salons held performances filled with religious stereotypes.[45] On stage, in song, and on paper, clerics, priests, and theologians were burlesqued.[46]

The satirical tradition continued well into the late twentieth century. But by the twenty-first century, lampooning Islam became uncomfortable, dangerous, and even lethal, particularly when the jokes involved the prophet Muhammad. By then, the number of Third World immigrants had swelled in Europe, and continental leaders had passed new laws or resurrected old ones to stifle criticism of Islam and Muslim leaders. Many of these changes were driven by demands of Muslims who had different understandings of satire, parody, slander, and blasphemy from their Western neighbors.[47]

Europeans have been arrested and fined for criticizing Islam. This stifles a full-throated discussion of the Caliphate. A Dane wrote, "The ideology of Islam is every bit as loathsome, nauseating, oppressive and dehumanizing as Nazism."[48] This candor cost him 1,600 kroner (the equivalent of about $250) in a criminal fine.[49] French prosecutors used a nineteenth-century law to charge a French journalist with the newspaper *Le Figaro* for comments he made in a radio debate about Islam.[50] In 2014, a British candidate for European parliament was arrested for quoting a passage from Winston Churchill's early book *The River War* describing the author's opinion of Muslims.[51]

Much more common than being arrested, fined, or imprisoned is being fired for insensitive comments. This leads to self-censorship. Eric Zemmour, the popular French political commentator, was fired from his job at a TV station.[52] As in Europe, many Americans are confused about the implicit speech codes and unspoken assumptions. While Americans cannot be imprisoned for objectionable political speech, they can be fired. Baseball great Curt Schilling was fired from a sports network for comments suggesting Islam was violent.[53]

Clever mathematics cost a German professor his job. At the Berlin School of Economics and Law, a statistician asked his students to calculate the rate of female genital mutilation in Egypt. He also asked his class to probe correlations between Muslims and acts of terrorism. An investigation on charges of racism began immediately. The professor's response: "I'm anti-Islamic as I am also anti-communist and anti-fascist."[54] He was fired.

Western media outlets censor themselves to avoid offending Muslims and sometimes fire those who give offense. Molly Norris, a Seattle-based cartoonist, obtained a notoriety that she neither expected nor wanted when she doodled sketches of Muhammad portrayed as household items. Meant in warm jest, Norris portrayed Muhammad as a cup of coffee, a spool of thread, and a tomato. But some Muslims thought that this was blasphemous, and they ordered her killed.[55] Her newspaper, the *Seattle Weekly*, fired her, and, in the words of one of her colleagues, she became a "ghost."[56]

US government agencies have redacted words, even those connected to mass murders, that might cast Islam in a bad light. For example, the FBI released a transcript of Florida killer Omar Mateen's conversation with law enforcement.[57] In the initial release of his oath to the

Islamic State and its leader, the FBI redacted the words "Abu Bakr al-Baghdadi" and "the Islamic State." The unredacted transcript read, "I pledge allegiance to Abu Bakr al-Baghdadi may God protect him [in Arabic], on behalf of the Islamic State."[58]

American media very gingerly describe terrorist attacks. The culprit of the Nice attack, Mohamed Lahouaiej-Bouhlel, was described by the *New York Times* as a "Frenchman of Tunisian origin" and not as a Muslim Frenchman. In the United States, ten Muslims who were convicted of providing material assistance to the Caliphate were identified as "Minnesota men." When describing Caliphate-endorsed attacks, particularly those committed by lone wolves, American media outlets add the qualifier "killer's motives, worldview not clear," just as the Associated Press described Lahouaiej-Bouhlel's attack.[59]

After a French priest was murdered at the altar of a Norman church in July 2016, media analyst Blain Tamrin examined same-day and early-next-day headlines of major media outlets and divided them into what he described as left- and right-oriented media.

Left-leaning outlets:
    Al Jazeera English—"Priest, 84, 'killed with blade' in French church attack"
    BBC—"Priest killed in French church attack"
    CNN—"Hollande: Deadly church attack in France carried out in name of ISIS"
    Deutsche Welle—"Hostage situation in French church"
    Huffington Post—"Police kill 2 attackers who took hostages in Normandy church"
    NY Times—"Attack on church in France kills priest, and ISIS is blamed"
    Washington Post—"French president: Church attackers were affiliated with ISIS"
Right-leaning outlets:
    Breitbart—"'Islamic State' chanting attackers 'behead' priest during morning mass in France"
    Fox News—"ISIS hit in France, attackers hit church, slit priest's throat during Mass"[60]

Tamrin underscored the nuanced differences in the headlines. In his judgment, the conservative outlets more directly confronted the Islamic element, while the outlets he designated as left-oriented tended to be more ambiguous and used the passive voice more frequently.

Other times, websites vanish. This was the case with the Facebook account of Stop the Islamization of America, a group with over 50,000 members,[61] run by the controversial Pamela Geller, a critic of Islam. The site was pulled on the day of the Orlando massacre.[62] Reddit censored coverage of the Florida killing in June 2016, even blocking requests for blood donors.[63] Facebook banned the page of gay magazine *Gaystream* after it published an article critical of Islam in the wake of the Orlando massacre.[64] Wikipedia plucked the Orlando shooting from the "Islamist Terror Attack" list because, in the words of its editor, "The fact that ISIL has, via their media agency, made such a claim does not make it true."[65]

Western artists feel the pressure to shy away from any Islamic themes. In spring 2016, the Royal Theater in Copenhagen scotched the proposed performance of *The Satanic Verses*, a play based on Salman Rushdie's provocative novel that set Islamic passions aflame throughout the world. Said Morten Kirkskov, head of the theater, "Fear played no role in our decision. It never crossed our mind." Some are skeptical.[66]

In 2015, there was an exhibit in London called *Passion for Freedom*. London artist "Mimsy" offered a lightbox tableau as artistic parable. It portrayed smiling hedgehogs, squirrels, and rabbits gamboling in a sylvan setting. Threatening on the border was a band of black-clad, weapons-toting, and scowling mice. The rodent terrorist group was called "MICE-IS."[67] Some viewers thought it was clever. The organizers of the event scrapped the exhibit because of "a number of serious concerns regarding the potentially inflammatory content."[68]

There have been British plays about the Caliphate, including *Another World: Losing Our Children to Islamic State*. Staged in London in 2016, the play was based on verbatim testimony of a cross section of Western politicians, diplomats, and Muslims.[69] But other plays are spiked. In London, one play wrestled with the attraction the Islamic State holds for young Britons. The play's theme and its aborted engagement speak volumes about the Eurabia–Islamophobia dispute, as discussed below.

PROFILE SIX: HOMEGROWN—
"OUR VOICES WERE SILENCED TODAY"

Artists have struggled with Islamic radicalism in Britain and with the popularity of the Caliphate. Many are fearful of Islam—period. A few British writers, such as Sir Salman Rushdie, have even been threatened with death. On the continent, some comics and critics have been killed and others have gone underground to survive. Nonetheless, men and women of letters have tried to put in print, on film, in song, or on stage the ambient European anxiety.

One play to grapple with the lure of the Caliphate was *Homegrown*, a reference to homegrown Islamic radicalization. It was a play about youth and was to be put on by the National Youth Theatre (NYT) in London.[70] Some famous actors have come out of NYT, including Dame Helen Mirren, Daniel Craig, Colin Firth, and Daniel Day-Lewis.[71]

The play billed itself as exploring the "stories and communities behind the headlines and the perceptions and realities of Islam and Muslim communities in Britain."[72] The play's creative team had been preparing for six months, and the cast of 112 was looking forward to opening night. But the play was canceled two weeks before the curtain was to rise. Why had it been scrapped?

A statement published in the *Guardian* read, "The production of *Homegrown* will no longer go ahead. After some consideration, we have come to the conclusion that we cannot be sufficiently sure of meeting all of our aims to the standards we set and which our members and audiences have come to expect. All purchased tickets will be fully refunded."[73]

Some saw this statement as bureaucratic babble. A Londoner who claimed to live in Bethnal Green and study drama said, "I don't know what causes teenagers to be radicalised and join Islamic State. But I do think it's important that we have a conversation about it. I call upon National Youth Theatre to reinstate *Homegrown*."[74] The writer and director accused the theater of "self-censorship," because NYT "feared controversy."[75] The Metropolitan Police denied any involvement in the cancelation.[76] Members of the cast were crestfallen, and they took to social media. One of the actors, Qasim Mahmood, tweeted: "Our voices were silenced today."[77]

Weaponized Humor

Some American leaders have turned to Hollywood to develop a propaganda strategy against the Caliphate. This action has precedent; presidents have partnered with movie studios to face an external enemy before,[78] including during World War II, when films boosted morale on the home front[79] and many celebrities went to war against the Axis powers. Three generations later, Hollywood is being recruited by the Obama administration to battle the Caliphate.[80] In February 2016, Secretary of State John Kerry turned to Hollywood producers, executives, and actors for strategic advice.[81]

Hollywood had some answers. The rock band U2's lead singer, Bono, long an advocate for political causes, suggested that the White House build a team including comedian Sacha Baron Cohen and others who connect with millennials. They would joke and make sarcastic comments about the Caliphate. But some are skeptical that that would make for effective propaganda. "Bono says fight extremism with comedy? Yeah Bono, like that worked for *Charlie Hebdo*."[82]

In Canada, a trio of Middle Eastern–raised Muslims host the *Weekly Show*, which lampoons hot issues in the Arab world, including sexual harassment and the Caliphate. One host explains, "Our message to young Muslims is that ISIS is using Islam in a sick way."[83]

Western civil servants look to undermine the popularity of the State by drawing in moderate Western Muslims. In Europe, some governments have subsidized anti-Caliphate popular culture. Belgian authorities funded a play entitled *Djihad*, in which three Belgian Muslims stumble their way to Syria to fight for a cause they don't understand. One of the militants is an Elvis impersonator. Belgian educators liked the play and subsidized its performance because young people thought it was funny.[84]

Elsewhere in Europe, government officials occasionally serve as talent scouts for entertainers who can keep the young away from the Caliphate. Britain's Humza Arshad is a popular Muslim comedian.[85] An eighteen-year-old woman explained that his popularity is a result of his warm empathy and wit. She said, "A lot of students look at police and think they don't know what they're talking about, or they don't see things from our perspective. But Humza . . . we've grown up watching him. He raises awareness in a way that we can understand."[86] For this reason, police have hired him to fight the attraction of the Caliphate.

In Britain, funny-lady Shazia Mirza used comedy in her acclaimed 2015 one-woman show, *The Kardashians Made Me Do It*,[87] in which she asks why so many young Western Muslim girls choose to run away to join the Islamic State. She crafted her script from public hearings of three teenage girls who left Britain for the Caliphate. Mirza was intrigued by what one of the girls took with her: "an epilator, a packet of new knickers, and body lotion. I thought, 'You're going to join a barbaric terrorist organization and you are thinking of your bikini line?'"[88]

In Germany, satirists had fun with the Green Party's focus on nonlethal force to stop the flurry of migrant violence. In one sketch, an actor dressed as a German police officer speaks to the camera, endorsing a new, nonlethal response to the random stabbings and machete slashings. He demonstrates a new tactic as a burly man, dressed in black and wielding a two-bladed axe, charges him. The police officer ducks, hugs his assailant, and says, "I love you."[89]

The Iraqi government promotes parody on national television. One sketch portrays a coy European-looking journalist, anticipating the interview of her life, asking Caliph Abu Bakr if he had slaughtered a sheep in her honor. He replies, "A sheep? I slaughtered 300 men in your honor."[90]

There is also far more stark satire, unlike anything presented in the West. A roaming band of avant-garde poets and activists travels to Iraqi towns reciting poetry in absurd situations. Wearing orange jumpsuits, they perform from a prisoners' cage, an ambulance, even body bags. The poets kneel down with their hands tied behind their backs and orate. They burlesque the killing fields of their homeland and taunt the Caliphate through verse in what has been called "poetry of the absurd."[91]

Cringe Humor, Gallows Humor, and Caliphate Humor

Some American comedians have fun with the Caliphate, too, but few joke about its Islamic component. It might be that they find nothing funny about Sharia or that they do not want to meet the fate of the French satirical cartoonists. A late-night entertainer, Bill Maher has been a leading celebrity critic of the Caliphate, but he often feels alone. He admits, "I just don't understand how liberals who fought the battle for civil rights in the '60s, fought against apartheid in the '80s, can then just simply ignore Sharia law in forty countries."[92] Milo Yiannopoulos, editor of the conservative Breitbart news outlet, said that it is "obscene that the political left . . . is happy to pander to and mollycoddle people that want me [referring to his homosexuality] dead . . . And I'm tired of being polite about it. . . . The problem is Islam."[93]

Some Caliphate-connected humor has panicked the audience. In May 2016, there was no laughing when guests at a swanky hotel in Cannes, France, fled for their lives after a boat with a black flag and six men landed on the Riviera. Guests at the tony Hotel Du Cap Eden-Roc scrambled, hid, prayed, and clutched each other while sneering men in commando dress and make-believe suicide vests roamed the area. But it turned out that this was a publicity stunt by a French internet startup company, which received the attention it wanted.[94]

Far from the Riviera, many suffer the reality wrought by the Islamic State. Some use humor as both an escape and a means of protest. Hundreds of thousands of displaced persons subsist in the haunts and despair of vast refugee camps in the Levant. Some are under attack from all sides of the conflict.[95] Mohammed is one of them, as shown below.

PROFILE SEVEN: SNICKERING FROM THE REFUGEE CAMP— "WE ALSO KILLED THE DENTISTS"

The unrelenting despondency of Caliphate-created refugee camps offers both opportunities and challenges for Syrian comics. An example of Mesopotamian cringe comedy comes from funnyman "Mohammed," a refugee who penned a yarn for an American audience. First he apologized for being late in blogging his heartbreak at the death of Cecil the Lion, who was killed by a wealthy American dentist on an African bow-hunting safari. The death of the feline made world news. Wrote Mohammed, "Not Cecil the Lion! Not him! Truly, is there no innocence left in this world?"[96]

Refugee Tent City in Syria

In thinly disguised mockery, Mohammed explained that he couldn't use his email to communicate his sorrow at the lion's death because Americans had bombed the local power plant, plunging his village into complete darkness. He wrote that he had had to walk for two days to reach an internet café, ducking fighters along the way, hopscotching over decomposing corpses of old friends, avoiding the blasts of Syrian barrel bombs, watching State soldiers decapitate boys, and wiping the tears off of the faces of girls who had had acid thrown at them. His journey was interrupted when "ISIS discovered my brother was gay and . . . they forced [me] to throw him off a building."[97] Mohammed then had to bury his daughter, who had died of cholera. He did not have to feed his wife because she had been carted off as a sex slave months ago.[98]

Mohammed could brave all of this. But the death of Cecil the Lion was too distressing to endure. Finally, stepping out of comedic character and now deadly serious, Mohammed wondered, "What is wrong with America?" and concluded, "You do not hear stories like this in Syria, partly because we already killed all our lions but also because we killed all our dentists."[99]

Academia—Coping with the Islamic State

Popular culture—movies, television, comedy, art, drama—has explored the Caliphate and so has academia. There have been myriad panels, discussion groups, speaking engagements, and resolutions passed on university campuses. Some see it as a campus craze. This is important because universities prepare future generations of journalists, public intellectuals, and scholars for leadership around the world. Professors and other intellectuals shape popular debate. On television, radio, the internet, and in social media, professors are a key source of informed comment regarding the Islamic State. Today's university students are tomorrow's political and cultural leaders.

Arguments about the Islamic State are often framed in a broader context of Western–Islamic relations. In universities' Middle East Studies and liberal arts departments, there is general agreement that Western policies have provoked Muslims around the world. Some of this consensus reflects the red-green campus alliance, which is an informal and confusing solidarity of left-oriented professors and Muslims. As discussed earlier, leftists and Islamists seem strange bedfellows, given their often-clashing views on women, homosexuality, religious piety, and some democratic norms, but both converge in Antonio Gramsci's concept of the establishment of a "cultural hegemony," and both are highly critical of existing Western values.[100]

Within this campus alliance, there is far-reaching agreement that Western foreign policy in the Middle East has been usually ill-advised, counterproductive, and often unjust. Many professors see the popularity of the Caliphate as an unintended consequence of American-led wars in Iraq and general American belligerence. These acerbic themes are underscored in academic publications, conferences, and campus-based advocacy. For example, according to celebrated American scholar Noam Chomsky, the root causes of the terrorist attacks in Paris were the invasions of Iraq and Afghanistan.[101]

This was also the case with Columbia professor Hamid Dabashi, who equated "ISIL's atrocities [with] Trump's vulgarities." The behaviors of both the Caliphate and the presidential aspirant were "pornotopic." Dabashi explained to al Jazeera that the word "pornotopic" refers to "the spatial formation of biopolitics in modernity, a dreadful exhibitionism transcending the false binaries we usually make between democracy and terrorism, between modern and medieval, between normative and barbaric."[102]

But other professors have rebuked the Caliphate. Yasir Qadhi (also spelled Kazi), an assistant professor at Rhodes College in Memphis, made clear, "ISIS does not represent my faith, their actions are in contradiction to my faith, and I'm appalled at what they are doing in the name of my faith."[103] Qadhi *literally* risked his life by making this statement. The Caliphate offered a reward, retrievable in the "afterlife," to anyone who kills him. Qadhi is now marked for death.

Many university professors who do not teach Middle East studies are confused about the Caliphate, and Joyce Carol Oates is one of them.

A perennial hopeful for the Nobel Prize and recipient of numerous prestigious literary awards, Oates—a novelist, professor, short-story writer, and literary critic—tried not to judge the Islamic State prematurely. Less than two weeks after the November 2015 Paris massacre, she asked, "All we hear of ISIS is puritanical & punitive; is there nothing celebratory & joyous? Or is query naïve?"[104] Salon-set sarcasm erupted immediately.[105] One responded, "Yes Joyce, they celebrate and find joy in killing, raping, beheading and mass-murdering 'infidels.' Got it now?"[106] But another blogger, Mortimer, had a more substantive and elevated response, citing verses of the Koran, the Hadith, and a canonized biography to demonstrate that Muhammad was "joyful" when his enemies were killed or tormented. The sacred verses include: "Muhammad smiled when loot was brought to him (Sahih Muslim 8.76.433); Muhammad smiled when he heard of the violent crimes of his companions (Ibn Ishaq, p. 502); Muhammad laughed violently when a prisoner was tortured (Al-Tabari, Vol. 7, p. 150); Muhammad smiled while slaves were beaten before him (Abu Dawud 10:1814)."[107]

University life has given opportunities to prankster activists. James O'Keefe, conservative provocateur, trained his sights on the academy. Pretending to be a Muslim, O'Keefe requested that Cornell University's assistant dean for students invite a Caliphate "freedom fighter" to lead a campus "training camp" under the cover of being a "sports camp." The dean agreed to allow this.[108] After the gag was revealed, O'Keefe opined that Cornell owed "people an apology, or at least an explanation."[109] But Cornell's president offered neither.[110]

At a similar sting at Catholic University, an undercover student journalist represented herself as a spokesperson for "Sympathetic Students in Support of the Islamic State of Iraq and Syria." She confided, "I want to start fundraising efforts on campus, and what I want to do is raise funds to send overseas." She was given sympathetic consideration.[111] At Barry College, a faculty adviser agreed to allow fund-raising for the Islamic State, too.[112]

This campus kerfuffle is typified by two scholars with clashing opinions. Both Mark LeVine and Daniel Pipes have much to say about the Caliphate and political Islam, as discussed below.

PROFILE EIGHT: HALLS OF IVY—
MARK LEVINE AND DANIEL PIPES: A GENERATION GAP
IN MIDDLE EAST STUDIES

Heavy Metal and the Caliphate

Mark LeVine, rock guitarist, activist, and associate professor at the University of California at Irvine, has made a reputation in the classroom and as a lead guitarist on the Middle Eastern rock-and-roll scene. The local newspaper, the *Orange County Register*, gushed that he was "a regional scholar fluent in the Bible and the Koran" and that he'd played with Mick Jagger and B. B. King. He has written ten books about the Middle East, one of which is *Heavy Metal Islam*, a travelogue of his academic and musical explorations from Morocco to Pakistan.[113]

The professor is also an activist. For over a decade, LeVine has tried to persuade American leaders "to declare a truce with the Muslim world and radical Islam, in particular."[114] He explained that "a truce . . . rather than an increasingly dangerous 'clash of civilizations,' is the only way to avoid a long, ultimately catastrophic conflict."[115]

LeVine is a regular commentator in Middle Eastern and American media. Why did Caliphate-endorsing Muslims kill *Charlie Hebdo* cartoonists? Some might find the professor's answer baffling: "Decades of the combined onslaught of extreme capitalism and extreme religion have shaped a necropolitics of the oppressed that is the mirror image of the necropolitics of local and Westerners governments, and the oppression and violence they've imposed."[116]

As for the Caliphate, he sees it as the "new resistance": "If world leaders don't want Chibok, Raqqa, or Mosul to be the new model for resistance, what are they prepared to do to foster a truly democratic, just, and sustainable model for the region, and the world?"[117] And the Islamic element of the State? "The Islamic State is as real a form of expression of Islam as the violent and chauvinist Israeli settler movement is to Judaism or as extreme Hindu nationalism, and militant Christianity are to their religions."[118]

Daniel Pipes—A Conservative

Daniel Pipes, also a scholar, has a different personal style and academic bent. The Harvard PhD is seventeen years older than LeVine.[119] He is the author of sixteen books and offers pro-American and pro-Israel viewpoints on Middle-Eastern affairs. He is a Republican and has advised Republican presidents, which is not the norm in academia today.[120]

His view on the Caliphate? He agrees with LeVine that the Caliphate's vitality reveals the failure of US policy, which cost the West thousands of lives and over a trillion dollars.[121] He critiques Republicans as having unfairly blamed the development of the Caliphate on President Obama. He writes, "This is basically a Middle Eastern problem and outside powers should aim to protect their own interests, not solve the Middle East's crises. Tehran, not we, should fight ISIS."[122]

But Pipes would not agree with LeVine that the Caliphate is a bent, twisted, and largely unrecognizable version of Islam. Pipes asserts, "Anyone with eyes and ears realizes that ISIS, like the Taliban and Al-Qaeda before it, is 100 percent Islamic. Over time, they are increasingly relying on common sense to conclude that ISIS is indeed profoundly Islamic."[123]

Campus Activism and the Caliphate

In Europe, many universities are aflame with hatred of the West and support for the Caliphate. In the United Kingdom, Islamists trapeze between campuses, assailing Western norms and advocating for Sharia. When speaking to largely Islamic audiences on campus, students and instructors have advocated female genital mutilation and stoning.[124] Apologists for the Caliphate are common on campus, and a string of student bodies have refused to participate in the government's antiextremism strategy.[125]

Unsurprisingly, British and continental universities are rich environs for the Caliphate's recruiting. Some Western students and professors neither support nor condemn the Caliphate. The British National Union of Students (NUS) refused to pass a motion condemning the State on the grounds that to do so would be, in its words, "Islamophobic."[126] The activist who helped spike that resolution became president of the NUS in mid-2016. The first black female Muslim president of the NUS said that condemning "ISIS would be blatant Islamophobia."[127] The NUS comprises 600 student organizations with a student population of more than seven million.

In Western universities, professors of Middle East Studies are often reluctant to condemn the Islamic State without also criticizing the West. They offer guarded and equivocal explanations for Caliphate-directed or -inspired attacks in the West, such as the killing in San Bernardino. The director of Duke University's Islamic Studies Center decried America's "deadly fetish" and "gun obsession."[128]

The Western Working Class and the Caliphate

Far from the Ivy League and Oxbridge, the common man and woman are afraid. Many Americans did not know how to respond or how to prepare themselves after the killing sprees in cities as distant from each other and as culturally diverse as Paris, San Bernardino, Orlando, Fort Hood, Brussels, and Nice and the many other venues of butchery. Republican presidential candidate Donald Trump called for a "total and complete" ban on Muslims entering the United States "until our country's representatives can figure out what is going on."[129] Some look to firearms for protection. In Sweden, demand for firearms licenses is increasing and memberships in shooting clubs are soaring.[130] After the

2016 New Year's Eve mass sexual molestations, German stores cannot keep pepper spray in stock; they are sold out as soon as a new shipment arrives. Worried adolescent girls and young women are enrolling in self-defense classes.[131] Gun sales in the United States, too, have climbed. A feisty Florida gun-shop owner declared his property to be a "Muslim-free zone." In his view, Muslims overwhelmingly support the Islamic State. "I'm not going to be politically correct."[132] He said that he was prepared for lawsuits, and he got them.

A Missouri educator has a similar view and published an Islamic State coloring book. Wayne Bell insists the book *ISIS: A Culture of Evil* shows the world "the hideous reality" in which the terrorists live.[133] The images depict genocide, "people thrown off buildings, kids recruited, and women and children about to be killed."[134] It includes color-ins of the now-deceased Jihadi John and of gay people being thrown off roofs.[135]

Many Westerners simply want to avoid the Caliphate controversy, and some business owners are caught in the political crossfire. One owner of a Denver book-and-gift store had his property repeatedly vandalized in 2015. Specializing in spirituality items, Isis Books & Gifts was named after the Egyptian goddess of healing.[136] A British lingerie chain, Ann Summers, was similarly caught off guard. A spokesperson issued an apology for releasing a line of sexy underwear under the name "Isis." The erotic items included black-and-white bras and thongs, the colors of the Caliphate's flag.[137]

Summary

The drama of the Islamic State is alive in Western popular culture. In academia, the Middle East bursts with controversy, and scholars and students try to understand what drives the Islamic State. Many professors with scarlet leanings argue that ISIS's agenda is largely a response to the West's predatory and cruel history in the Middle East. Other social leaders caution against conflating radical Islam with peaceful Islam. David Petraeus, former director of the CIA, opined, "The terrorists' explicit hope has been to try to provoke a clash of civilizations—telling Muslims that the United States is at war with them and their religion."[138] Some public intellectuals defend the West and criticize values that underplay the element of Islam in the State's agenda and falsely blame the West, largely America, for the Caliphate's savagery.[139]

Notes

1. Christian Wilhelm Kindleben, Gaudeamus Igitur—English Translation, http://www.users.on.net/~algernon/gaudeamus/translation.html.

2. Some historians were not convinced by President Obama's historical analogy. "I don't think the president knows very much about the crusades," Thomas Madden, a historian at the University of St. Louis said. "Even Simon, Historians Weigh In on Obama's Comparison of ISIS Militants to Medieval Christian Crusaders," *Yahoo News*, February 6, 2015, http://abcnews.go.com/Politics/historians -weigh-obamas-comparison-isis-militants-medieval-christian/story?id=28787194.

3. "Kerry Brands ISIS 'Apostates,'" *The Daily Star* (Lebanon), February 6, 2016.

4. Johanna Markind, "DHS and the Dearborn Muslim Community: A Relationship on the Rocks?" *American Thinker*, February 6, 2016.

5. "The Center for the Study of Islam & Democracy Holds a Discussion on ISIS," *Political Transcript Wire*, March 6, 2016.

6. Reyhan Guner, "Interview with Professor John Esposito: On ISIS, the Middle East, and Terrorism," *Journal of Turkish Weekly*, October 24, 2014.

7. For a comprehensive study on this topic, read Martin Kramer (Washington, DC: Washington Institute for Near East Policy Publication, 2001). A review to read is Robert D. Kaplan and Patrick Clawson, "Ivory Towers on Sand: The Failure of Middle Eastern Studies in America (Brief Article)," *Middle East Quarterly*, Spring 2002.

8. Manuel Valls, "There Is 'No Reason' to Grant French Citizenship to Tariq Ramadan," *Morocco World News*, May 22, 2016.

9. Guy Benson, "Hillary: Muslims 'Have Nothing Whatsoever to Do with Terrorism,'" *Townhall*, November 20, 2015.

10. Denis Staunton, "Two Sides Lay Out Cases over Military Action in 10-Hour Commons Debate; Cameron Describes ISIS as 'Woman-Raping, Muslim-Murdering, Medieval Monsters,'" *The Irish Times*, December 3, 2015.

11. David Cameron, "This Is Not Islam; It's a Perverted Ideology and We Must Fight It," *Times of Israel*, June 26, 2015.

12. "Obama: Stigmatizing Muslims 'Plays into Hands' of Jihadists," *AFP*, March 26, 2016.

13. "West's Willful Bias against Islam," *Arab News* (Jeddah, Saudi Arabia), February 27, 2015.

14. Andrew Desiderio, "SNL's 60 Minutes Lampoons Obama's ISIS Response and Secret Service," *Mediaite*, October 4, 2014, http://www.mediaite.com/tv/snls -60-minutes-lampoons-obamas-isis-response-and-secret-service-failures/.

15. Charlie Peat, "Islam Inspires ISIS Fanatics to Commit Horrific Terror Attacks, BBC Religion Chief Claims," *Express*, June 2, 2016.

16. Bernard Haykel and William McCants, May 2015 Faith Angle Forum, Ethnic and Public Policy Center, accessed June 19, 2015, https://eppc.org/programs /the-faith-angle-forum/.

17. On June 30, 2014, Abu Bakr Al-Baghdadi declared a caliphate. The group considers itself a sovereign political entity that dispenses law and order, health

care, welfare, education, religion, and more, according to Sharia law, in the areas it controls in Iraq and Syria.

18. Robert Spencer, "Muslim Leader Says Muhammad Protected Rights of Christians, Ignores His Persecution of Them," *Jihad Watch*, August 28, 2015.

19. Michael Copeland, from Robert Spencer, "US Envoy: To Defeat the Islamic State, We Must 'Tell the Story of How We Celebrate Islam,'" *Jihad Watch*, October 14, 2014.

20. Raymond Ibrahim, "ISIS: The Latest Phase of the Jihad," *Strategika*, February 1, 2016.

21. Mehdi Hasan, "How Islamic Is Islamic State?" *New Statesman*, March 13, 1996.

22. Youtube.com/watch?v=rOCnw-nVoGY, December 3, 2014.

23. For example, State soldiers split a woman in two with cars. They tied the hands of one woman to the back of a car and her legs to another car and they split her into two. In several other Islamic countries there are beheadings.

24. "'They put women and children under the ground,' he said. 'They were alive. I still hear their screams.'" "Report: Islamic State (ISIS/ISIL) Split Woman in Two with Cars, Buries . . .," September 12, 2014. . . . IS, ISIL. "Report: ISIS Terrorists Split Woman in Two with Cars, Bury Yazidis Alive." Pamela Geller, "Report: Islamic State Split Woman in Two with Cars, Buries non-Muslims Alive," September 12, 2014, http://pamelageller.com/2014/09/report-islamic-state-isisisil-split-woman-two-cars-bury-non-muslims-alive.html/.

25. "Daesh Beheads 2 Women in Syria," *AFP*, June 30, 2015.

26. John Hall and Robert Verkaik, "ISIS Bans Pigeon Breeding—Punishable by Public Flogging—Because Seeing Birds' Genitals Overhead Offends Islam," *Mail Online*, June 2, 2015.

27. Yaron Steinbuch, "Musicians Beaten by ISIS Religious Police for "Un-Islamic" Instruments," *Daily Mail Online*, January 20, 2015.

28. Hisham Melhem, "Keeping Up with the Caliphate: An Islamic State for the Internet Age," *Foreign Affairs* 94, no. 6 (November 2015): 148–153.

29. "Egyptian Researcher Ahmad Abdou Maher: ISIS Implements Islamic Heritage Taught by Al-Azhar," *MEMRi*, December 21, 2015.

30. George Orwell, "What is Fascism?," *The Tribune*, 1944, http://www.orwell.ru/library/articles/As_I_Please/english/efasc.

31. Roger Cohen, "The Char Lie War," *Vanity Fair* 57, no. 8 (August, 2015): 84.

32. Barbara Bennet, "Liberalism and its Discontents (Review)" *Presidential Studies Quarterly*, June 1, 1999.

33. "In Defence of the Term 'Islamofascism.'" *Winnipeg Free Press*, October 24, 2007.

34. Rosa Brooks, "Author, Law Professor and National Security & Foreign Policy Expert" (blog).

35. John McCormack, "DoD Hires LA Times Columnist Who Belittled Al Qaeda Threat," *Weekly Standard*, April 16, 2009.

36. Rosa Brooks, "It's Had Some Military Success, but the Islamic State Is No Existential Threat," April 16, 2015.

37. "Jessica Stern and J. M. Berger Explore the Origins and Tactics of the Group in a Bid to Understand Its Future," *The Washington Post*, 2015.

38. Rosa Brooks, "Can Gay Marriage Defeat the Islamic State? A Few—Admittedly Sappy—Thoughts on the Power of #LoveWins," *Foreign Policy*, June 26, 2015.

39. Rosa Brooks, "Can Gay Marriage Defeat the Islamic State? A Few—Admittedly Sappy—Thoughts on the Power of #LoveWins," *Foreign Policy*, June 26, 2015.

40. Robert Spencer, "Foreign Policy Think Tweeting Photos of Gay Marriage Supporters Will Defeat the Islamic State," *Jihad Watch*, June 27, 2015.

41. "Jessica Stern, the executive director of the International Gay and Lesbian Human Rights Commission, told the [United Nations] council that courts established by ISIS in Iraq and Syria claimed to have punished sodomy with stoning, firing squads and beheadings and by pushing men from tall buildings." "Islamic State Has Killed at Least 30 People for Sodomy, UN Told," *The Guardian*, accessed August 25, 2015.

42. "It has been suggested that the Islamic extremists flung four men from a rooftop before allowing them to plunge to their deaths to 'celebrate' the occasion." Jamie Lewis, "Horrific Moment ISIS Kill Four Gay Men by Throwing Them from a Roof," *Mirror*, June 27, 2015.

43. "Don't Let's Be Beastly to the Germans" was a satirical World War II song written by Noel Coward in 1943 about proposed treatment of Germans. It was banned by the BBC.

44. Lindsay Wise and Jonathan Landa, "After Texas Shooting: If Free Speech Is Provocative, Should There Be Limits?," *McClatchy*, May 4, 2015.

45. Philip M. Soergel, "Scheming Papists and Lutheran Fools: Five Reformation Satires," *Renaissance Quarterly*, December 22, 1995.

46. A. J. Caschetta, "Humor Could Be an Effective Weapon," *South Florida Sun*, May 23, 2016.

47. For many in the West, "slander" refers to false comments about someone. The truth is the absolute defense, as ruled by the Supreme Court in a succession of cases from the *John Peter Zenger* case of 1734 through the *Hustler Magazine v. Falwell* case of 1988. In European and Commonwealth countries, slander is more plaintiff-friendly.

48. Sheikyermami, "The Ideology of Islam Is Every Bit As Loathsome, Nauseating, Oppressive and Dehumanizing As Nazism" *Winds of Jihad*, http://sheikyermami.com/2016/02/the-ideology-of-islam-is-every-bit-as-loathsome-nauseating-oppressive-and-dehumanizing-as-nazism/.

49. "Blasphemy: Denmark Fines Citizen for Facebook Post That Was Critical of Islam," *The Rebel*, February 13, 2016.

50. Peter Allen, "French Journalist Is Prosecuted Under Nineteenth-Century Press Law for Questioning Islam during a Radio Debate," *Daily Mail*, October 9, 2013.

51. The young Churchill's scathing commentary about Islam in the Sudan in the late nineteenth century was deemed hate speech in the early-twenty-first

century. Muslims in Weston's audience called the police, and Weston was taken to jail and booked. Weston quoted Churchill: "Improvident habits, slovenly systems of agriculture, sluggish methods of commerce, and insecurity of property exist wherever the followers of the Prophet rule or live. . . . No stronger retrograde force exists in the world. Far from being moribund, Mohammedanism is a militant and proselytizing faith." Roland Quinault, "Churchill and Black Africa: Roland Quinault Examines the Career, Speeches and Writings of Churchill for Evidence as to Whether or Not He Was Racist and Patronizing to Black Peoples," *History Today*, June 1, 2015.

52. Eric Zemmour is the author of *The French Suicide*, which rocked the charts by lambasting both Muslims and federal bureaucrats. According to Zemmour, the decline of France began in 1968 and was accelerated by immigration and homosexuality. Benjamin Haddad, "New Charlie Hebdo Book Blames Victims: An Inane Essay by a Radical Left-Wing French Writer Claims Supporters of Charlie Hebdo Are Essentially Islamophobic Fascists," *The Daily Beast* (New York), October 18, 2015.

53. He tweeted, "It's said only 5–10% of Muslims are extremists. In 1940, only 7% of Germans were Nazis. How'd that go?" That tweet got him immediately fired by ESPN, despite his offering a public apology. Des Bieler, "Curt Schilling Removed from ESPN Baseball Coverage for the Rest of the Regular Season," *Washington Post*, September 3, 2015.

54. Chris Tomilson, "German Maths Professor Fired Over Islam Criticism," Brietbart.com, May 29, 2016, http://www.breitbart.com/london/2016/05/29 /german-maths-professor-fired-over-islam-criticism/.

55. "Dueling Fatwas; War Comes Home in the Internet Era," *The Washington Times*, October 5, 2010.

56. Jack Cashill, "First They Came for Molly Norris," *WND*, January 7, 2015.

57. Joel B. Pollack, "Loretta Lynch: Islam ISIS to be Scrubbed from Orlando 911 Tapes," *Breitbart*, June 19, 2016.

58. "Breaking: DOJ Releases Unredacted Transcript after Criticism," *The Right Scoop*, June 20, 2016.

59. "Name the Enemy: Jihadis Are Driven by a Twisted View of Islam," *Pittsburgh Post-Gazette*, July 24, 2016.

60. Blain Tamrin, "How Do News Outlets from Around the World Identify Jihadi Murder in Their Headlines," *Jihad Watch*, July 27, 2016.

61. Allum Bokhari, "Facebook Deletes Pamela Geller's 'Stop Islamization of America' Page after Orlando Attack," *Breitbart*, June 12, 2016.

62. Pamela Geller, "Facebook Removes "Stop Islamization of America" (SIOA) Page in Wake of Gay Jihad Slaughter in Orlando," June 12, 2016.

63. "Reddit Censorship," *Jihad Watch*, June 13, 2016.

64. Chris Tomlinson, "Facebook Bans Gay Magazine Critical of Islam," *Breitbart*, June 17, 2016.

65. Lucas Nolan, "Wikipedia Removes Orlando Shooting from 'Islamist Terror Attack' List," *Breitbart*, June 30, 2016.

66. "Copenhagen Caves In: Danes Cancel 'Satanic Verses' Play to Please Muslims," *Sputnik*, May 26, 2016.

67. Claire Armitstead, "Artwork Showing Sylvanian Families Terrorised by ISIS Banned from Free Speech Exhibition," *Guardian*, September 26, 2015.

68. Ibid.

69. Matt Wolf, "Harold Pinter and Tracy Letts Revivals, and ISIS on Stage in London," *New York Times*, May 6, 2016.

70. Matthew Hemley, "Revealed: The Unseen NYT Email That Shut Down ISIS Play Homegrown," *The Stage*, September 3, 2015, https://www.thestage.co.uk/news/2015/revealed-unseen-nyt-email-shut-isis-play-homegrown/.

71. Hannah Ellis-Petersen, "Immersive Play in East London School to Explore Motives of Radicalised Youth," *The Guardian*, June 2, 2015.

72. Ibid.

73. Hannah Ellis-Petersen, "Controversial Isis-related play cancelled two weeks before opening night," *The Guardian*, August 4, 2015.

74. Kristian Carter, "Reinstate the ISIS-Related Play, Homegrown," *Change.org*, accessed August 18, 2015, https://www.change.org/p/ucl-academy-north-london-reinstate-the-isis-related-play-homegrown.

75. Jay Akbar, "Theatre Accused of Self-Censorship after It Cancelled Play about Radicalised Muslims Which Explored Why Youngsters Are Attracted to Extremist Groups," *Mailonline*, August 15, 2015.

76. David Huthchison, "Police Deny Role in NYT ISIS Play Cancellation," *The Stage*, August 7, 2015.

77. "Play Exploring Radicalisation of Young Muslims Axed Two Weeks before Opening," *East End Review*, August 5, 2015.

78. Kirk Baird, "Hollywood War Movies Have Ranged from Pro to Con," *Las Vegas Sun Post-Tribune* (Indiana), March 28, 2003.

79. "Private Ryan to Rank among War Movies," *Post-Tribune* (Indiana), August 9, 1998.

80. Jim Korkis, "The Story Behind 'Der Fuehrer's Face,'" *Jim Hill Media*, accessed February 27, 2016, http://jimhillmedia.com/alumni1/b/wade_sampson/archive/2004/04/19/1219.aspx.

81. Brenda Gazzar, "John Kerry Turns to Hollywood for Help Fighting ISIS," *Daily News* (Los Angeles, CA), February 16, 2016.

82. "The Funforgettable Fire; Bono Says Send Schumer, Rock and Baron Cohen to Fight ISIS with Jokes," *The Mirror* (London), April 14, 2016.

83. Chris Cobb, "Students' Online Show Opens Satrice Front Against Jihadists," *Ottawa Citizen*, November 7, 2015.

84. Teri Shultz, "A Belgian Playwright Tackles Muslim Radicalization with Comedy," *NPR Weekend Edition*, January 17, 2016.

85. Charlie Rose, "This Morning Police in Britain Have a New Tool in Their Struggle against a Wave of Young People Joining ISIS," *CBS This Morning*, April 23, 2015.

86. Griff Witte, "Muslim Comedian's Anti-Extremist Message a Big Hit with British Teens," April 1, 2015; "Humza Arshad Has Become Britain's Most Potent New Force in the War with the Islamic State for Hearts and Minds," *The Washington Post*, April 1, 2015.

87. "Laughter Helps Us Learn," *The Western Morning News*, February 27, 2016.

88. Homa Khaleeli, "Shazia Mirza: 'Look at Me—ISIS Would Stone Me to Death," *Guardian*, August 18, 2015.

89. Baron Bodissey, "A Kinder, Gentler German Police Force," *Gates of Vienna*, July 23, 2016, accessed July 24, 2016, http://gatesofvienna.net/2016/07/a-kinder -gentler-german-police-force/.

90. Audie Cornish, "Anti-ISIS Satire Lampoons Militant Group's Hypocrisy," *All Things Considered*, November 10, 2014.

91. "Poets' Militia" Relives Victims' Plight While Reciting Anti-ISIS Poetry," *Mayadeen TV* (Lebanon), November 24, 2015.

92. Daniel Nussbaum, "Bill Maher: Liberals Protested Apartheid in One Country, Ignore Sharia in 40 Countries," *Breitbart*, February 10, 2016.

93. Charlie Spierling, "Milo Fires US Trump Supporters in Cleveland," *Breitbart*, July 18, 2016.

94. Selina Sykes, "Terror in Cannes: A-List Guests Flee as Masked Men Wear 'Suicide Vests' in Sick Stunt," *Express (Online)*, May 14, 2016, http://www.express .co.uk/news/world/670337/Cannes-terror-scare-France-Cannes-Film-Festival -ISIS-sick-stunt-Paris-attacks.

95. Luc Mathieu, "Tension, Paranoia Grows in ISIL's Syrian Stronghold of Al-Raqqah," *Paris Liberation Online*, September 17, 2015: 4–5.

96. I Will Always Remember Where I Was When Cecil the Lion Was Killed," Duffel (blog), August 3, 2015, http://www.duffelblog.com/2015/08/will-always -remember-cecil-lion-killed/.

97. I Will Always Remember Where I Was When Cecil the Lion Was Killed," Duffel (blog), August 3, 2015, http://www.duffelblog.com/2015/08/will-always -remember-cecil-lion-killed/.

98. Ibid.

99. Ibid.

100. William Pfaff, "American 'Hegemony'? The Influence Has to Be Welcome," *International Herald Tribune*, May 12, 1997.

101. Noam Chomsky, "Paris Attacks Are Result of Western Policies in Middle East," *FARS News Agency*, December 14, 2015.

102. "How is this related to anything pornographic? All these symptoms point to a psychopathological condition characterized by the compulsion to display one's genitals in public to mark contested territories and claim virulent domination." Hambid Dabashi, "Pornotopia: From ISIL to Donald Trump," *Al Jazeera Online*, September 3, 2015, http://www.aljazeera.com/indepth/opinion/2015/08 /pornotopia-isil-donald-trump-150830125017487.html.

103. Kaitlyn Schallhorn, "ISIS Targets U.S. Professors for Condemning Charlie Hebdo Terror Attacks Campus Reform," March 2, 2015, http://www.campus reform.org/?ID=6325.

104. Daniel Victor and Joyce Carol Oates on Twitter, *New York Times*, November 23, 2015.

105. A *New York Times* blogger parodied the professor: "All we hear about the Khmer Rouge is the massacres, the re-education camps, the piles of skulls; was there 'celebratory' in beginning society anew, with fewer intellectuals and bespectacled people?" Unknown blogger in Ross Douthat, "The Joy of ISIS," *New York Times*, November 23, 2015.

106. Robert Spencer and Joyce Carol Oates, "Is There Nothing Celebratory & Joyous about ISIS," *Jihad Watch*, November 24, 2015.

107. Mortimer also offered several canonized verses that illustrate Muhammad's sense of humor on lighter, nonviolent themes: Muhammad smiled when his wives fought one another (Sahih Muslim 31:6131); Muhammad laughed after telling a woman to suckle an adult male (Sahih Muslim 8:3424); Muhammad laughed when someone drank his own urine by mistake (Al-Tabari 39:199). Mortimer for Robert Spencer and Joyce Carol Oates: "Is There Nothing Celebratory & Joyous about ISIS," *Jihad Watch*, November 24, 2015.

108. Carl Campanile, "Cornell Dean Says ISIS Welcome on Campus in Undercover Video," *New York Post*, March 24, 2015.

109. "ISIS Club at Cornell? School Official Supports Inclusive Club for Terrorists," *Ben Shapiro's Truth Revolt*, March 25, 2015.

110. Eric Owens, "Cornell U. President Defends Dean Who Encouraged Campus ISIS Club, Charges Trickery," *Daily Beast*, March 27, 2015.

111. David Martosko, "Catholic University Officials Caught on Secret Video Approving Student Club Devoted to Raising Money for ISIS, Saying: 'We're Here to Get That Done,'" *Daily Mail*, March 30, 2015.

112. Ibid.

113. He quotes a founder of the Moroccan heavy-metal scene: "We play heavy metal because our lives are heavy metal," *Heavy Metal Islam* homepage. Mark LeVine, "Heavy Metal Islam: Rock, Resistance, and the Struggle for the Soul of Islam," Audible, May 15, 2012, https://www.amazon.com/Heavy-Metal-Islam-Resistance-Struggle/dp/B0083LJ7WK.

114. Mark LeVine, "Why Charlie Hebdo Attack Is Not about Islam," *Al Jazeera*, January 10, 2015.

115. Robert Spencer, "Mark Levine: Noam Chomsky as Rock Star," *Frontpage Magazine*, December 7, 2004.

116. Mark LeVine, "Why Charlie Hebdo Attack Is Not about Islam," *Al Jazeera*, January 10, 2015.

117. Ibid.

118. Cinnamon Stillwell, "Pros Blame ISIS on 'Islamophobia' and 'Grievances,'" *Frontpage Magazine*, November 25, 2014.

119. Pipes has taught at Harvard, Pepperdine, the US Naval War College, and the University of Chicago. He has served in various capacities in the US government. For the purposes of full disclosure, the author (Silinsky) has written several book reviews for Pipe's publication *Middle East Quarterly*.

120. Pipes founded the Middle East Forum (MEForum.org), an independent 501©3 organization, in 1994. The forum has a US$4 million annual budget. Its mission is promoting American interests through publications, research, media outreach, and public education. It publishes the *Middle East Quarterly* and sponsors *Campus Watch*, *Islamist Watch*, *The Legal Project*, and *The Washington Project*. Daniel Pipes, "Biography on Dr. Pipes," *Middle East Forum*, accessed June 25, 2015, http://www.meforum.org/.

121. The fancy façade of $53 billion in American-sponsored institutions, from failed hospitals to the Iraqi National Symphony, have been exposed as the fiascos they are. Images of ISIS soldiers standing triumphant atop US-supplied military

equipment brings home the folly of once-high American hopes for "a stable, democratic, and prosperous Iraq." Daniel Pipes, "ISIS Rampages, the Middle East Shakes," *National Review Online*, June 12, 2014, http://www.danielpipes.org /14473/isis-iraq-mosul.

122. Ibid.

123. Daniel Pipes, "ISIS Is Not Islamic?," Cross-posted from *National Review Online, The Corner*, September 10, 2014. http://www.danielpipes.org/blog/2014 /09/isis-is-not-islamic.

124. In 2014, on British campuses, Saleem Chagtai, who equated apostasy with "treason," and Yusuf Chambers, who "supports the death penalty for homosexuality," spoke to applauding students. Azzam Tamini described suicide bombing as "a noble cause" and added "the Koran tells me if I die for my homeland, I'm a martyr, and I long to be a martyr." Asim Qureshi made statements that *Sharia Watch* have called "direct incitement to engage in acts of terror." Qureshi called upon all Muslims to "support the jihad of our brothers and sisters" when they are "facing the oppression of the west." "Learning Jihad: New Report on Campus Extremism Has Launch Event Cancelled by the University of West London," *States News Service*, November 11, 2014.

125. Moore Fraser, "Muslim Preacher Who 'Said Husbands Should Hit Their Wives' Allowed to Tour UK Universities," *Express*, January 9, 2016.

126. Neither did a neighboring university vote to commemorate the annihilation of Europe's Jews. Goldsmiths University's student assembly in London rejected a motion to commemorate Holocaust Memorial Day by a margin of 60–1. Elliot Friedland, "UK National Union of Students Votes Not to Condemn ISIS," *Clarion Project*, October 21, 2014.

127. Lea Speyer, "Threatening to Break Ties with National Student Union over New President Accused of Antisemitism, Supporting ISIS," *Algemeiner*, April 22, 2016.

128. Cinnamon Stillwell, "Academia on San Bernardino Attack: No Jihad Here," *Campus Watch*, December 11, 2015.

129. "Donald J. Trump Statement on Preventing Muslim Immigration," (Press release) Donald J. Trump for President, December 7, 2015.

130. Nicholai Sennels, "Post-migrant Sweden: 'For the First Time, I Feel Scared to Live Here Now,'" *Jihad Watch*, December 15, 2015.

131. Marc Geppert, "Germany's Secret Islamic Horror: How Blind Elites Are Destroying a Once-Great Nation," *Brietbart*, July 17, 2016.

132. Kim Bellware, "Anti-Islamic Gun Shop Owner Offers 9/11 'Muslim' Discount, the Shop Owner Says People Need Guns to 'Combat Islam,'" *The Huffington Post*, September 14, 2015.

133. The book is available at ColoringBook.com.

134. Mary Chastain, "ISIS: A Culture of Evil' Adult Coloring Book Shows 'Hideous Reality' of Terrorists," Breitbart.com, November 2015, http://www .breitbart.com/big-government/2015/11/12/isis-culture-evil-adult-coloring-book -shows-hideous-reality-terrorists/.

135. Mary Chastain, "'ISIS: A Culture of Evil' Adult Coloring Book Shows 'Hideous Reality' of Terrorists," *Breitbart*, November 12, 2015.

136. "Colorado Spirituality Bookstore Named Isis Vandalized," *AP World-stream*, November 18, 2015.

137. David Harding, New York Daily News, August 23, 2014 August 26, 2014, http://www.nydailynews.com/news/world/ann-summers-lingerie-line-isis -draws-fire-linked-terror-article-1.1914235.

138. Jonah Bennett, "David Petraeus; Be Nice to Muslims, or They Might Blow Us Up," *The Daily Caller*, May 13, 2016.

139. Abraham H. Miller, "Academic Apologists for ISIS Blame America [incl. Sherene Seikaly and Adam Sabra]," *The Washington Times*, June 15, 2015.

4. BLUE-EYED JIHAD: THE CALIPHATE'S FOREIGN LEGION, PART ONE

Introduction

Earlier chapters set the background to examine foreign fighters. Chapter 4 explains the draw of the Caliphate. Who is an average foreign fighter? A think tank with the US Military Academy at West Point processed 4,000 captured records of foreign fighters. The average age was twenty-six, but the age range went from teenagers to men in their sixties. Many were uneducated, but several had advanced degrees. About 60 percent were single, but some were married with families. A third had gone to high school, and a quarter had some college education. Most are laborers.[1]

Westerners have heard the Caliphate's call and have come by the thousands. There are three basic draws to the State—utopia, Jihad, and psychosocial factors.

Black Utopia—Heaven on Earth

I left to build us all a house in heaven, Allah promised us heaven if we sacrifice our world life. . . . I'm not coming back.

—A London-raised mother writing from Raqqa, October 2014[2]

Some European foreign fighters go to the Middle East to build a paradise. Well-to-do as well as out-of-luck Western Muslims see limitless prospects in a society they can help create. The world they envision is ordained and described by Allah as the perfect society. It is an Islamic utopia, a heaven on earth.

Other religions and civilizations have imagined perfect worlds. In his 1516 masterwork, Thomas More wrote of a pretend island named Utopia, translated as "happy land." Its upbeat citizens dressed plainly, eat communally, and owned no private property.[3] A darker utopic vision was crafted in the steamy, disease-ridden jungles of Paraguay in 1886. New Germany was to be protected from the contaminants of modernity, materialism, and racial spoilation.[4] But it collapsed, and little remains today but a scattering of German family names and Nordic appearances in South American jungles.[5] The Islamic State's philosophy bears little resemblance to these societies. However, it shares some characteristics of totalitarian dystopias of the 1930s and 1940s: the Soviet Union and the Third Reich.

Three Utopias

Like the Soviets and Nazis, today's Islamist State adherents see their utopia as void of significant political or social faults. The Soviets sought to build a workers' paradise of equally divided goods and services. They saw the major defects in the world the result of unfair distribution of national and political wealth. The Nazis' paradise was to build on the foundations of a pseudoscience of race.[6] As with the Soviets, the Nazis envisioned a society in which its citizens would enjoy health care, education, nutrition, and wealth.

All three philosophies are atavistic. Like the Marxists and Nazis, Jihadists want to eliminate the roots of war and to re-create elements of a largely mythical past. The Caliphate hopes to return to a period of "rightly guided" Muslims, which is the first generation of Muslims. Though embellished by modern technology, it would be a socially primitive society in which all human activity is circumscribed by Islamic law and Koranic revelation.[7] A young Indonesian explained, "The Islamic State is like a dream come true for me and all Muslims. Now is the time to return to Islamic glory, like . . . in the old days."[8] The State would provide all the basic necessities for Muslims.

All three philosophies are romantic. Nazis hoped to re-create a pure Aryan society, as expressed in German mythology and folklore. Similarly, Marxists hoped to re-create a world without private ownership of property.[9] Islamists, too, look to a distant, largely imagined past.[10] Jessica Stern and J. M. Berger, writers on terrorism, speak of the Caliphate's hope to return Islam to an imaginary ideal of original purity.[11] Harvard's Noah Feldman, a scholar of Islam, adds, "The more medieval the practice, the more they like it."[12]

Like the Soviets and the Nazis, the Caliphate sees itself as constantly threatened by internal and external enemies. Yehuda Bauer, a scholar of the Nazi period, notes common elements of other twentieth-century utopias. "All three—Nazis, Stalinists, Islamists—aspired, or aspire, to rule over the entire world, promising a utopia and an apocalyptic end to history. All three were, or are, genocidal."[13]

Blogging the Life in Utopia

Power is in tearing human minds to pieces and putting them together again in new shapes of your own choosing.

—George Orwell, *1984*, 1949

The utopic aspirations of the State's foreign fighters can be gleaned from their blog entries. Blogging is a large part of the Caliphate's information operations. In 2011, before the creation of the Islamic State, a blogger on the al-Tahaddi Islamic Network described utopia as a "divine system, the Islamic system," which is completely absent of discrimination, injustice, or any social flaws. "It is not Arab nor regional, rather, it is Islamic."[14] This captures the utopic goal of the Caliphate today.

A reoccurring word in the Caliphate's literature is "freedom," which is promised in abundance in the Islamic State. But its usage contrasts with the Western understanding of freedom, which generally means the unfettered ability to say, believe, vote, and, often, behave as one would like. For the Caliphate, freedom is the ability to practice Islam unconstrained and to live in an exclusively Muslim society. This Islamic world has no legally defined borders because it aspires to global dominance. There is no clearly articulated concept of individual freedom in Islamic law, or Sharia. Islamic utopia is predicated on religious conformity.

But many of the world's Muslims support a level of religious freedom that would be antithetical to the State. In 2013, a Pew poll concluded that most Muslims around the world express support for democracy, and most say it is a good thing when others are very free to practice their religion. At the same time, many Muslims want religious leaders to have at least some influence in political matters.[15]

The media arm of the Caliphate, Al Hayat Media Center, promotes utopic themes for the State.[16] Its high-quality publications are far more sophisticated than those of al Qaeda.[17] The online magazine *Dabiq* has translations in several European languages. It features detailed articles on theology, international relations, popular culture, and life in the Caliphate.

Charlie Winter, a researcher at a British think tank, notes the Caliphate's attempts to make life appear attractive and family friendly.[18]

Table 4.1. Widespread Support for Democracy, Religious Freedom

	Prefer democracy over strong leader	Say religious freedom is a good thing
Sub-Saharan Africa	72	94
Southeast Asia	64	93
Souther Eastern Europe	58	95
Middle East -North Africa	55	85
Central Asia	52	92
South Asia	45	97

Source: "The World's Muslims: Religion, Politics, and Society, Pew Research Center, April 30. 2013.

Girls and women are recruited with promises of adventure, piety, security, and romance. A young Australian woman prattled that "the lifestyle here is amazing, it is something you have to see for yourself."[19] A thirtysomething Italian woman, Maria Giulia Sergio, explained that the Islamic State is a "perfect country" and that when the group beheads people, it is simply obeying Sharia law.[20] A convert to Islam, she determined to become a part of the collective of believers; the following profile tells her story.

PROFILE NINE: MARIA, FATIMA, AND ALESSANDRA

By the time she was in her early twenties, Muslim convert Maria Giulia Sergio had become famous in the country of her birth—Italy. She was also well known in her new home, the Islamic State, under her new name, Fatima. The former biotechnology student at the University of Milan said, "I can't wait to die as a martyr," according to *L'Espresso* magazine. Sergio celebrated the *Charlie Hebdo* killings. "When we behead someone, we're obeying Sharia Law."[21]

For Maria, Jihad became a family affair. She persuaded her entire Catholic family to convert to Islam. She also had success with her in-laws. This made news because the general pattern of family radicalization begins with parental pressure. But it was the young Maria who made Muslims of her family. She then traveled to Syria and beckoned her father, "Dad, you are called by Islam, you are the master at home: bring mum here in Syria. You are her husband: She's obliged to obey."[22] Her mother and father tried to do so but were held by police. Five Albanian in-laws connected to Sergio's husband were arrested for planning to join their daughter-in-law.[23]

While she was still living in Italy, Maria tried to make a case for Islam to her Italian compatriots. But not all Italians are enamored of Maria and her Islamist designs. In 2009, the fiery Muslima met her match with El Duce's granddaughter, Alessandra Mussolini. In the 1980s, Mussolini posed for European men's magazines, sometimes without wearing a top. Decades later, the two sparred on television. Hijab-clad Maria lectured Mussolini on feminine decorum, insisting that women should never wear revealing clothes that might excite men. But Mussolini, today a right-oriented European parliamentarian, was unconvinced. She, as well as her maternal aunt, Sophia Loren, made no apologies for the beauty of a woman's form.

Jihad—Duty, Honor, Caliphate

There's no life, no life without Jihad.

—Briton found guilty of terrorism in 2014
explaining his motives to a court in London[24]

Some of the Caliphate's recruiting tropes have timeless and universal appeal. These refrains are duty, honor, and country. Pericles's funeral oration of the Athenian dead of the First Peloponnesian War saluted the fallen and praised the living. It set a historical model for other Democratic leaders. Napoleon's farewell to the Old Guard acknowledged the nation of France's sacrifice.[25] Both contained patriotic and martial themes that are used in the Caliphate's information operations.

Duty, honor, and country are also woven into the Caliphate's general call for Jihad, which is the second general attraction. Jihad is a core tenet of Islam and has been called the sixth pillar of Islam. Some have likened Jihad to self-improvement or spiritual yoga. This is the Greater Jihad, which often means becoming more pious.[26]

Generally, however, Jihad has meant defending Islam, expanding Islam's domain by conquest, or subjugating cultures under its sway.[27] It is a matter of obligation and honor for all Muslims to heed this call and migrate to the Islamic State. This has been the general Western, as well as consensus Islamic, view. Tocqueville wrote, in 1838, "Jihad, Holy War, is an obligation for all believers. The state of war is the natural state with regard to infidels." The late political scientist Samuel Huntington referenced "Islam's bloody borders" in the context of Jihad.[28] Bernard Lewis said, "The Muslim Jihad was perceived as unlimited, as a religious obligation that would continue until the entire world has adopted the Muslim faith or submitted to Muslim Ruler."[29] This is the Caliphate's view.[30]

The late-twentieth-century activist/theologian who rallied the Islamic world to Jihad was Abdullah Azzam, a Palestinian. He became the theorist of global Jihad in the 1980s. In the absence of a Caliphate, individuals could make their own Jihad. He was later killed, perhaps on the orders of Osama bin Laden, but his voice and writing gave individual Muslims a prominent role in the current anti-Western Jihad.[31] Today, European-raised propagandists beckon Westerners to the Jihad.

For the first two years of the Caliphate's existence, it was easy for Westerners to travel to its cities. Security services did not expect the lure of the Caliphate, and many border controls in Europe had been removed. From 2014 until early 2016, it was simple for those with support and guidance to journey from most European cities to the Caliphate.

A *Daily Mail* undercover sting operation, undertaken with the coordination of the London police, shows the ease of travel and the assistance rendered to the traveler at each step of the journey. A journalist pretending to be a fixer for the State advertised on Twitter, Kik, Surespot, and Telegram. A young woman living in Syria responded and asked the uncover journalist to help transport her sixteen-year-old sister to Syria. The fixer and the Jihadi's sister would meet at a fast-food restaurant in niqabs, book a holiday to Basle, Switzerland, and pay with it on the fixer's credit card. They would pack in secret and leave before dawn, dressed in Western clothes. From Switzerland, they would book a one-way trip to Istanbul. From Istanbul, they would take a bus to Gaziantep, where they would be met by the State's fixers. They would be escorted to a safe house, where they would be introduced to the man who would be the girl's husband.[32] But police were monitoring this from the beginning and made arrests as a result.

It is not expensive to travel from Europe. A cheap flight from the continent to Turkey can cost as little as $150. In 2014, 2015, and 2016, a visa was generally not necessary to enter Turkey, which is the gateway to Syria. Smugglers ferrying pistachios, food, sugar, and fuel also transport Jihadis.[33] Some of the smugglers act out of solidarity, others have mercenary motives, and still others do it because the State pressures and threatens them.

Women Hear the Caliphate's Call

Keep it Halal and get married.[34]

There has long been a mystique associated with European women and the Islamic world. Stories of young, blonde beauties netted by Muslim pirates and imprisoned in harems were imagined in penny dreadful Victorian novels and on the canvasses of Jean-August Dominique Ingres and Eugène Delacroix.[35] Mozart had some musical fun with a harem in his opera *Abduction from the Seraglio*.[36] Fair-skinned, blue-eyed, blonde-haired girls and women were historically prized captives for Muslims.[37]

And today, European-appearing female captives fetch a handsome price in the Caliphate as sex slaves.[38] However, only rarely did women voluntarily forgo European or American lifestyles to live as traditional Muslims in the Islamic world. But history does record several.

Margaret Marcus was a well-to-do New Yorker who, as an adolescent, dreamed of a "new golden age" of Jews and Muslims. In early adulthood, she became tormented by schizophrenia. She converted to Islam and tried to build a new life in Pakistan, but her mental illness continued to stalk her there, too.[39]

A love-smitten twentysomething, Phyllis Chessler followed her poetry-reciting Afghan sweetheart to Kabul and found herself trapped in a harem. She escaped to write a memoir about it. So did Betty Mahmoody, who fled from Iran, as recounted in the docudrama *Not Without My Daughter*.[40] These women learned, too late, that their husbands, like many men in the Islamic world, held deeply ingrained traditional Islamic values.[41]

This makes the allure of the Islamic State perplexing. In the Islamic world and in Western Islamic enclaves, girls and women can be psychologically or physically tormented for wearing fashionable clothes and makeup, for befriending non-Muslim schoolmates, and for demanding to chart their life's course. Most horrific are "honor killings," in which family members collude to snuff out the lives of women and girls, often in the flower of their youth. Flirtations, idle chatting with boys or men, and being seen with males to whom they are not related can be serious, sometimes capital, offenses for girls and women in traditional Islamic families.[42]

Women journey to the Caliphate, nonetheless. Some come to Raqqa to find husbands, expecting an avalanche of manly suitors. Others travel to assume leadership and skill. As an analyst notes, "The girls go around making cookies. It's almost like a Jihadi Tupperware party."[43] Anne Birgitta Nilsen, an associate professor at Oslo University College, researched the Facebook activity of European women who want to join the State. She pointed out the "gentle" day-to-day nature of information operations.[44] The Caliphate's media operations show children playing in school yards.[45] And then there is sex.

Sexual Jihad

There are a lot of things about us women that sadden me,
considering how men see us as rascals.

—Lysistrata, from the play *Lysistrata* by Arisotphanes[46]

As the Greek play went, Athenian women were fed up with the war against the Spartans. Lysistrata organized a sex strike to force their men to stop killing Spartans, who, according to plan, would stop killing Athenians in turn. The older Athenian women seized the state treasury. The men, without money to buy wine or women to enjoy, made peace with each other, laid down their arms, and reveled in both Bacchus and women. But this is not the story with the Islamic State.

In the Caliphate, sexual Jihad is the obligation for women and girls to provide male Jihadis with sexual outlets to relieve the pent-up frustrations brought on by combat. Sexual intercourse is a recurring theme in Islamic sacred texts—when to have it, with whom to have it, where to have it, and the consequences of having it improperly. All kinds of advice about sex are given by the Islamic State. Posters in public places in Mosul read, "We call upon the people of this country to bring their unmarried girls so they can fulfill their duty in sex Jihad for their warrior brothers in the city."[47]

There is the "groupie" effect. Some women are drawn to the sexual Jihad because of the charisma and derring-do of the Caliphate's alpha males. The Caliphate's propagandists use "Jihotties" to play on the hormonal drives of young women and girls.[48] The British comedian Shazia Mirza, mentioned earlier, stresses, "This is not about radicalization; its sexualisation."[49] The repressed, sexually driven teenaged girls have built a fantasy world around their longing for romance and adventure. Mirza argued that for them State fighters promise "no-guilt halal sex of which Allah approves."[50]

The matrimonial pairing is sometimes facilitated by a "fixer," who acts as a matchmaker. There is also an electronic facilitator, "Jihad Matchmaker."[51] Women desiring husbands can send a picture of themselves and men can make a selection. Women already living in Syria have more options. As one female Jihadi tweeted, "They'll get a male foreign fighter in room and the girls will all walk up and down covered and the fighter will have the opportunity to look at their face and he will choose one."[52]

Photographs of young men with bandoleros crisscrossing their chests populate the Caliphate's websites. This led a Saudi woman to divorce her husband and smuggle herself and her two children into Syria and then Iraq. Her aim was to marry Abu Musab Al-Zarqawi, the paladin of al Qaeda in Iraq.[53]

Another example is the case of a young Dutch woman who was arrested upon her return to Holland from Syria. Earlier, she had gone to Raqqa to marry a Dutch-Turkish jihadist who had served in the Dutch military. She found him irresistibly attractive. The young woman's mother explained her daughter's overheated imagination: "She saw him as a sort of Robin Hood."[54] The mother made the dangerous trip to fetch her daughter from Syria. She succeeded, and the romantic adventure was over.

The call for sexual Jihad has had some successes and failures. Besotted women have trekked to the Middle East, but their sojourns usually do not end in the Gothic romance they expected.[55] Some are initially glad to sexually service the warriors, but most soon regret their decision.[56] Many of those who leave the relative comforts and security of the West soon begin to tweet their regrets to their parents and friends.[57]

Some of these Western women become widowed soon after marriage. Many cannot mourn men they did not know. One explained, "In the whole year I probably saw him for less than one month altogether. Then he was martyred."[58] She then married an Egyptian, who left her to return to Egypt. She did not love either man.[59]

Western widows, particularly the less attractive ones, need to wait for new husbands. But many widows see the wait as an act of piety. "It's not hard [the wait] because it's for the sake of Allah, we are happy to observe it. When one husband gets martyred, it's like a celebration."[60] But others enjoy the lifestyle and do not mind the replicable husbands. One of them is Aqsa Mahmood.

PROFILE TEN: AQSA MAHMOOD—"YOU ARE A DISGRACE TO YOUR FAMILY AND THE PEOPLE OF SCOTLAND"

I will become a martyr.

—Aqsa Mahmood

The Mahmood family of Glasgow, Scotland, was taken completely by surprise. The parents could not explain why their daughter, twenty-year-old Aqsa (also spelled Aksa), vamoosed for Syria to kill for the Caliphate. Aqsa's mother and father became particularly alarmed when they saw a photograph of her holding a severed head as a trophy.

A girl of relative privilege, Aqsa had studied at a tony all-girls' school, where, it is thought, she developed radical beliefs.[61] Her friends in high school described her as "ambitious and talented" and as a "normal girl."[62] In her final year of school, as she was preparing to begin a radiology course, she began to wear a hijab. In November 2013, she dropped out of university and moved to Syria.[63] Something had happened to her.[64]

By September 2014, Mahmood had a new family in Syria and was encouraging her Facebook fans to follow her lead: "The family you get in exchange for leaving the ones behind are like the pearl in comparison to the shell you threw away into the foam of the sea."[65] She married an Islamic State fighter in Syria, who was killed in battle, and she penned a survival guide for Jihadi war widows. Her blog commentary soon became morbid, and she became a leader of an all-women morality police force.[66] She saluted her sisters' "desires and cravings to participate in the battlefield and give away your blood."[67] She was in her element.

Aqsa developed an international fan club, but her parents have yet to become members. Her mother and father openly and repeatedly pled to Aqsa to return home, where she would be forgiven and loved. They whispered that they had raised her "with love and affection in a happy home."[68] But she no longer loves her parents; she belongs to the Caliphate. In her words, "I [belong] only to our beloved Ameer, destroyer of the enemies, Abu Bakr al-Baghdadi and to the Islamic State."[69]

Aqsa's parents' initial hope turned to anger and then despair. They called her a "bedroom radical."[70] They also sent a message to Aqsa: "You are a disgrace to your family and the people of Scotland, your actions are a perverted and evil distortion of Islam."[71] Mr. Mahmood is haunted by the last words his daughter said to him. She promised, "I will see you on the day of judgement. I will take you to heaven, I will hold your hand. I will become a martyr."[72] According to her father, "That's what she said."[73]

Deadly Women

Some women, like some men, are sadistic and power hungry, and the Islamic State provides them with opportunities. The British "White Widow" Samantha Lewthwaite married one of the perpetrators of the 2005 London bombings. She developed a sinister and legendary status as one of the world's most wanted women. The London University dropout is credited with killing over 400 people in coordination with the terrorist group al Shabaab.[74] A senior Somali official called her "an evil person, but a very clever operator."[75] She is not known to be currently associated with the Caliphate.

The middle-aged Belgian Muriel Degauque blasted herself into history, if only in a footnote, as the first known European Muslim female suicide bomber.[76] American Colleen LaRose, known as "Jihad Jane," was sent to prison for planning to kill Swedish cartoonist Lars Vilks.[77]

These three women represent a cross section of Western society. Intelligent Lewthwaite attended university; ordinary Degauque was from the industrial working class; and pathetic LaRose had a pitiable childhood. All turned to Islam to fill a spiritual void, as has happened with many other Western women.

Psychological and Social Drivers—
Peace Symbols and Black Flags

The heart's longings lead the mind and the existential filler
of ISIS nourishes the desperate and vulnerable soul,
however much one is surrounded by material comfort.

—Collective judgments of four psychiatrists referring to
why Westerners are drawn to the Caliphate, 2015[78]

The draw of utopia and the compulsion of Jihad explain two of the broad lures of the Caliphate. The third group of motivators is grounded in psychology and social themes. Anger at perceived discrimination, alienation, fatalism, and a need to belong to a mass movement are psychosocial drivers for some Western Muslims. Today's generation of Western Muslims is more attracted to Jihad than that of their parents or grandparents.

Western youth joining the Caliphate are usually eager to make war. For young men, there is a hypermasculinity and virility. The State's recruiting themes cultivate the image of the heroic horseman who is master of his environment and admired by his fellow warriors. Elizabeth van der Heide, of the Dutch Center for Terrorism and Counterterrorism, said young males see the war as a video game: "Those are primarily young people who relocate to the war game in Syria and Iraq from a video game."[79]

Another study observed that the most effective recruitment approach is to target a candidate's sense of self-worth. The study cited the Florida killer Omar Mateen as "the perfect fit" for the Caliphate's approach.[80] Young men who felt neglected or weak as boys can become a part of something powerful and victorious. One young man who was not weak but still needed a purpose in life was Thundercat, profiled below.

PROFILE ELEVEN: THUNDERCAT! "A PRINCE OF A MAN"

[He was] a prince who everyone on the street knew and greeted.

—A friend of Thundercat, 2015[81]

One Jihadi who fought for the State did not have an apparent need to validate his masculinity. He had proven it, repeatedly, in the ring as a two-time Thai boxing world champion from Germany. Valdet Gashi traveled to Syria with three other Thai boxers to fight with weapons, rather than fists.[82]

Gashi arrived in Germany from Albania as a six-year-old boy and was raised in a relatively secular home. As a young man, he shot up the kickboxing ranks, and the local boys described him as a "prince who everyone on the street knew and greeted."[83] He fought 152 fights under the name Thundercat.[84] Some of his fights were posted on YouTube, and his speed and style are clearly devastating.

Thundercat married his local sweetheart and then sired two daughters. But the fighter was drawn to the German Islamic Salafist program called Read, and he developed a moral obligation to leave his wife and daughters and join the Caliphate to fight for Islam. He said he would rather die for Allah than live as a coward.[85]

In an interview in May 2015, Thundercat declared his respect for the State, which, in his view, was deeply misunderstood in the West. As a Muslim, he could only be happy by "doing something good for Islam."[86] But many of his fans were disappointed, and some Muay Thai fans hoped to strip him of his championship titles.[87] His father was fed up, too. Enver Gashi said, "Valdet's place is with us—with his children, his wife, and his parents.... I want him to stop this nonsense, and I hope he'll come back to us one day, because his place is here and nowhere else."[88] But Thundercat never came home.

The champ tweeted from Syria that he was patrolling the Euphrates River to intercept smugglers. "If I die while doing good, I am sure I will be happy."[89] He did die, killed in a mission in July 2015. His brother eulogized him on social media and prayed that he may rest in peace. Thundercat's fights were over.

The Caliphate as a New Beginning—Antisocials in a New Society

> *Bar girl to Johnny: "Hey, Johnny, what are you rebelling against?"*
> *Johnny to bar girl: "Whaddya got?"*
>
> —From the film *The Wild One*, 1953[90]

> *If you're scrambling for your identity, ISIS is the bright flame to follow.*
>
> —Raffaello Pantucci, director of International Security Studies
> at the Royal United Services Institute, 2015[91]

Young Westerners with troubled biographies look to the Caliphate for a new beginning. Some try to shed their past, embrace a new religion, take an Islamic name, become part of a new religious family, and move to a new land. Often these young people were very troubled before their radicalization. Sometimes they drank excessively and abused and sold drugs. Later in life, many shed this lifestyle and image.[92] Those who travel to Syria leave behind criminal records, dissolute lifestyles, toxic family associations, and weak employment prospects

A case in point is the Spaniard "Nabil," who shifted in and out of legitimate and criminal behavior. His profile is similar to some of the more antisocial and marginally functional characters who have joined the State. A small-time drug dealer in his youth, Nabil later joined the army, where he began to traffic narcotics.[93] Soon, he was investigated for "psychological-physical deficiencies," and eventually he was cashiered for stealing and dealing medicine. He then turned his criminal energies to helping the Caliphate through smuggling and logistical support. He married a Muslim convert, and at age twenty-nine, he was arrested by Spanish authorities before he left for Syria. The troubled Nabil was the first Spanish soldier arrested for aiding the Caliphate.[94]

There have been many similar examples. Another young Westerner who left for Syria for a new start was Damian Boudreau, a Canadian.[95] As a young man, he was haunted by hallucinations of demons and tried to kill himself by drinking antifreeze. He recovered and retreated to his bedroom, where he found Islam on the internet. He told his mother that he was leaving for Egypt to study Islam, and he went to Syria to fight and was killed there.[96] At first, Damian called and e-mailed his mother regularly, but the frequency and tone of his correspondence changed. He invited his half-brother to join him in battle. Damian wrote in stilted prose, "As for how you worry about me and love me, it is known to me. These are not new pieces of information." His mother confided, "That's when I realized that my son disappeared, that there was somebody new that's in his body."[97] His mother, Christianne, described her pain: "It's like being in a really black, dark movie and you can't get out; it's like some sort of prison. No questions ever answered."[98]

Lukas Dam, a working-class boy from Copenhagen, followed a path similar to Damian's. He suffered from both Asperger's syndrome and attention deficit disorder. He, like Boudreau, went to Syria to join the State, where he started a new life. Soon, his new life was over; he was killed in combat.

Other forms of radicalization move quickly. According to the French minister of interior, the man who drove a truck through a crowd in Nice, killing eighty-four people, Mohamed Lahouaiej-Bouhlel, redis-covered his faith very quickly.[99]

As with men, young women try to reinvent themselves before trudging to the Middle East. This is what happened to the rebellious and tattooed "Betsy." At twenty-one years old, Betsy's dream was to become a hip-hop superstar: Holland's Eminem. She enjoyed narcotics and the nightlife. Then Betsy found religion and began dressing in full Muslim robes. After a family fight, she left for Syria. Her mother said, "I don't blame Islam. I blame the people who made her believe in a radical way of life."[100]

The Caliphate uses its Western-raised recruits to spot emotional vulnerabilities through social media. Its cells in the West draw lonely hearts to the Caliphate's cause, but they also attract young men and women who appeared perfectly normal to most of those who knew them.

PROFILE TWELVE: SALLY—KRUNCH AND CARNAGE

Sally Jones, a former rocker in an all-girl band, would appear to be an unlikely candidate for Jihad. Born in Kent and white, Jones enjoyed some wild times in her youth. In a performance from the early 1990s posted on YouTube, Sally plays lead guitar, wearing a leather miniskirt, in a group called Krunch.[101] She also dabbled in the black art of witchcraft. One neighbor described her as "scatty," but others remember her as an animal lover with a particular affection for cats. Long-term employment proved difficult for her. She went on welfare and accepted relief from churches.[102]

Forty-something Sally took up with the computer-savvy Junaid Hussain, who was originally from Birmingham and was twenty years her junior. By summer 2014, Jones became known to the world as Umm Hussain al-Britani. She and her husband moved to Syria, where her bloodlust jolted her to the headlines of Britain's tabloids. She tweeted, "You Christians all need beheading with a nice blunt knife and stuck on the railings at Raqqa . . . Come here I'll do it for you!"[103] There was more. Umm chirped her love for Osama bin Laden and contempt for Jews.[104]

And when her cyber-hacking husband was killed by allied forces, she tweeted to the world that she had become a "black widow."[105] She would follow the path of the Chechen woman, Hawa Barayev, who exploded herself among Russian Special Forces, killing twenty-seven of them. As for her invitation for Christians to come to be beheaded, as of this writing, there have been no takers.

Mental Health of Foreign Fighters— "Crazy Eyes" and "Holy Anger"

Some observers of the Caliphate have speculated that its ranks are over-represented with sociopaths and people with other severe emotional disorders. The bloodletting in Syria and Iraq may have attracted emotionally unstable or sadistic personalities. According to Nicholas Sennels, a Danish psychologist, violence is much more accepted in European Muslim households than in European non-Muslim households. He argues that exposure to violence and the inculcation of hate, particularly at very young ages, increases the risk of psychiatric disorders.[106] He concludes that Islamic culture is more likely than Western ethos to create criminal and antisocial behavior.

Ostentatious displays of anger in the West are signs of weakness and of brittle personalities. In Muslim culture, he argues, anger is much more accepted, and being able to intimidate people is seen as strength and a source of social status. It is seen as "holy anger," which is a venomous blend of religious fanaticism and emotional instability. Finally, there is, according to Sennels, the demonization of the non-Muslim. Killing another person is easier if you hate him and do not perceive him as "fully human."[107]

But other mental health professionals are not persuaded that this cohort contains a statistically significant higher level of psychopathology or psychosis than is found in general European populations. Persons with significant psychotic disorders usually cannot perform satisfactorily in a military or paramilitary setting. By definition, persons experiencing psychosis are often unable to distinguish fantasy from reality. Their tortured minds are haunted by auditory or visual hallucinations, which explains their often-eccentric behavior. In regimented structures, such as the military, they would be quickly identified as acting inappropriately or communicating incoherently. Observers might remark about their abnormal facial expressions, such as unfocused or "crazy" eyes, or their jumbled and mumbled conversations with flat affect or out-of-context outbursts of anger. In the Caliphate, persons exhibiting this behavior would be noticed immediately and would likely be restrained or killed. In the Caliphate and in other Sharia-based countries, people are killed for sorcery and witchcraft. Many Muslims believe in evil spirits called "jinns."[108] What can be seen in Western states as idiosyncratic or strange-but-innocuous behavior can be interpreted as demonic possession in parts of the Islamic world. This could bring a swift death sentence.

The legal definition of insanity differs among Western countries and in different states in the United States. In the United States, to be proven innocent by reason of insanity in most courts, a defendant needs to convince the court that he or she was compelled by an irresistible impulse to commit the crime. This is also known as the "policeman-at-the-elbow" defense.[109] To be innocent by reason of insanity a person needs to be unable to resist the drive to kill and would have killed the victim even if a police officer had been at the scene.[110] Another standard is the "wild beast test." To be found innocent, a defendant needs to have a mental deficiency in "understanding and memory" and would need to act like a "wild beast."[111] By this standard, there are few Western Jihadis who would qualify. But there are dangerous psychotics who kill because they hear voices and commands that they cannot resist. Some believe they are killing on God's orders, as profiled below.

Profile Thirteen: Beware the Smiling Nanny

The Moscovites could not believe their eyes. Maybe a studio was filming a horror movie near the subway station in Moscow. Maybe it was a sick prank. A dark-skinned, Central Asian-appearing, middle-aged woman was brandishing the head of a child and yelling "Allahu akbar." Then she smiled and yelled in Russian, "I am a terrorist."[112] She was the nanny of the four-year-old girl whom she had beheaded because voices told her to do so. Allah had spoken to her.

Gyulchekhra Bobokulova was raised in Uzbekistan. Unlucky with men and an unmarried mother herself, she became an increasingly devout Muslim. At some point, probably in late adolescence, she began to hear voices. Her mental health deteriorated, and she was hospitalized for schizophrenia in her native country. She told friends that she wanted to go to live in Syria but did not have the money to do so.[113] Instead, she connected with the Caliphate online.[114]

She went to Moscow to work as a nanny, and her ward was a handicapped four-year-old girl. Bobokulova was taken into the hard-working young couple's home as part of the family who were kind to her, by all accounts. But she kept hearing voices, and people who observed her noticed that she smiled and giggled for unknown reasons.[115]

When interrogated by police, she explained, "Allah ordered me to [sever the head]."[116] Russian authorities and mental health care professionals declared her insane. As of summer 2016, she will not be tried for murder. Instead, she will be incarcerated for madness. As for the child she killed, those who loved her, as well as passersby, paid tribute to her at the Oktyabrskoye Pole metro station in Moscow. People laid many flowers and placed dolls and teddy bears at a make-shift memorial.

Interspecies Predators—Psychopaths and Foreign Fighters

I'm glad I've lived to see an enemy prepared to die for something other than their bank balance.

—Ian Brady, infamous British Moors murderer,
referring to the Caliphate, 2016[117]

Sometimes called "psychopaths," sometimes called "sociopaths," historically called "evil," they are men and women without any feelings of remorse.[118] Though they are not necessarily mentally ill, they do not have a conscience. Lacking empathy, they can harm, betray, or kill people, even family members. But there is no current expert consensus that Westerners who fight for the Caliphate are *significantly* more psychopathic than other cohorts.[119]

Nevertheless, many of the foreign fighters display several classic traits of the psychopath. They enjoy hurting people and lie about activities and conditions in the Islamic State. Some have poor behavioral skills and act impulsively. They were juvenile delinquents and indulgent in parasitic lifestyles in their Western homes. They have not shown remorse when they hurt people.

There are also female sadists, some of whom capture headlines in European tabloids. Some display great pleasure at the suffering of non-Muslims, much like the Nazi concentration camp guards. These "emotional vampires" sometimes brag about killing non-Muslims and regale their electronic audience with the details of torture. It is difficult to explain this sadism exclusively in religious terms because they take ostentatious joy in torture. Nonetheless, they justify mass murder, rape, and enslavement with Koranic verses. As with their male counterparts, some of the women have fun chuckling about bloody beheadings, regretting only that they did not commit the murder themselves.[120] The husband-and-wife San Bernardino couple who killed their coworkers and abandoned their young child relished in the planning and execution of their killing spree.[121]

However, other Westerners who serve the Caliphate are not abnormally antisocial in the context of life in the Islamic State. They cooperate with their companions in the Caliphate. A psychopath would not likely risk death for a cause that did not directly benefit him or her.[122] Psychopaths are driven only by advancing their personal interests.[123] Further, many foreign fighters in the Caliphate are protective of their fellow soldiers. Some have exposed themselves to danger for the Islamic State. Some have been self-sacrificial. Many more have emotionally bonded with their comrades, and a psychopath would not. But there are some psychopaths in the Caliphate, and they are profiled below.

PROFILE FOURTEEN: VERY CRUEL MEN

Mehdi Nemmouche

If there were a club for sadists in the Caliphate, Mehdi Nemmouche would certainly be a prominent member. By his own account, he relished torture. Well known to French police authorities, Nemmouche had been in and out of prison much of his twenty-nine years. That is where he was radicalized.[124] Some of his convictions were petty, such as driving without a license, but he was also sentenced for armed robbery, which landed him a five-year sentence. Sometime in early 2013, Nemmouche went to Syria to fight for the Jihad.[125] He flourished there.

He was more than a garden-variety thug-turned-Islamist. Nemmouche was particularly sadistic toward captives, even by the brutal standards of the Caliphate's foreign legion. Nemmouche delighted in torturing European captives: "The torture went on all night, until prayers at dawn," a French survivor wrote in *Le Point* magazine. "The howls of the prisoners alternated with shouts in French."[126] He is also supposed to have serenaded his captives with his own rendition of Charles Aznavour love songs.

But at some point, Nemmouche fell from the favor of the Caliphate's leaders. French criminologist Alain Bauer says, "ISIS did not like him at all." Bauer compares him to Zacarias Moussaoui, sometimes called "the twentieth hijacker" from the 9/11 plot, who was so crazy that al Qaeda leadership didn't know what to do with him.[127] In June 2014, French police in Marseilles arrested Mehdi Nemmouche for mass murder. He was the primary suspect in the Brussels Jewish Museum attack of May 2014, in which three Jews were shot dead.[128] Today, Nemmouche sits in prison.[129]

Mohammed Emwazi

I've seen it before, you all squirm like animals, like pigs.

—Mohammed Emwazi referring to beheadings[130]

Like Nemmouche, Kuwaiti-born Mohammed Emwazi enjoyed hurting people. He certainly displayed the classic signs of psychopathy: lack of empathy, grandiosity, glibness, and a need for power. He was sadistic by any standard, and it was he who cut off the heads of Western captives for a global audience on YouTube.

Emwazi's family moved to Britain when he was six years old. He was smart enough to complete a college degree in computer science, and his primary- and secondary-school teachers remember him as quiet, lonely, and quick to take offense. In high school, Emwazi underwent anger management therapy after fighting with fellow students, and when he drank he had difficulty controlling his temper.[131, 132] He found Islam and became a leader in an Islamist sleeper cell, "The London Boys" and he raised money for the Jihadis.[133]

If he was uncomfortable in Britain, he appears to have been in his element in Syria. A released hostage related that the British John Cantlie and American Jim Foley were forced to compose a song titled "Welcome to the Lovely Hotel Osama." They sang it to the mocking delight of the three British Jihadis who guarded them most of the time. These three were called "the Beatles." Mohamed Emwazi was dubbed "Jihadi John" after John Lennon. Another Jihadi, dubbed "George," was particularly fond of the song: "George shouted, 'Anyone who doesn't know the words, I'll kick to death.'"[134] Another torturer was Najim Laachraoui. He would leave the Middle East and travel to Europe, where he would die in the Brussells airport attack in 2016, which killed thirty-two people and injured more than 300.[135]

Jihadi John enjoyed torturing other captives. The group's twenty-three hostages suffered constant beatings and degradations, and one survivor likened their condition to that of former presidential aspirant Senator John McCain at the hands of the Vietnamese communists. They called their digs the "ISIS Hilton."[136]

Emwazi fathered a son in Syria, who is entitled to British citizenship.[137] But the boy will never know his father, who was "vaporized" in an air strike in November 2015. "Vaporized" is current slang for killing people through drone-launched munitions. Emwazi knew he was being hunted by British and US Special Forces. He knew that modern technology and first-rate policing revealed his identity, despite his camouflage. But in his skyscraping vanity, he repeatedly gave away his positions. A New York baseball cap, his signature piece of apparel, may have identified him to targeteers, according to one British tabloid.[138]

Two MQ-9 Reaper drones locked in on him and flashed the "Beatle's" image to Creech Air Force Base in Indian Springs, Nevada. As Emwazi got in a car at the Islamic courts, two Hellfire missiles exploded atop his car. Few were surprised when the twenty-seven-year-old former Londoner was "vaporized."[139] The State later eulogized him as an "honorable brother."[140] But a military spokesperson for the country that killed him had a different take: "This guy was a human animal, and killing him is probably making the world a better place."[141]

Summary

Westerners will still be drawn to the Caliphate. There will always be a desire among the young to live in a perfect society—a utopia. However, the image of Raqqa as an Islamic utopia, or even a habitable environment, has been tarnished. Some will be driven by Jihad and will come to fight. Some, like Thundercat, will die in battle and, in the words of the Islamic State, be finally at peace with Allah.

1. Ruadhan Mac Cormaic, "Leaked Islamic State Records Give New Insights into Its Fighters' Background; ISIS Records Obtained by Media Show an Organisation Learning from Its Mistakes," *The Irish Times*, April 23, 2016.

2. "London: Mother Who Took Toddler to Raqqa Convicted by UK Court," *AFP, North European Service*, January 29, 2016.

3. Daniel Hager, "Utopia versus Utopia," *Ideas on Liberty*, March 3, 2003.

4. Russell Lemmons, "Old Dreams of a New Reich: Volkish Utopias and National Socialism. (Brief Article)," *The Historian*. January 1, 1994.

5. Katherine Ellison, "19th Century Vision of Master Race Is History in Paraguay's 'Forgotten Fatherland,'" *The Buffalo News*, May 31, 1998.

6. Freddy Gray, "Great Red Hope. The Forsaken: An American Tragedy in Stalin's Russia (Book review)," *The American Conservative*, November 3, 2008.

7. V. S. Naipaul, "V. S. Naipaul Says ISIS Is Now the Fourth Reich," *Mail On Sunday*, March 21, 2015.

8. Jonathan Kaiman, "Islamic State's Influence Stretching Thousands of Miles to Indonesia," *Los Angeles Times*, August 8, 2015.

9. Marx was influenced by the Swiss philosopher Rousseau's view that property was theft and that there once existed a harmonious society without the division of property. This was an overly romantic view of Indian life in pre-Revolutionary War America.

10. A scholar at the British think tank Quilliam clarified that Jihadists today have "a very romantic, idealized idea [among some Muslims] that Islamic State is some kind of utopia and a state of justice and paradise on earth." Emily Dugan, "Why Are There Pockets of Sympathy for ISIS in Some Parts of Modern Britain? The Increased Feeling of Isolation for Many Muslims in Britain Plays a Key Role," *The Independent*, June 16, 2015.

11. "Book Review: ISIS, the State of Terror," *Mint*, July 24, 2015.

12. Noah Feldman, "Islamic State's Medieval Morals," *Bloomberg View*, August 16, 2015.

13. Yehuda Bauer, "Nazis, Communists, and Radical Islamists," *Jerusalem Post*, November 29, 2002.

14. Steven Corman, "De-Romanticizing the Islamic State's Vision of the Caliphate," in *"Multi-Method Assessment of ISIL," A Strategic Multilayer Assessment (SMA) Periodic Publication*, eds. Hriar Cabayan and Sarah Canna, December 5, 2014.

15. "The World's Muslims: Religion, Politics, and Society," *Pew Research Center*, April 30, 2013.

16. Smadar Perry, "ISIS Magazine Preparing Young Muslims for an Apocalypse," *Ynetnews*, June 15, 2015.

17. Olivia Becker, "ISIS Has a Really Slick and Sophisticated Media Department," *Vice News*, July 12, 2014.

18. "UK Source Says ISIL Propaganda Trying Present 'Semblance of Normality' within ISIL-Held Territories," *London Independent Online*, March 20, 2015.

19. "Why They Become a Jihadi Bride," *Johannesburg City Press*, April 19, 2015.

20. "Italian Jihadist Defends 'Perfect' Islamic State," *The Local*, July 7, 2015.

21. Ibid.

22. "Italian Jihadist Defends 'Perfect' Islamic State," *The Local,* July 7, 2015.

23. Gianluca Mezzofiore, "ISIS: Family of Italian Maria Giulia Sergio Arrested in Antiterror Operation," *International Business Times,* July 1, 2015.

24. Ben Eccleston, "Coventry Man Guilty of Terrorism Offences," *Coventry Telegraph,* May 26, 2015.

25. Napoleon wrote, "I have sacrificed all of my interests to those of the country. I go, but you, my friends, will continue to serve France." April 20, 1814. Complied by Tom Holmberg, "Napoleon's Addresses: 1814 Campaign," Research Subjects: Napoleon Himself, http://www.napoleon-series.org/research /napoleon/speeches/c_speeches13.html.

26. For others it means "to strive, to exert one's self, to struggle" and is not confined to "Jihad of the sword." It also means "Jihad of the tongue" and "Jihad of the pen." Abdul Karim Khan, "Jihad in Classical and Modern Islam: A Reader. (Book Review)," *Journal of World History,* March 1, 2003.

27. Lee Harris, "Jihad Then and Now. (The Legacy of Jihad) (Book review)," *Policy Review,* October 1, 2006.

28. Bruce Thornton, "Nothing to Do with Islam," *Frontpage,* August 18, 2014.

29. Norvell B. De Atkine, *"Muhammad Taught Us How to Fight": The Islamic State and Early Islamic Warfare Tradition,* IDC Herzliya, Rubic Center, February 6, 2016.

30. David Motadel, "The Last Jihad Declared by Caliph Was in November 1914 to Mobilize Muslims against the Entente Powers of World War I, Jihad 1914," *History Today* 64, no. 9 (September 14, 2014): 41.

31. Daniel Pipes, "Jihad through History," *Jerusalem Post,* June 1, 2005.

32. "ISIS Plot Exposed to Lure British Schoolgirl, 16, to Syria as a Jihadi Bride," *London Mail Online,* May 22, 2015.

33. Tim Arango and Eric Schmitt, "A Path to ISIS, Through a Porous Turkey," *International New York Times,* March 1, 2015.

34. This is a play on words of the 1939 British moniker issued as World War II broke out: "Keep calm and carry on." "Instead the Jihad Matchmaker Site Puns, Dating Site Could Have Lured Yusra to Syria to Become a Jihadi Bride; New Lead as Mum Begs Teen to Return," *The Mirror* (London), October 2, 2014.

35. Zainab Bahrani, *Women of Babylon: Gender and Representation in Mesopotamia* (London: Routledge, 2001), 162.

36. A Spaniard entices an Ottoman pasha with wine so European sex slaves can escape their captivity. Inebriated, Osmin the Turk and the Spaniard toast the beauty of "blondes and the brunettas . . . and Baccus." The opera ends happily for fair-skinned ladies, who return to Europe.

37. M. H. Shboul, "Byzantium and the Arabs: The Image of the Byzantines as Mirrored in Arabic Literature," in *Arab-Byzantine Relations in Early Islamic Times,* ed. Michael Bonner (Burlington: Ashgate Publishing, 2004), 240, 248.

38. In September 2015, Saudi Sheik Yahya Al-Jana spoke of the joys of Paradise, saying that men will have the strength of a hundred men in Paradise and will be busy "tearing [the] hymens" of the virgins of Paradise, whose breasts are "like pomegranates," and that after Muslims will "rupture" the virgins' hymens Allah

will immediately repair their hymens to make them virgins again so true Muslims will never run short of virgins. Tarek Fatah, "Everything You Wanted to Know about Orgies in Paradise, but Were Too Afraid to Ask," Tarek Fatah Blog, October 8, 2015, http://tarekfatah.com/everything-you-wanted-to-know-about-orgies-in-paradise-but-were-too-afraid-to-ask/.

39. Pamela Constable, "Searching for Peace, from One Faith to Another," *The Washington Post*, June 5, 2011.

40. "'Not Without My Daughter' American Woman Trapped in Iran Relives 2-Year Trauma," *Post-Tribune* (Indiana), 1987.

41. Bradley S. Klapper, "Europe Failing to Protect Muslim Women from Islamic Extremists, Campaigners Say," *AP Worldstream*, April 18, 2005.

42. The United Nations Population Fund estimates that 5,000 women are killed each year for dishonoring their families. Chesler Phyllis, "Are Honor Killings Simply Domestic Violence? (Report)," *Middle East Quarterly*, March 22, 2009.

43. Alistar Bell, "Islamic State Attracts Female Jihadis from U.S. Heartland," *Reuters*, September 4, 2014.

44. Erlend Ofte Arntsen and Morten S. Hopperstad, "Norwegian Security Service Fears Country's ISIL Brides Recruit Others Online," *Oslo VG Nett*, July 5, 2015.

45. "UK Source Says ISIL Propaganda Trying Present 'Semblance of Normality' within ISIL-Held Territories," *London Independent Online*, March 20, 2015.

46. Aristophanes, "Lysistrata," The Eserver Drama Collection, http://drama.eserver.org/plays/classical/aristophanes/lysistrata.txt.

47. "ISIS Issues Orders in Mosul: Give Over Girls for 'Sex Jihad,'" *Clarion Project*, June 29, 2014.

48. "'Horny' Jihadi Brides Are Just Suckers for Hairy Bad Boys, Says Muslim Comic," *Agence France-Presse*, February 22, 2016.

49. "'Horny' Jihadi Brides Are Just Suckers for Hairy Bad Boys, Says Muslim Comic," *Agence France-Presse*, February 22, 2016.

50. Ibid.

51. Stefanie Marsh, "I Can't Wait to Have My Own Jihadi Baby: The British Women Joining ISIS," *Time Online*, December 1, 2014.

52. Ibid.

53. Abdulrahman Al-Rashed, "Opinion: The Reality of 'Sexual Jihad,'" *London Asharq Al-Awsat Online*, March 4, 2015.

54. "Dutch Teen Who Married IS Jihadist in Syria Returns Home," *BBC News Europe*, November 19, 2014.

55. If Islamic men can have endless sex with their female slaves, can Islamic women have sex with male slaves? Palestinian-Jordanian cleric Sheikh Mashhoor bin Hasan Al-Salman, pondering this question, answered "no." The sheik quoted Muhammad's reference to life in paradise where "the woman gets a man of full virility, with a penis that never bends. So she can have sex with this strong man." As reasoned by the sheikh, women must be satisfied with just one "strong" man. "Cleric: A Woman Must Not Have Sex with Her Slave; She Can Marry Him, Turning Him into Her Master," *MEMRI TV*, June 7, 2015.

56. In December 2014, the Iraqi Ministry of Human Rights had announced that one member of ISIS had killed at least 150 females, including pregnant women, for refusing to participate in sexual jihad. "Jihad-al-Nikah or Sex Jihad: 10 Interesting Facts," *India TV News Desk*, September 12, 2015.

57. Tunisians returned from their sexual Jihad pregnant, abused, degraded, and often physically injured. This has been condemned by Muslims and non-Muslims, referring to the practice as forced prostitution. Some have been referred to as "comfort women," a reference to the Japanese incarceration.

58. Sherine Tadros, "Escaped Islamic State Wives in Hiding in Turkey," *Sky News Online*, April 20, 2015.

59. Ibid.

60. Michelle Shephard, "Why It's Wrong to Underestimate the Islamic State's Female Recruits," *Toronto Star*, March 28, 2015.

61. David O'Leary, "Hands Off Our Husbands and Bring Thermal Undies, Tweets Jihadi Bride," *The Scotsman*, November 22, 2014.

62. "From Matilda to Martyrdom; She Took Just Months to Transform from Normal Glasgow Schoolgirl to Bride of Islamic State Fighter Study but She Her of Term Her Layth," *Daily Record* (Glasgow, Scotland), September 3, 2014.

63. "ISIS Brit Girl on How to Be Jihadi Widow," *The Mirror* (London), January 26, 2015.

64. "From Matilda to Martyrdom."

65. "I'll Kill or Be Killed; Scots Jihadi's Chilling Vow Fanatic Wants to Murder and Die a Martyr the Family You Get in Exchange for Leaving the Ones Behind Are Like the Pearl in Comparison to the Shell You Threw Away Disowned Mum and Dad Turn Back on Scots Girl Jihadi Who Wrote," *Daily Record* (Glasgow, Scotland), September 12, 2014.

66. "Report: 60 British Women Joined All-Female Islamic State Brigade," *Jerusalem Post*, September 8, 2014.

67. "Brit Woman Calls for War on the Streets in Her Diary of Hate," *The Mirror* (London), September 3, 2014.

68. "Syria-Bound London Teenagers 'May Have Been Recruited by Scottish Woman," *BBC*, February 21, 2015.

69. Khaleda Rahman, "'I Will Only Come Back to Britain to Raise the Black Flag': Scottish 'Private School Jihadist' in Warning to West's Muslims as She Rejects Appeal to Return," *Daily Mail*, September 11, 2014.

70. "'Bedroom Radical' Aqsa Mahmood Left UK to Become ISIS Bride," NBC News, September 4, 2016.

71. "Syria-Bound London teenagers."

72. Leary, "Hands Off Our Husbands."

73. Khaleda Rahman, "'I Will Only Come Back to Britain to Raise the Black Flag': Scottish 'Private School Jihadist' in Warning to West's Muslims as She Rejects Appeal to Return," *Daily Mail*, September 11, 2014.

74. Stewart Whittingham, "White Widow Samantha Lewthwaite 'Has Killed 400 People in Reign of Terror against the West,'" *Mirror*, May 17, 2015.

75. Ibid.

76. RAF CASERT, Associated Press writer. "Belgians shocked to learn Baghdad suicide bomber was local woman." AP Worldstream Press Association. December 1, 2005.

77. Simone Roworth, "Australia: Editors' Picks for 2015 Australia's Caliphettes, Canberra," *The Strategist*, December 29, 2015.

78. Omar Sultan Haque, Jihye Choi, Tim Phillips, and Harold J. Bursztajn, "Why Are Young Westerners Drawn to Terrorist Organizations Like ISIS?" *Psychiatric Times*, September 10, 2015.

79. "Dutch Antiterror Expert Urges Use of ISIL Deserters' Narratives against Group," *Hilversum*, September 22, 2015.

80. Robert Pape and Walker Gunning, "ISIS and the Culture of Narcissism—Using Hollywood's Methods to Make Young Westerners Think They're Starring in a 'Hero's Journey,'" *Wall Street Journal*, June 29, 2016.

81. John Hall, "Thai Boxing World Champion Abandons Life in Germany to Fight for ISIS in Syria . . . Where He Admits Attending the Terror Group's Brutal Public Executions," *Daily Mail*, June 12, 2015.

82. Johnlee Varghese, "Syria: Two-Time World Thai Boxing Champion from Germany, Valdet Gashi, Joins Isis," *International Business Times*, June 4, 2015.

83. Hall, "Thao Boxing World Champion Abandons Life in Germany."

84. Margit Hufnagel, Dieter Loeffler, and Wolfgang Wisler, "Avldet Gashi, the ISIL Fighter from Lake Constance," *Augsburger Allgemeine Online*, June 21, 2015.

85. Varghese, "Syria: Two-Time World Thai Boxing Champion from Germany."

86. John Hall "Thai boxing world champion abandons life in Germany to fight for ISIS in Syria," *Daily Mail Online*, June 12, 2015, http://www.dailymail.co.uk /news/article-3121659/Thai-boxing-world-champion-Valdet-Gashi-abandons-life -Germany-fight-ISIS-Syria-admits-attending-terror-group-s-brutal-public -executions.html#ixzz4KW6GhpYr.

87. "World Muay Thai Boxing Champion from Germany Joins ISIS in Syria," *Russia Today*, June 4, 2015.

88. Ibid.

89. "World Champion Joined ISIL," *Tirana Shquiptarja*, July 6, 2015.

90. "The Wild One—1953" IMDb, Accessed September 15 2016, http://www .imdb.com/title/tt0047677/quotes.

91. Katrin Bennhold, "ISIS Telling a Potent Tale in Britain," *International New York Times*, July 29, 2015.

92. Nicolai Sennels, "Dutch Researcher: 'The Better Integrated, the Higher the Risk of Radicalization,'" April 3, 2015.

93. Andros Lozano, "From the Spanish Army to the ISIL's Jihad," *Madrid Elmundo*, July 27, 2015.

94. Ibid.

95. American journalist Julia Ioffe profiled Westerners' mothers whose sons sought emotional relief and spiritual fulfillment in the Caliphate. Julia Ioffe, "Mothers of ISIS Recruits Fight Their Own Battles Back Home," *Huffington Post*. Accessed September 17, 2016, http://highline.huffingtonpost.com/articles/en /mothers-of-isis/.

96. Julia Ioffe, "Mothers of ISIS Their Children Abandoned Them to Join the Worst Terror Organization on Earth. Now All They Have Is Each Other," *Huffington Post*, accessed August 13, 2015, http://www.huffingtonpost.com/entry/the-mothers-of-isis_us_55cb80ace4b0f1cbf1e71061.

97. Ibid.

98. David Maher, "Irish Mum Tells of Pain as Son Dies Fighting with ISIS in Syria Eire Region," *The Daily Mirror*, May 5, 2016.

99. "Urgent—Nice France Attacker Radicalized Quickly," *CNN Wire Service*, July 16, 2016.

100. Anthony Faiola and Souad Mekhennet, "Europe's Converts to Islam Hearing the Call to Jihad," *The Washington Post*, May 6, 2015.

101. Leon Watson, "Revealed: How Sally Jones of Chatham Went from Being All-Girl Rock Band Member to 'Wife of ISIS Jihadi Fanatic Who Threatens to Behead Christians by Herself with a Blunt Knife,'" *Daily Mail*, August 31, 2014.

102. Rebecca Perring, "ISIS Jihadist Dubbed Mrs. Terror Who Wanted to Behead Christians Lived on Church Aid," *Express*, August 17, 2015.

103. "Female Recruits 'Revel in Gore and Brutality,'" *Western Mail* (Cardiff, Wales), February 21, 2015.

104. Watson, "Revealed: How Sally Jones of Chatham."

105. "Suicide Bomb Wish for ISIS 'Black Widow' Warped Terror Bride Hoping for a One Way Trip to 'Paradise,'" *Birmingham Mail* (England), November 30, 2015.

106. Nicholai Sennels, "Psychologist: Poor, Insane Muslim Terrorists with Family Problems Are Still Muslim Terrorists," *Jihad Watch*, July 18, 2015.

107. Nicholai Sennels, "Psychology: Why Islam Creates Monsters," *10news*, December 15, 2014.

108. "Hate Preacher Omar Bakri Instructs Followers to Convert Aliens to Islam," *Daily Mail*, January 3, 2009.

109. Nor are those who suffer psychosis significantly more violent than those in healthy populations. According to a Harvard 2001 study, "'Findings have been inconsistent about how much mental illness contributes to [violence].'" The combination of mental illness with substance is, according to Harvard researchers, a dangerous cocktail. "Mental Illness and Violence," *Harvard Mental Health Letter*, Harvard Health Publications, 2011.

110. One of the more infamous and successful uses of the irresistible impulse was the Lorena Bobbitt case of 1994, in which the defendant was found not guilty of cutting off her husband's penis in a fit of rage.

111. "From Daniel M'Naughten to John Hinckley: A Brief History of the Insanity Defense," *Frontline*, Accessed September 17, 2016, http://www.pbs.org/wgbh/pages/frontline/shows/crime/trial/history.html.

112. "Nanny Accused in Russia Girl's Murder: Allah Ordered It," *CBS/AP*, March 2, 2016.

113. Maria Tsvetkova and Andrew Osborn, "Nanny Who Beheaded Russian Girl Cites Revenge for Putin's Syria Strikes," *Reuters*, March 3, 2016.

114. Will Stewart, "Killer Nanny Who Beheaded Four-Year-Old Girl 'Kept Her Schizophrenia a Secret and Was Kicked on to Streets after a Divorce,'" *Daily Mail*, March 14, 2016.

115. Maria Tsvetkova and Andrew Osborn, "Nanny Who Beheaded Russian Girl Cites Revenge for Putin's Syria Strikes," *Reuters*, March 3, 2016.

116. "Nanny Accused in Russia Girl's Murder."

117. Leda Reynolds, "ISIS Has a New Super Fan—Sadistic Moors Murderer Ian Brady Who Wants Britain Attacked," *Express (Online)*, May 9, 2016.

118. According to the widely used Psychopathy Checklist, the defining traits of psychopathy are:

- glib and superficial charm
- grandiose (exaggeratedly high) estimation of self
- need for stimulation
- pathological lying
- cunning and manipulativeness
- lack of remorse or guilt
- shallow affect (superficial emotional responsiveness)
- callousness and lack of empathy
- parasitic lifestyle
- poor behavioral controls
- sexual promiscuity
- early behavior problems
- lack of realistic long-term goals
- impulsivity
- irresponsibility
- failure to accept responsibility for own actions
- many short-term marital relationships
- juvenile delinquency
- revocation of conditional release
- criminal versatility

Robert Hare, "Without Conscience," Accessed September 17, 2016, http://hare.org/.

119. Greg Eghigian, "A Drifting Concept for an Unruly Menace: A History of Psychopathy in Germany," *ISIS: Journal of the History of Science in Society* 106, no. 2 (2015): 283–309.

120. "I wish I did it," said one woman, referring to the murder of US journalist Steven Sotloff. "My best friend is my grenade. . . . It's an American one too. May Allah allow me to kill their Kanzeer [pig] soldiers with their own weapons," said another. "UK Experts Claim Women Joining ISIL Not Victims," *Paris AFP (North European Service)*, January 28, 2015.

121. Ryan Mauro, "Forensic Psychiatrist: Fascinating Insights into Orlando Shooting," *Clarion Project*, July 11, 2016.

122. There is a counterargument that obtaining virgins in heaven as a martyr is a very compelling reward for young sex-starved men.

123. Nicolai Sennels, "Psychiatrist: Paris Jihadis Aren't Psychopaths, They're Islamic Fundamentalists, An Interview with Henrik Day Poulsen, Psychiatrist, Ph. D.," *10news*, posted on *Jihad Watch*, January 10, 2015.

124. Elaine Ganley, "Arrest Shows Europe's Challenge to Track Jihadi," *AP Online*, June 3, 2014.

125. "Belgium Thwarts Islamist Attacks—Report," *AFP*, September 20, 2014.

126. Matthew Campbell, "French Journalist Tells of Being Tortured in Syria by Islamic Terrorist," *The Times*, September 15, 2014.

127. Christopher Dickey, "French Jihadi Mehdi Nemmouche Is the Shape of Terror to Come," *Daily Beast*, September 9, 2014.

128. Terrorism Research and Analysis Consortium, "Mehdi Nemmouche—Individual Profile," accessed August 10, 2014.

129. Betsi Fores, "Megyn Kelly Talks to Former Islamic Radical: Calling Them Psychopaths Lets Them Off Too Easily," *Rare Staff*, September 3, 2014.

130. R. Siva Kumar, "Squirm Like Animals" Neweveryday.com, March 16, 2016, http://www.newseveryday.com/articles/11137/20150316/squirm-animals-released-hostage-recalls-horrific-torture-jihadi-john-sadist.htm.

131. Anthony Mason and Charlie D'Agata, "British Intelligence Officers Are Reportedly Questioning Teachers from Emwazi's Former High School after One Came Forward Last Night and Said as a Student, Emwazi Had Trouble Controlling His Anger Too," *CBS This Morning*, 2015.

132. Jane Miller, "Jihadis in London," *In These Times*, May 1, 2015.

133. "Emwazi Tried to Recruit at 12 Mosques," *The Mirror* (London), March 23, 2015.

134. "IS Captives Taunted by Song 'Welcome to Hotel Osama,'" *The Mirror* (London), March 23, 2015.

135. "Dead Airport Bomber Beat ISIS Hostages Held in Syria Edition 3," *The Times*, April 23, 2016.

136. "Jihadi John 'Held a Blade on My Neck,'" *The Mirror* (London), March 16, 2015.

137. Emma Glanfield, "Jihadi John Fathered a Secret Son in Syria Who Is Now Entitled to British Citizenship," *Mail Online*, November 14, 2015.

138. Marco Giannangeli, "Jihadi John Pinpointed by SAS for US Airstrike Because of Baseball Cap He Always Wore," *Express*, November 15, 2015.

139. Glanfield, "Jihadi John Fathered a Secret Son in Syria."

140. "ISIS Obit for Jihadi John," *Daily Record* (Glasgow, Scotland), January 20, 2016.

141. That is what Colonel Steven Warren, a US Army spokesperson, said. Jamie Schram and Danika Fears, "How the US Wiped 'Jihadi John' off the Face of the Earth," *New York Post*, November 14, 2015.

5. BLUE-EYED JIHAD: THE CALIPHATE'S FOREIGN LEGION, PART TWO

We have the unborn martyrs in our wombs.

—A woman shouting at Muslim Day Parade in New York City, 2015[1]

The previous chapter focused on the Islamic State's foreign legion of Westerners. Chapter 5 will continue to discuss this cohort with attention to parental involvement and disillusionment in the Caliphate's cause and comrades.

Level One—Family Are Primary Drivers

Oh Allah, I ask for a death in your path, and I ask for death in the country of your prophet . . . heaven, heaven, heaven . . . I swear, I can't wait.

—An Italian woman converted to Islam by her Tunisian husband, 2016[2]

There is a wide range of family involvement in the radicalizing of their children. Some parents and other family members promote their child's radicalization; some are unaware of the transformation; and some are aware and try to dissuade them from joining the Caliphate.

On the first level, parents or family members are involved in radicalization and have actively encouraged and/or facilitated their kin's participation in the State. As mentioned earlier, many Muslims feel segregated in Europe. At home and in school, children are "fed on a diet of Islam," as revealed in British investigations.[3] After the Second World War, Western European schools stressed assimilation and liberalism, but many European schools today foster segregation, and some pro-mote Islamist supremacy. This isolation is encouraged by some Muslim families.

Some entire families leave Europe to fight in the Caliphate. Their neighbors notice that, one day, they simply vanish. Local children won-der why their playmates stopped coming to class and ask what happened to them. Rumors circulate, particularly if the families seemed very re-ligious and aloof from non-Muslims. Some of the missing have turned up on social media with stories and photographs of their new lives.[4] For example, a British family of twelve made a statement in July 2015, from Raqqa, that they had escaped the "so-called freedom and democracy that was forced down our throats."[5] Safely ensconced in Raqqa, they asked their former British neighbors to join them there.

Sometimes it is hard to determine the parents' agenda for their chil-dren. For example, the father of a "Jihadi bride" was unmasked when he was filmed marching in solidarity with Islamist radicals, including the killer of the British soldier Lee Rigby. Further, he took his daughter with him on the march.[6]

Other times secular-oriented parents become legally entangled in a sordid spectacle their children created. A case in point is the arrest of the parents of the white British Muslim convert Jack Letts, dubbed "Ji-hadi Jack."[7] Initially, the parents, John and Sally, middle-class Oxford residents, were shocked that their son had joined the State.[8] The police warned them not to support their son, but John and Sally tried twice to send him 1,000 pounds. After the second attempt, they were arrested for "fundraising and arranging availability of money and property for use in terrorism."[9] Their son's response? Jack said he hated them because they were nonbelievers. "I call them to Islam."[10]

Other times, the children suffer. After a Caliphate-bound British mother was imprisoned in spring 2016, her three children were sent to live with relatives. In a family court at Old Bailey, the judge told the mother, "You knew perfectly well of your husband's dedication to ter-rorism."[11] The children were kept from the Islamic State, but their lives were changed forever.

Level Two—Family Were Unaware of Radicalization

ISIS is stealing our children, draining our life force.

—Veronique Roy, whose French son was killed in the Islamic State, 2016[12]

On the second level of family involvement, family members were un-aware of the person's plans to leave for the Caliphate. These family mem-bers are usually shocked and emotionally traumatized when they learn what has happened. Despite therapy, some do not fully recover and are unable to shake an overwhelming sense of betrayal and loss. Many blame themselves.

An Australian man was distraught when his twenty-six-year-old Australian ex-wife abandoned their children and left for Syria. Jasmina Milovanov, a convert to Islam, left her children with a sitter, promising she would soon return. She never came home. Her ex-husband explained, "I can't believe that she left these beautiful children."[13] Similarly, a British Muslim was completely blindsided when his wife took their children to the Middle East on Valentine's Day, 2015.[14] Despairingly, he asks, "My question is why did she go there? She has two kids, she has a family, and this house is in her name. Why has she left everything?"[15]

Mario Sciannimanica was born in Italy and raised in Germany. His mother was shaken when Mario left for the State, where he recruits fellow Europeans in both German and Italian publications. Desperate to hear from her son, the mother wrote to Germany's leading Salafi website: "Please, I beg you, anybody who is close to him, let us know how he is and whether we can do anything for him. In the name of God."[16]

Sometimes parents are able to rescue their children. But even these initially joyous events can become tragic. A Tunisian military physician went to Turkey to retrieve his son, who had joined and then left the Caliphate. Earlier, the son had been a lighthearted medical student. "He used to spend time with my daughters, laughing and joking, but that stopped," said a cousin. But he became withdrawn and hateful toward nonreligious Muslims. He joined the Caliphate and left for Iraq but soon changed his mind and asked his father, a general in the Tunisian military, to get him out. The father's connections and persistence worked, and the general went to Turkey to bring his boy home. As the general was transiting the airport in Istanbul on June 28, 2016, he was killed in the Caliphate-directed terrorist attacks there. The general was buried with full military honors in his Tunisian home. The local newspaper noted, "ISIS attracts a son . . . and kills a father."[17]

Siblings and friends of Western foreign fighters are surprised, too.[18] They cannot explain the sadism they see meted out by their sons, daughters, or former friends. Maxime Hauchard, twenty-two, from a village in Normandy in northern France, was filmed decapitating a Syrian prisoner. Those who knew him in France could not understand why he would hurt anyone. A former neighbor speculated that Maxime must have been drugged.

In Australia, one couple agonized about their daughter, grandchildren, and great grandchild. Australians Karen and Peter Nettleton's daughter converted to Islam and, with her husband, took their five children to the Caliphate.[19] The Nettletons' heart-rending case is presented below.

*I accept that some will be critical of my daughter, who followed her heart
and has paid an enormous price. Mr. Abbott, I beg you,
please help bring my child and grandchildren home.*

—Karen Nettleton to then Prime Minister Abbott[20]

Australian grandmother Karen Nettleton wrestles with her memory to grasp what went wrong with her daughter, Tara. What caused it? How did it happen? A next-door neighbor described Tara as polite and attractive and not very different from other girls in the neighborhood.[21] One day the neighbor noticed that Tara was wearing Islamic apparel. He said to her, "You are too pretty to wear those things." After that, Tara never spoke to him again.

Tara met a Muslim when she was still a teenager and had his baby when she was seventeen. They were high school sweethearts. Her heart-throb was Khaled Sharrouf, a man with a troubled past, drifting into and out of petty crime and abusing drugs. He was mentally ill, diagnosed first with depression and later with schizophrenia.[22] The son of Lebanese parents and raised in a dysfunctional family, Sharrouf served time for stockpiling weapons. Before release, he was put on medication, and in early 2009 physicians commented on his "remarkable recovery."[23] Later, both Tara and Khaled embraced fundamentalist Islam and left for the Caliphate to build a life. And they, along with their children, became famous.

"That's My Boy!"

Karen Nettleton still cannot comprehend her daughter's descent into sadism or her delight in global publicity. Partnering with her husband, Tara enslaved, raped, beat women. They made this a family affair. One of their sons, a seven-year-old, held a severed head for a photo. Bursting with pride, Khaled shouted, "That's my boy!" That caught the world's attention when it was posted on Facebook.

At age thirty-one, Tara succumbed to complications from appendicitis. Her husband, Khaled, may be dead, or he may be alive; Western authorities are not sure. The eldest daughter, Zaynab, who had a child of her own, was killed by a drone.[24]

Four of Tara and Khaled's five children and one granddaughter are still alive, according to reports, probably in Raqqa, and Karen is desperate to rescue them.[25] She is concerned that the girls will be turned into sex slaves or beggars. "I am devastated because I wasn't able to be at my daughter's side. I'm not able to be there for my grandkids and great-grandchild, who are suffering traumatic events outside their control."[26]

Level Three—Family Were Active Dissuaders

It's better not to live than to be the mother of a terrorist.
You realize what a monster you gave birth to.

—Shakhla Bochkaryova[27]

The third level of family involvement is that of family members who intervened and tried to stop the radicalization. One unsuccessful mother, Shakhla Bochkaryova, chained her twenty-year-old daughter, Fatima, to the apartment's radiator to keep her from fleeing Siberia and becoming the fourth wife of a Jihadi. Like other similarly distraught mothers, Shakhla saw the irreversible transformation from a fashion-conscious, head-turning young woman to a Caliphate-bound, hate-spewing Jihadi, but the mother was powerless to leash her daughter. Said the mother plaintively, "I looked at her, and I could no longer see my child. She was simply a shell of my daughter, no soul, no thoughts, no heart."[28] From Raqqa, Fatima cursed her mother, calling her an infidel murderer and threatening to kill her when the Caliphate conquers Europe.

Sometimes parents will brave the dangers of Raqqa to fetch their daughters back home. Nineteen-year-old Aicha fell hard for a charismatic Dutch Jihadi after seeing him on television. She converted to Islam and left with him for Raqqa but soon called her mother, Monique, to take her home. "Monique," fully aware of what she would likely encounter, set out to Raqqa undercover and in a burka to bring her daughter home, at great risk to both of them. Monique said, "Sometimes you do what you have to do."[29] Monique rescued her daughter, but most stories do not have warm endings.

In the United States, the parents of Shannon Maureen Conley had evidence that their girl was preparing to fight as a Jihadi. Only after they exhausted their pleas to their daughter did they contact the FBI, knowing she would be arrested. Her story, and that of a Russian college student, is told below.

PROFILE SIXTEEN: AN AMERICAN AND A RUSSIAN: HALIMA AND AMINA

Shannon/Halima

Christian-raised Shannon Maureen Conley, a nineteen-year-old Denver suburbanite, planned to make herself useful to the Islamic State after she became a Muslim. Shannon changed her name to Halima, which is loosely translated as "mild mannered" and "generous." She announced to the world that she had become a "slave of Allah."[30]

All this was a surprise to some of those who had known her as a girl, well before she became Halima. Her neighbors commented that Shannon had undergone a drastic transformation late in high school. A neighbor related, "I would see her in shorts and, then, all of a sudden, she started wearing those [Islamic] clothes."[31] She found a new identity in Islam as she entered adulthood.

Halima did not keep her newfound faith to herself. At Faith Bible Chapel, near her home, she made her presence known. Wearing a hijab and a backpack, she gained the pastor's attention by acting with a curious hostility. A volunteer at the church's small café noticed that Conley ordered biscuits and gravy one morning. But Shannon became angry when she found out that her meal contained meat, and she hurled it into the trash.[32] She also made political comments that alarmed churchgoers.[33] She was asked not to return.

The FBI intervened, interviewed her and her parents, and advised her not to make statements that could easily be construed as threatening. But she told the FBI, "If they [churchgoers] think I'm a terrorist, I'll give them something to think I am."[34] The FBI kept their eyes on Halima and spoke to her nine times. They understood that she intended to travel to Syria.[35] They were right.

There was an element of romance, of sorts, to Shannon's road to Jihad. She fell hard for a man she had never met in person. On the internet, she spooned her affections to a man she believed to be a fellow traveler. Her paramour and coconspirator boasted that he was an active Caliphate fighter. In turn, she crowed that she had attended US Army Explorers camp and would use that training to wage Jihad against nonbelievers.[36] She was also certified in shooting skills by the National Rifle Association. They had much in common. He proposed marriage, and she accepted. They dreamed of meeting and marrying in Syria and then fighting for the Caliphate. She would cook and nurse injured Jihadis; he would kill the enemies of the State. But before traveling to Syria, Conley needed to prepare.[37]

Shannon's father discovered his daughter's plan and notified the FBI, who arrested her at the Denver airport. In her luggage, the agents found several CDs and DVDs labeled "Anwar al-Awlaki," who was a leading propagandist of Islamic violence. She also carried a list of contacts, one of whom was the man she planned to wed. Shannon did not make it to the Middle East or get married. She was sentenced to four years in a federal prison.[38] And the reaction of those who knew her? The church volunteer who served Shannon the biscuit that she had chucked in the trashcan with scorn said of Shannon, "I feel sorry for her. She needs a lot of prayer."[39]

Amina

A young Russian woman took a path similar to Shannon's. With a soft smile and a broad, Slavic face, the nineteen-year-old Varvara Karaulova looked more like a Russian coed than a Jihadi aspirant. She was both. Varvara was enrolled in one of Russia's most respected universities, Moscow State University, where she studied Arabic and philosophy. She had already mastered French and English, and her intellectual curiosity led her to the Middle East. Her Facebook profile says she likes authors J. R. R. Tolkien and leading Russian writer and poet Mikhail Lermontov. But in late May 2015, she would be arrested, with other Russians, while trying to infiltrate into Syria from Turkey.[40]

Her father, Pavel, commented with confusion, "She's always home studying . . . she's so trustworthy. But somehow she got twisted into this."[41] Varvara's friends noticed that she began acting and dressing differently after she started taking Arabic classes at her university. She had become more distant from non-Muslims and began to wear the hijab. Then, a week before she left, Pavel noticed she wasn't wearing her cross necklace. "She said the chain broke," he said. She changed her name to Amina and left for Syria.[42]

Interpol detained her when she tried to cross illegally from Turkey to Syria.[43] Varvara was deported back to Russia. Her father was relieved but despaired. "I just had no idea. This should be a lesson for all of us."[44]

WANTING TO COME HOME

The Revolution is like Saturn. It devours its own Children.

—Georg Büchner, *Danton's Death*, 1835[45]

My iPod is broken. I want to come back.

—A young French Jihadist's tweet to his parents in France[46]

The first three parts of this chapter discussed the broad groupings of reasons why Westerners travel to the Caliphate. The chapter will now turn to reasons why some of them want to leave the Caliphate and return to their former homes.

Some Westerners who have traveled to the Caliphate are happy there and do not want to leave. They have built new lives and found important positions. Some Westerners have died, often in combat, and are buried in what became their homeland. But many have not found what they had hoped to find in the Caliphate and want to return to the West, after grim living. The diehard British Jihadis fighting for the State call their homesick comrades "mummy-boys." It is hard to gauge how many or what proportion of those Western émigrés want to leave the Caliphate. Those who try to break out are often killed or threatened. Some are caring for their children and would not escape without ensuring their safety. There are three groupings of reasons why they want to come home: disappointment, fear, and that cruelty was not in their nature.

Reason One—Disappointment and Discomfort

*Syrian woman backbiting us [me and my Australian sister]
while we're sitting in front of her, thinking that I don't speak Arabic.*

—A British woman called Umm Rayyan[47]

For some Westerners, there is a gap between what they expected in the Caliphate and what they found. Many did not find the enchanting village they were promised. The roasting temperatures and inadequate air conditioning are enervating. An Australian woman, "mother of the seeker of martyrdom," carped about the blazing summer sun: "The heat in sham [Syria] is shocking. I'm thinking to change my kunya [name] to Umm [mother] Sweat. Over this heat."[48]

The stabbing heat provides the perfect climate for exotic bugs and diseases, including tropical diseases that are largely unknown in the West, to flourish. Many Europeans in Syria today do not understand the cause of their skin sores. For example, a deadly flesh-eating bug, Leishmaniosis, is a sand fly, and it feasts on the corpses strewn in the street by the State's fighters. After devouring the dead, the bugs bore into the living.

The searing temperatures, boutique diseases, and sand flies are not advertised in the Caliphate's recruitment brochures. Nor is the mundanity awaiting many Western recruits. Some have blogged that their assigned tasks are menial or unfulfilling. There are few luxury goods or cars. Male fighters are offered beautiful and nubile brides as well as sex slaves, but many are not as eye-catching or sexually enthusiastic as promised.[49] An Australian recruiter preparing to leave for Syria and join his comrades canceled his plans when he heard about the squalid conditions in which he would live. They slept on "spongy" mattresses and took showers with dirty buckets of water. Further, they had no toilet paper.

Those who come dream of becoming warriors but instead launder clothes and cook and clean up after others. One fighter complained about having to clean weapons and transport dead bodies from the front. He said, "Winter's arrived here. It's begun to get really hard." A South African returning from the Caliphate commented, "Much of the attraction of the Islamic State to outsiders is built on half-truths and propaganda. It's no surprise that the reality did not live up to the illusion."[50]

An American Jihadi escaped from Syria, in part, because he was forced to study Islam for eight hours each day. A Virginian, he had earned a degree at community college and worked as a teller at a local bank, but he was not academically inclined. He hoped to fight for Islam in the State but was forced to study the religion instead. He was captured by the Kurdish Peshmerga and confessed he could not endure the daily all-day Koranic memorization and regurgitation. It became maddening. He also missed smoking.[51] "My message to the American people is that life in Mosul, it's really, really bad."[52]

Beyond the weather, diseases, and tedious lifestyle, many Westerners are also astonished by the hatred the locals show them. Westerners expect to be welcomed as liberators but are seen as occupiers and thieves. They have heard comments such as "You are here to sabotage my country; you are coming to force something on us."[53] Leaders of the State explain to new Western recruits that some Syrians are not delighted by their presence. A Caliphate-produced book, *Culture Clash: Understanding the Syrian Race*, tries to lessen the culture shock.[54]

In addition to the brutality, some Westerners are repulsed by the manners of their compatriots. They find the Middle Easterners, particularly the Arabs, to be vulgar and inconsiderate. One Briton blogged about the initial shock and then steady fatigue he experienced trying to grapple with the boorish table manners, peevish behavior, and brazen theft of personal property.[55]

Others who want to leave are killed by their fellow fighters. This probably happened to "Florent," a Cameroonian who immigrated to Germany, where he was raised Christian. He converted to Islam at fourteen and left for Syria the following year.[56] Dead at seventeen, his German hometown didn't know whether to hold a Christian or Islamic memorial service. His former Christian pastor decided to have a Muslim service in his church to show "learning and respect among religions."[57]

A Woman's World within a Man's World

It's not Sharia that men scream or talk to us in the street. It's not.
I feel more and more sad here now. There is so little respect for us.

—A foreign fighter[58]

I know it may be shirk [idolatry] but sometimes I do miss Starbucks.
The coffee here is beyond wretched.

—Western woman called GreenBirdofDabiq[59]

By their own accounts, many female foreign fighters travel to the Caliphate to escape unwanted attentions of men. But, according to many tweets, Western women do not find the sanctuary they expect.[60] For example, in August 2015, a Swedish woman moaned, "Seriously, I am getting so tired of many men muhajirin [emigrants] now. I feel harassed so often now. Women can't do this or that. What is the point?"[61]

British girls are urged to take lingerie with them as they travel to Syria to marry Islamic State fighters.[62] One blogger suggests that women should bring as much milk as possible, but that hair straighteners and deodorant are available.[63] Many Western women never fully adjust to Jihadi living. They do not like to share their husbands with other women. Young women in search of benevolent and "caring" mother figures may be similarly lured. Sometimes they find them. But cowives are not always friends; they compete against each other for their husband's affections and lovemaking and for prestige and place in the household. Some of the household chores have a morbid twist; for example, the more talented seamstresses are impressed into sewing suicide vests.

Sometimes Western girls and women are trapped in the Caliphate. Two early Western Caliphate volunteers were Samra Kizinovic (sometimes spelled Kesinovic) and her friend Sabina Clemovic (sometimes spelled Selimovic). Samra was sixteen and Sabina fifteen when they left their homes in Vienna in April 2014. First, they wanted to find husbands.[64] The girls were very pretty, particularly Samra, who was given the moniker "Caliphate's queen of beauty."

The promised adventure soon turned sour. When they realized they had made a mistake, they contacted their parents and pled to go home. They never would return. According to Kurdish sources, Samra, the fair-haired, blue-eyed young beauty, was dead by summer 2015. Her friend would die, too. According to the source, they were beaten to death.[65]

One woman who did make it out had a similar experience. Convert Sophie Kasiki, whose French husband was an atheist, traveled to Syria to live in "paradise." She took their four-year-old son to look for "ISIS Prince Charming." What she found was a prison, from which she eventually escaped. "I will always feel bad about taking my son to this hellish nightmare."[66]

Reason Two—Fear

A second reason for wanting to leave the Caliphate is fear. Some Western men and women live in constant fear and would like to escape the Caliphate. One young man wrote, "They want to send me to the front, but I don't know how to fight."[67] Westerners discover, often too late, that fellow Jihadis are killed for trivial offenses. Those who ask to return home are sometimes forced into suicide operations.[68] The Islamic State kills anyone from their own cadre who tries to leave. It has executed at least one hundred of its own foreign fighters who tried to flee Raqqa.[69] Some make it out of Syria, but some are stranded in Turkey, where they are hunted down by agents of the State.[70] By summer 2016, they were killing relatives of escapees. As one man said, "They got stricter as they worried we'd rebel, burning people alive and cutting people's throats."[71]

Western fighters do not know whom to trust. One described the situation: "It [the Caliphate's security and intelligence service(s)] is a highly organized body, with very strong discipline. Everybody spies on everybody else."[72] There is cybersecurity. In the shadowy world, cybercafes are often the only means by which Westerners can communicate with their friends and family. For this reason, the Caliphate's security operatives have installed software that records keystrokes.[73]

In summer 2015, the Caliphate tightened surveillance over Raqqa, the Caliphate's capital. One year later, Raqqa was under regular and gunmen guards, increased checkpoints, and tightened security. The Caliphate has counterintelligence capabilities and uses double agents to unmask those persons and groups they consider subversive or untrustworthy. They deploy members of the cadre in the streets and cybercafes to penetrate underground networks that organize foreigners' departures. They regularly use double-agent operations to trap would-be deserters.[74] Without passports or an ability to speak Arabic, some Westerners are too scared to try to leave. Others just disappear.

This was the case with Zora, a girl from the French suburbs who left for Syria after she turned fourteen years old. She had been recruited by three other women and, as of late 2015, lived in a communal setting with about fifty other girls and young women, mostly from Europe. They were heavily guarded and rarely allowed to leave their tight living confines. She and other females were, according to Zora, forced to watch beheadings and were often awoken by bomb blasts. She hoped to return to France, and her father offered to pay anything. He sent her a scanned birth certificate in case she would escape. But he stopped hearing from her. "I call every morning. I'm waiting for her to get back online."[75]

Most escapees need to reach Turkey, where there are consular offices that can help them.[76] Defections began as a trickle and then poured by spring 2016. Defectors arrive in singles, doubles, or small groups, usually disheveled and desperate.[77] As one would-be defector explained in June 2016, "We don't know where to go. We want to go further away, but Europe is too expensive," he said. "We know people are after us and want to kill us. We feel lost."[78]

Mohimanul Alam Bhuiya, a twenty-five-year-old former Brooklyn resident, is also certain that Caliphate gunmen are determined to kill him. From Syria, he emailed the FBI to "extract" him and bring him home.[79] In high school he wrote glowing term papers on World War II leaders of democracy, Churchill and Roosevelt. Then he found Islam and the Caliphate; today he misses democracy.

Reason Three—Cruelty Was Not in Their Nature

The third reason Westerners want to come home is the realization that they are not emotionally suited for the cruelty of the State. Some Western Jihadis relish the brutality they inflict on their enemies. Sadists are comfortable in the Caliphate today. But many people cannot witness this cruelty without becoming traumatized. The reality of war is not what they expected.[80]

The State requires recruits to prove allegiance by hurting people. Some eagerly do so. One Caliphate supporter prepared to kill humans by slitting the throats of rabbits. Later, he would stab to death a French police officer and his wife in Paris in summer 2016.[81]

Many recruits realize that killing people would be too difficult. In the words of one recruit, "They told us, 'When you capture someone, you will behead them.' But as for me, I have never even beheaded a chicken. It is not easy . . . I can't do that."[82] A New Yorker who joined and then left the State in 2016 warned his fellow Americans to "avoid the worst decision" he ever made. "I did see severed heads placed on spiked poles . . . I just blocked them out."[83] Some beheadings are shown on the Caliphate-produced snuff films with names such as "Harvest of the Apostates."

Sadism has its own dark humor in the Islamic State. A deserter described a prank at a water well in a small town called Hute. State security personnel would take blindfolded prisoners and tell them that they were free to leave but not to remove the blindfold until they had been walking for a few minutes. When the prisoners took a few steps forward, they would fall into a deep well, to the laughing delight of Caliphate spectators. They would die quickly or slowly. "It smells horrible because of all the corpses inside the well. I know that over 300 people were thrown into that well."[84]

For many Western recruits, there is first an initial shock, followed by the numbing effect created by constant carnage, and sometimes feelings of guilt.[85] One woman cannot escape the memory of the pained expressions on the faces of women whom she hurt. She is remorseful that she served al-Khansaa, an all-women religious enforcement brigade, and hurt people as an enforcer of virtue.[86] She flogged women, sometimes delivering sixty lashes, for failed escape attempts. Wearing inappropriate clothes brought forty hits. "What upset me most was lashing old women when they weren't wearing the proper clothes."[87] She said, "We'd lash them and humiliate them."[88]

Al-Khansaa militants disfigure women by pouring acid on their faces.[89] There is also a dehumanization of girls and women that many Westerners have not experienced. Among the most horrific illustrations is the sexual slave market, which splits mothers from daughters. Girls are priced according to their attractiveness. Then they are raped and discarded.[90] A Syrian woman, racked by guilt for her earlier support of the State, warned, "The Caliphate is not what you think it is. Women are whipped, sold, and stoned. Corpses are on display publicly for weeks."[91]

Sometimes it is difficult to know the truth. Those who are arrested upon return have every incentive to downplay their militancy and emphasize their compassion. A twenty-five-year-old German joined the Caliphate and then slipped back into Germany, where he was betrayed to police. He confessed his service for the State, but said that he never took the oath of loyalty and that he only fired a single round in combat, which was aimed at an empty building. German prosecutors could not prove that he had hurt anyone in the Middle East. Had he done so, it is not likely that he would have volunteered the information and risked a stiffer prison sentence.[92]

Some Westerners break out of the Caliphate. One British escapee explained, from hiding in Turkey, that she feared for her life every day. She was convinced that the State is tracking her down as a traitor. "I am a young girl. I want to live my life. I want to travel, go to cafes, meet friends like any normal girl."[93] Another said, "This is not the 1001 Nights."[94]

Psychological and social drivers will continue to attract and repel West-erners. Those who are sadistic or driven to kill non-Muslims will find ample opportunities to do so in the Caliphate. For women who want to perform the sexual Jihad, there will be men available in Syria and Iraq. But many Western women will find life in the Caliphate onerous. Shukee Begum, a thirty-three-year-old British mother and university graduate, warns of the "gangster kind of mentality among the single women there."[95] She explained, the Caliphate was not "me cuppa tea." By summer 2016, the State responded to the Western flight by burying defectors alive, burning them to death, shooting them, or being maca-brely creative with their killing skills.[96]

But some Westerners are elated with their new lives in the Caliph-ate, finding the prestige, power, and comradery that eluded them in the West. In Raqqa, a young woman phoned her European mother, who was weeping at the other end of the line, and said that she had not traveled to Syria just to return to Europe. She was at home in the Caliphate, and she was there to stay.

Notes

1. Ralph Sidway, "Do the Muslims Love Their Children Too: Reapplying Sting Cold War Anthem to a New War," *Jihad Watch*, June 13, 2015.

2. "Woman Detained in Italy 'Wanted to Be a Terrorist,'" *The Local*, June 7, 2016.

3. "Teachers Get Indefinite Classroom Bans over Pupils 'Fed a Diet of Is-lam,'" *Press Association*, February 19, 2016.

4. "UK Sources Dismiss New ISIL Video Purportedly Showing Killing of 'Spies' for Britain," *The Sun Online* (London), January 4, 2016.

5. "Missing UK Family of 12 'Feel Safe after Joining ISIS,'" *Guardian*, July 4, 2015.

6. Joshua Baker and John Simpson, "Father of Islamic State Runaway Had Taken Her on Protest March." *The Times*, UK News, April 6, 2015.

7. "Jihadi Jack: Is Oxford Youth First White Briton to Join IS?" *Hindustan Times* (New Delhi, India), January 24, 2016.

8. "Family Say Jihadi Jack 'Not with IS,'" *The Mirror* (London), January 25, 2016.

9. Richard Kerbaj and Dipesh Gadher, "UK Source Says Police Have Arrest-ed Parents of 'Jihadi Jack' for Trying to Send Him L1,000 in Syria," *Sunday Times Online*, February 7, 2016.

10. Joe Kasper, "I'm Not in ISIS Edition 2," *Daily Star*, July 26, 2016.

11. Ben Hurst, "Children Living with Relatives after ISIS Mum Sent to Pris-on," *Birmingham Mail*, May 28, 2016.

12. Lara Marlowe, "France's Lost Generation: ISIS Is 'Stealing Our Children, Draining Our Life Force'; A Small Town Mourns a Muslim Convert Who Joined Islamic State," *The Irish Times*, January 26, 2016.

13. "Lured by Jihadi Bride Recruiter, Mom Abandons Kids to Join Islamic State," *Firstpost*, May 26, 2015.

14. Matt Watts, "Minicab Driver Begs Wife to Return after She 'Fled to Join IS with the Couple's Children,'" *London Evening Standard*, March 23, 2015.

15. Amanda Williams, "Boy, Eight, on His Way to Join ISIS with His Mother and Sister Had Scrawled 'Jihad' on His Garden Shed before Leaving," *MailOnline*, March 24, 2015.

16. Paolo Biodani and Piero Messina, "A Boxer for the Caliph," *Rome L'Espresso*, May 21, 2015.

17. "Tunisia Buries Army Doctor Killed in Istanbul Looking for ISIS-Linked Son," *Tunis Mosaique FM Online*, July 16, 2015.

18. Duncan Gardham, "Young Mother Who Stole Her 'Party Girl' Twin Sister's Passport so She Could Join ISIS in Syria for a Second Time Is Spared Jailed [sic] so She Can Be with her Young Child," *Mailonline*, July 31, 2015.

19. Sarah Crawford and Taylor Auerbach, "Peter Nettleton Says Bring His Aussie Terror Grandchildren Home Now," *The Daily Telegraph*, August 12, 2014.

20. Lillian Radulova, "'My Daughter Made the Mistake of a Lifetime': ISIS Extremist Khaled Sharrouf's Mother-in-Law Begs for Her Daughter to Be Allowed to Come Home With Her Five Children After Australian Terror Deaths," *Daily Mail*, June 23, 2015, http://www.dailymail.co.uk/news/article-3136285/My-daughter-mistake-lifetime-Mother-ISIS-terrorist-Khaled-Sharrouf-s-wife-begs-allowed-return-Australia-five-children-reports-Mohamed-Elomar-killed.html.

21. Sarah Dean, "Living Next Door to the Devil: The Red-Brick Home of the Aussie Jihadist Who Raised His Boy to Hold Up Severed Heads—and the Kindly Old Neighbour Who Remembers the Terrorist Getting Home at 3am," *Daily Mail*, August 13, 2014.

22. Patrick Odysseus, "Australian Jihadist Has History of Mental Illness," *The Washington Post*, August 30, 2014.

23. Susie O'Brien, "Unthinkable We'd Let Evil Return," *The Cairns Post*, May 29, 2015.

24. Ibid.

25. Bernard Lagan, "'Get My Orphaned Grandchildren out of the Caliphate,'" *The Times*, February 13, 2016.

26. Ninemsn, "Fate Unknown for Five Aussie Children Orphaned in Syria," *9News*, February 11, 2016.

27. Will Stewart, "'I Gave Birth to a Monster': Russian Mother of ISIS Poster Girl Chained Her Daughter up to Try to Stop Her Marrying Jihadi . . . But Could Not Stop the Girl Reaching Syria Where She Praises Terror Atrocities," *Daily Mail*, February 23, 2016.

28. Ibid.

29. Chris Perez, "Ma Rescues Daughter from ISIS," *The New York Post*, November 19, 2014.

30. Honorable Bob Goodlatte Chairman House Judiciary Committee Committee on House Judiciary Subcommittee on Crime, Terrorism, Homeland Security and Investigations, "Congressional Testimony, 'Isil And Domestic Terrorism:Bob Goodlatte, Federal Document Clearing House, February 26, 2015, https://www.highbeam.com/doc/1P1–232908557.html.

31. P. Solomon Banda and Dan Elliott, "Shock, Sadness after Teen's Arrest in Terror Case," *AP Online*, July 3, 2014.

32. P. Solomon Banda and Dan Elliott, "Shock after Teen's Arrest in Terror Case," *The Charleston Gazette* (Charleston, WV), July 3, 2014.

33. P. Solomon Banda and Dan Elliott, "Shock, Sadness after Teen's Arrest in Terror Case," *AP Online*, July 3, 2014.

34. Ibid.

35. Dina Temple-Raston, "When Americans Head to Syria, How Much of a Threat Do They Pose?" *NPR Morning Edition*, December 12, 2014.

36. "Deal May Be Near for Colorado Woman Accused of Aiding Islamist Insurgents," *Arab American News*, August 5, 2014.

37. "Arvada Woman Sentenced for Conspiracy to Provide Material Support to a Designated Foreign Terrorist Organization," *States News Service*, July 23, 2015.

38. "Judge Hands Down 4 Year Sentence to 'Jihad Shannon,'" *CBS Denver*, January 23, 2015.

39. P. Solomon Banda and Dan Elliott, "Shock after Teen's Arrest in Terror Case," *The Charleston Gazette*, July 3, 2014.

40. Mairbek Vatchagaev, "Moscow College Student Caught Crossing into Turkey to Join IS," *Eurasia Daily Monitor* 12, no. 110, June 10, 2015, http://www .jamestown.org/single/?tx_ttnews%5Btt_news%5D=44026#.V-RAcIWcG7M.

41. Sophia Jones, "Missing Russian Student, Suspected of Trying to Join ISIS, Detained While Trying to Cross into Syria," *The World Post*, June 5, 2015, http:// www.huffingtonpost.com/2015/06/05/varvara-karaulova-found-isis_n_7518530 .html.

42. Ibid.

43. "'ISIS Recruit' Moscow Philosophy Student Was among 13 Russians on Their Way to Syria," *Russia Today*, June 5, 2015.

44. Sophia Jones, "Missing Russian Student, Suspected of Trying to Join ISIS, Detained While Trying to Cross into Syria," *The World Post*, June 5, 2015.

45. Georg Buchner, "Revolution Is like Saturn, It Devours Its Own Children," Accessed September 17, 2016, http://www.brainyquote.com/quotes/quotes/g /georgbuchn403255.html.

46. Harriet Alexander, "My iPod Is Broken. I Want to Come Back." *The Telegraph*, December 2, 2014.

47. Twitter post. Twitter.com/Muhaajirah, September 4, 2015.

48. Twitter post. Twitter.com/al_Australi, no date available.

49. "No Jihadi Brides for 'Inferior' Indian ISIS Fighters," 2 *News* (India), November 25, 2015.

50. "South Africans Return Home from ISIS Held Territory," *Cape Town News24*, September 11, 2015.

51. Matt Zapotosky, "American ISIS Fighter Who 'Found It Hard' Returns to Face Criminal Charges," *Washington Post,* June 9, 2016.

52. Liam Deacon "Inevitable Clashes In Cultures': British ISIS Terrorist Complains About 'Angry, Rude, Lazy' Arabs," *Breitbart London,* September 16, 2015, http://www.breitbart.com/london/2015/09/16/inevitable-clashes-in-cultures -british-isis-terrorist-complains-about-angry-rude-lazy-arabs/.

53. Sarah Sinno, "The Defectors' Handbook to Destroying Islamic State UK Source Argues West Should Use Insiders Testimony of ISIL Defectors to Demolish ISIL's Appeal," *London Telegraph,* September 23, 2015.

54. Below are more excerpts from Omar Hussain's guide. British ISIS fighter Omar Hussain frequently gives advice on his Tumblr blog on various topics relevant to Westerners planning to join ISIS in Syria. This includes marital advice. "See MEMRI JTTM Report British ISIS Member Offers Advice on Marrying Jihadis from Twitter," March 30, 2015.

55. Jack Moore, "ISIS's 'Supermarket Jihadi' Complains about Fellow Fighters' Caliphate Conduct," *Newsweek,* September 17, 2015.

56. Oliver Lane and Chris Tomlinson, "Outrage as Church Holds Muslim Funeral for Islamic State Fighter," *Breitbart,* May 27, 2016.

57. Ibid.

58. Twitter post. Twitter.com/06_Haqqprevails, August 10, 2015

59. Twitter post. Twitter.com/GreenBirdofDabiq, May 28, 2015.

60. An attorney for several former French Jihadis explained that their clients, some of whom are trapped in the Caliphate, "can no longer stand it, their husbands are off fighting for weeks, with bombs raining down up to three times a day. They fear for the safety of their babies."

61. Twitter post. Twitter.com/Muhajirahumm6, August 10, 2015

62. "ISIS Militants Use 'Jihadi Cool' to Recruit Globally," *States News Service,* September 5, 2014.

63. John Simpson and James Dean, "Make Babies and Influence People: British Jihadist Brides Sent on Recruitment Drive," *London Times Online,* January 29, 2015.

64. "Interpol in Hunt for Austrian Jihadist Teenage Girls," *Al Arabiya,* April 18, 2014.

65. "Miss Terrorist ISIS Dies Due to Sexual Assaults," *Shafaq News,* July 26, 2015.

66. Joey Millar, "Western Women Are Just Wombs'—Woman Who Escaped ISIS Reveals 'Nightmare' of Jihadi Life," *Express,* January 10, 2016.

67. Harriet Alexander, "Jihadists in Syria Write Home to France: 'My iPod Is Broken. I Want to Come Back,'" *The Telegraph,* December 2, 2014.

68. John Hall, "The Unwilling Suicide Bomber: Teenager Weeps as He Is Ordered to Drive Armoured Vehicle Filled with Explosives—Moments before He Is Obliterated in Mushroom Cloud in Attack on Syrian Village," *Mailonline,* September 23, 2015.

69. "IS Has Executed 100 Foreigners Trying to Quit: Report," *AFP.* December 20, 2014.

70. Lauren Williams, "British Widow Who Left the UK to Join ISIL Now Stranded in Turkey and Desperate to Come Home," *Telegraph*, August 15, 2015.

71. Josie Ensor, "'I Fear for My Sister. ISIL Is Killing Relatives of Those Who Flee,'" *The Sunday Telegraph*, June 19, 2016.

72. Guiallaume Debre, "Syria: Former ISIL Cameraman Speaks to French TV," *TF1 News*, June 7, 2015.

73. Wi-Fi's have been banned from terraces to avoid unauthorized connections. Luc Mathieu, "Tension, Paranoia Grows in ISIL's Syrian Stronghold of Al-Raqqah," *Paris Liberation Online*, September 17, 2015, 4–5.

74. Ibid.

75. Noemie Bisserbe and Stacy Meichtry, "French Children Add to ISIS Ranks," *Wall Street Journal (Online)*, December 26, 2015.

76. Maria Abi-Habib, "World News: Western Recruits Try to Flee Islamic State—Defectors Seek Help Exiting Syria or Turn Up in Turkey; Dilemma for Home Countries," *The Wall Street Journal Asia*, June 8, 2016.

77. Ibid.

78. Louise Callaghan, "Defectors Pour from Crumbling Caliphate Eire Region," *Sunday Times*, June 12, 2016.

79. Adam Goldman, "I Am Fed Up with This Evil': How an American Went from Ivy League Student to Disillusioned ISIS Fighter," *Washington Post*, June 30, 2016.

80. "A Portrait of an ISIS Foreign Fighter," *The Daily Star* (Beirut, Lebanon), October 27, 2014.

81. Bradley Jolly, "Warped Paris Terrorist Larossi Abballa's Reign of Terror Began by Slaughtering Rabbits," *Daily Star (Online)*, June 22, 2016.

82. Natasha Bertrand, "Former ISIS Fighter Explains Why He Joined the Terror Army—and Why He Left after Just 3 Days," *Business Insider*, July 28, 2015.

83. David K. Li, "Ex-ISIS NYer: I Was an Idiot," *New York Post*, May 20, 2016.

84. Jamie Dettmer, "IS Deserters Flee Terror Group's Hypocrisy, Cruelty," *Voice of America*, December 21, 2015.

85. "11 Return from IS Following Disillusionment, Security Officials Monitoring Situation," *Johannesburg City Press*, September 13, 2015.

86. Sherine Tadros, "Escaped Islamic State Wives in Hiding in Turkey," *Sky News Online*, April 20, 2015.

87. Ibid.

88. Ibid.

89. Hazhar Mamuzini, "Islamic State Disfigure 15 Women with Acid," *BasNews*, February 9, 2015.

90. "10 Shocking Acts of Sexual Terror by Islamic State," *India TV*, September 14, 2015.

91. Eric Wenig, "Female ISIS Defector: 'Women Are Whipped, Sold And Stoned'" *The Daily Caller*, June 23, 2015, http://dailycaller.com/2015/06/23/female -isis-defector-women-are-whipped-sold-and-stoned/#ixzz4KXE7eFZa.

92. "Germany: 'Shahid S' From Leverkusen Confesses in Court to Junud al-Sham, ISIL Membership," *Die Welt*, June 24, 2016.

93. Nick Hallet, "Revealed: British School Girls Groomed by Specialist Islamic State Unit," *Breitbart* (London), May 28, 2015.

94. Marie-Amelie Lombard-Latune, "The French ISIL Female Militants," *Paris Le Figaro*, May 16, 2015.

95. "IS 'Not My Cup of Tea' Says Disillusioned Briton," *London Al-Araby al-Jadeed*, October 16, 2015.

96. Tom Batchelor, "ISIS in Crisis: Mummy-Boy Jihadis Fleeing Caliphate as Europe Braced for Terror Influx," *Express (Online)*, June 8, 2016.

6. SALAFIST DYSTOPIA: LIFE IN THE STATE

ISIS is dedicated to a contemporary holocaust.

—V. S. Naipaul, March 2015[1]

Introduction

Earlier chapters detailed the Caliphate's geography, philosophy, origins, and support base. They surveyed tensions between Muslim and non-Muslim communities in the West and observed the lures of the Caliphate. This chapter returns to Mesopotamia and walks the besieged streets of Raqqa, Mosul, and other Caliphate towns to examine the lifestyles of those under the sway of the Islamic State.

Daily Life

We are afraid to leave our house—they are degrading Islam.

—Maisaa, Raqqa resident[2]

It looked so beautiful the sisters and I joked around and called it the New York City of Syria.

—Umm Haritha, Raqqa resident[3]

This is what daily life is like. You wake up in the morning and if you don't hear the sound of shelling, or a jet breaking the sound barrier, you feel like it could be a good day.

—Abu Hadi, a resident of Raqqa, 2015[4]

Westerners who travel to Planet Caliphate find lifestyles very different from those they knew at home. With its bodies strewn in the streets, sex-slave auctions, public executions, random beatings, and deteriorated infrastructure, Raqqa is unlike anything most Europeans could imagine. Circumstances are often worse outside large cities because there are few public services.[5] Like something out of the Black Death of medieval Europe, rotting corpses are a common sight, and there is a constant reek of the dead in the streets. Some of the conditions are so vile that Caliphate cadre leave, if only temporarily, the towns they conquered because of the stench of decaying corpses.[6]

The Caliphate is often very open with its killings. In the twentieth century, some states used the fog of war to hide their butcheries. Behind the doors of Moscow's Lubyanka Prison or the gates of German concentration camps, Nazis and Communists veiled some of their slaughters. Not so the Caliphate. Its leaders bask in their flamboyant cruelty, regularly filming beheadings, shootings, stonings, and other methods of murder, including throwing people off buildings and setting them on fire. From spring 2014 to spring 2016, the Caliphate have executed over 4,000 people and often make little attempt to hide the acts.[7]

In some parts of the Caliphate, public killings have a circuslike atmosphere. Young boys, sometimes barely taller than the rifles they fire, shoot other boys at point-blank range to the applause of their Caliphate leaders. Smiling handicapped men in wheelchairs fire into groups of young men accused of spying in a disturbing promotion of the Caliphate's value of "equal opportunity," according to Human Rights Watch.[8]

Some infamous centers of brutality have developed their own sobriquets. Raqqa's central square has become known as Hell Square, which is where the State publicly executes people.[9] There was a celebrity torturer, known as "the Bulldozer" or "the Monster," who administered Caliphate justice until he was captured.[10] He boasted a fan club of admiring boys and young men. A mammoth of a man, he was the dean of the Caliphate's "Chopping Committee." He amputated hands or feet, and sometimes hands *and* feet, as well as heads.[11] In April 2016 he killed a man accused of being a magician.[12] The Bulldozer was caught in June 2016, tossed half-naked into the back of a truck, and hauled away by Syrian forces.

There was another pinup killer in the Caliphate, who, like the Bulldozer, enjoyed celebrity and had a short shelf life. The photogenic Caliphate killer known as the Desert Lion is profiled below.[13]

PROFILE EIGHTEEN: ABU WAHEEB—THE LION OF THE DESERT

Shaker Wahib, also known as Abu Waheeb, was a heartless man, dead at thirty, who lived his short life with a rage. Born in 1986, the former computer science student savored the brutality he delivered as a Caliphate leader. He basked in the heroic image his den of Caliphate cubs held of him. He was a tough Jihadist, and by his midtwenties he had been arrested by US authorities in Iraq. As a part of al Qaeda, he was captured by US forces in 2006. Later, he escaped from a high-security prison to become a leader in the Islamic State.[14]

He became a local celebrity in 2013 when he was photographed interrogating three Syrian lorry drivers by the side of the road. Seemingly spontaneously, he shot them in the back of the head, and viewers began to speculate as to why. Unlike other State soldiers, he often showed his face.[15] He challenged Western fighters to kill him. This vanity, like Jihadi John's, ultimately proved self-destructive.

Waheeb was al-Baghdadi's personal assistant, and they both survived a US drone attack in Nineveh. But in May 2016, his luck ran out. The Pentagon confirmed that he had been killed. A US Department of Defense spokesperson said, "On May 6, a coalition airstrike targeted Abu Waheeb. . . . It is dangerous to be an ISIL leader in Iraq and Syria nowadays."[16]

Mundanity, Fear, and Misery

Life is tedious and dangerous in the Caliphate. Well-paying jobs, scarce in the Caliphate's territory, are often unattainable for those unconnected to the leadership. For most of the Caliphate's residents, there is mundanity, fear, and misery. Basic services—electricity, waste management, potable water, road repair—are undependable. In the villages, electricity can be cut for an entire week. Only the wealthiest or most well-connected cadre have sustained access to private generators, and the price of petrol became out of reach for most residents after 2015.[17] For most households, basic services and medical items are scarce. As in other failed states, women wait in long lines for food, and men walk the streets in search of employment, taking whatever is offered.

The State feeds and houses its own. Depending on the cash flow, most of its soldiers earn several hundred dollars each month. They are paid more for each wife, child, and slave.[18] Teachers' salaries range between seventy-five and ninety dollars—only enough to buy a family bread for a month. But most teachers, other than religious instructors, are unemployed.[19] Others have lost hope. Many civil servants, who lost their positions after 2014, have fallen into destitution. Some have turned to subsistence farming to feed their families. Some men have despaired of work and commiserate with each other in cafés where they chat, read the papers, and network for jobs.

The rules for socializing at cafés have changed under the Caliphate. Historically a staple of Middle East popular culture, the café is a very male environment, filled with burbling water pipes, songs from the radio or television, and smiling men telling jokes and stories. No longer. Under the State, the water pipes were pulled, as were all forms of tobacco. If caught by the morality police, a smoker will be flogged, up to forty lashes. After a second offense, he will be whipped again and imprisoned. The third time brings prison and a crippling fine.[20] For café owners, the Caliphate is bad for business. One owner explained, "No customers come in. They do not enjoy a cup of coffee if they can't smoke a cigarette with it."[21] There are also shortages of coffee and food, and most music is forbidden.

Without smoking or sipping coffee there is little to do in cafés beyond chatting and watching television. Soccer has been popular in the Middle East for decades, and men and boys would gather to cheer their teams in cafés, but this now has its hazards. In May 2016, in the small town of Balad in northern Iraq, Caliphate assassins burst into a café and shot dead at least fourteen Real Madrid fans while shouting that soccer is un-Islamic. Local police caught one of the culprits, and the locals burned him alive.[22] Two weeks later, Islamic State killers struck again and killed men in a café watching soccer.[23] The Islamic State then went after the players themselves.[24] The soccer stars were well known and well liked, but in July 2016, the State gathered a crowd of children and beheaded these local sports heroes in front of their weeping fans.

Bureaucrats in Black

Though gainful employment is difficult to find for most residents of Mosul or Raqqa, there is no shortage of bureaucrats. The Caliphate's economic model is unique for a terrorist organization.[25] One European observer opined that the Caliphate was a functioning state because it had "an administration, infrastructures, an education system, and a complaints bureau."[26] A Paris-based think tank estimated the State's wealth at $2.2 billion in 2015.

The State's ownership of land, natural resources, and control of human capital give it a revenue stream, and Caliphate cadre serve as administrators and managers. They issue and inspect myriad permits required to obtain basic goods, apartment rentals, medical attention, and transportation. The religious police are ubiquitous. Pedestrians are stopped and forced to present identification; these are usually shakedowns. Civil servants extort money from passersby to help fund State operations and to provide themselves with some spending money. Some of these civil servants speak French, English, German, or other European languages. This is because some are Western Jihadis.

Bureaucrats were busy and creative in the early, victorious years trying to raise money for the State and pay themselves a livable salary.

An early source of income was a "repentance" fee from those unconnected to the Caliphate. In 2015, the new conquerors imposed a one-time tax on those whom they determined were insufficiently Islamic. If they paid and repented, they were issued a repentance card. If they didn't, they were beaten or killed.[27] Some individuals and families who raised a smugglers fee of several hundred dollars could leave.

By spring 2016, the Islamic State had lost about 30 percent of the revenues it drew in 2015 because oil sites had been bombed. Many of the people who had money that could be taxed in 2015 were much poorer one year later. However, bureaucrats continue to tax anyone and anything they can. They pull over truck drivers for tax and force a tax on anyone installing new satellite dishes or repairing broken ones. They stop men on the street and force them to recite the Koran; those who fail the test are fined or beaten. Sometimes they are shot.

Some entrepreneurs trade slaves on the internet.[28] The most attractive virgins are auctioned to the highest bidders. Non-Muslim women have been given as prizes in Koran-memorization competitions in Syria.[29] Non-Muslim women arriving at the jail are given two choices: convert to Islam or refuse and be subjected to rape, slavery, and slow death.[30] Women twenty to thirty years old are more prized and can fetch a price of $84 or a bottle of high-end, single-malt Scotch.[31] A girl can be sold and bought by five or six different men.[32] The phrase "smelling the girls" is slang for determining if their hymens are intact.[33] In a report by the British newspaper the *Independent*, surgery is forced on sex slaves to restore their virginity after every rape.[34] Many of the captives try to kill themselves, and some succeed.

Among the most notorious of the civil services is the all-women's al-Khansaa unit, named for a bard of the first generation of Muslims. Tumadir bint Amr, or al-Khansaa, was Muhammad's favorite poet.[35] Today, her name lives on as the al-Khansaa (often spelled Al-Khansaa or Al-Khansa) women's unit.[36] It was formed in early 2014 to expose men who dressed as women to escape.

Today, they enforce a morality code for women. Al-Khansaa's mission has expanded to include the operation of brothels and prisons and to recruit women to join the Caliphate's ranks.[37] There are many Western fighters in al-Khansaa. British women work as "recruiting sergeants" for the State.[38] Its leadership in 2015 and 2016 was heavily British.[39]

Women are terrified of members of the brigade who can stop, frisk, and beat any woman they choose. They sometimes inflict collective punishment. Some Al-Khansaa members operate covertly, pinballing between different shopping stands and waiting lines to listen in on conversations that might reveal hostility to the State.[40]

To keep Yazidi slaves sexually available, the State forces abortions. When birth-control pills are available, the prettier Yazidi sex slaves are forced to ingest them.[41]

Health Care—Deadly Medicine

Westerners accustomed to European health care standards are often shocked by the primitive conditions in their new Middle Eastern home. By 2015, most of the Caliphate's hospitals had fallen into disrepair. Citizens without money or influence receive the most rudimentary health care or none at all. In Raqqa, the hospital's dialysis machines and incubators stopped working soon after the Caliphate's conquest. Humanitarian aid was blocked from Raqqa because it came "from the infidels."[42]

The Caliphate's medicine is particularly agonizing for women giving birth. The State clamped down on Caesarean operations, which it considers Western and effete. The clerics determined that Muslim women should be stoic enough to endure childbirth pains without modern medicine. Muhammad's wives and daughters did not enjoy anesthetics or antibiotics, and they should serve as the exemplars.[43]

Women doctors are terrified by al-Khansaa, and most have stopped treating patients at the larger hospitals in Raqqa. They are too scared of being whipped.[44] After the clerics took control of the Raqqa National Hospital, only one woman doctor, Raheb, continued to practice there.

With health care in chaos and insufficient resources, physicians help boost hospital funding. Some harvest organs from the living or newly dead for sale on the underground market. This is legal according to the State's mullahs, as long as the organs come from non-Muslims or apostates. The Caliphate's Fatwa Sixty-Eight declared that "the apostate's life and organs don't have to be respected and may be taken with impunity."[45]

Health care administrators relieve their hospital's overcrowding by killing some of the patients. For example, HIV-positive fighters have been ordered to carry out suicide attacks, freeing the State of their medical costs. If there is a shortage of blood, Christians and Yazidis are forced to give blood for transfusions. A Christian woman said, "They even take our girls and old women's blood. They use it for their wounded ISIS fighters."[46] By summer 2016, State fighters in embattled Fallujah grabbed healthy-looking pedestrians off the streets or dragged them from their homes and forced them to give blood. This left some drained and dying in the city streets.[47]

Some of the medical services are healing; some are marginal; most are substandard; some are lethal. In the Caliphate, there is little room for "defectives." For example, the Caliphate issued a fatwa to kill babies and children with Down's syndrome. They were to be suffocated.[48] Medical clinics can be death centers for enemies of the State. Hospitals sometimes lure State opponents in for care and then inject them with poisons. Some of the victims had no idea that they were on a list of enemies until they began to die.[49]

Some medical experiments resemble those carried out by the Germans in World War II. The Caliphate's foreign fighters, particularly French, Tunisians, and Libyans, injected poisons into the veins of prisoners. One of the prison guards said that corpses taken out of these rooms "looked like skeletons, only an hour after being injected with the needles."[50]

By summer 2016, Caliphate militants began injecting severely injured soldiers with potassium chloride. Leaders calculated that pictures of injured, disfigured, or maimed soldiers might lower morale.[51]

Fashion in the Islamic State—Black Is the New Black

God loves women who are covered.

—A placard in a street in Raqqa[52]

The Caliphate takes dress seriously. Men and women must appear the way the first generation of Muslims were believed to have looked. Men who can't grow a beard need to improvise. "Nadhim," a thirty-year-old taxi driver, despaired because skin rashes prevented him from growing a beard or moustache. Nadhim pleaded his case to the religious police, but, he moaned, "they didn't care. . . . One of them told me I'd better stay at home if I shaved."[53] Men may not cut their hair, put gel in it, or wear it in anything that resembles a Western style.[54]

Still, men have more fashion freedom than women, who must always be covered in public. The tent-like niqab covers everything but the eyes, which must be covered with a veil. Schoolgirls must wear them, too.[55] Most women find this suffocating.[56] Only women may sell clothing to women. Women must not wear high heels. The few hair salons that are still open are required to black out the pictures of women on the packaging of hair dye solutions.[57]

If women do not dress in accordance with the State's morality codes they are beaten and, sometimes, severely tortured. Morality police are unforgiving. A nineteen-year-old-woman was placed in a cage "with some skulls" to teach her a lesson about inappropriate dress.[58] Women face particularly challenging obstacles should they require hospitalization, as even there they must remain completely clothed. An elderly

Types of muslim female headgear

| Hijab | Chador | Niqab | Burka |

Fashion in the Islamic World

woman suffering cardiac arrest was forbidden from removing any of her clothing, despite the pleas of attending nurses. She died.[59]

Those girls and women who escape the Caliphate cast aside their raven-colored coverings as soon as they can. This is what happened in summer 2016, when the State was driven from some Syrian towns and villages. For the first time in years, they could show their faces in the street, and they could wear whatever colors and styles of clothing they pleased.[60] A nineteen-year-old northern woman freed from State-controlled Syria ripped off the *khimar* (a long hijab) she had been forced to wear for two years, proclaiming, "I felt liberated. . . . They made us wear it against our will so I removed it that way to spite them."[61]

Entertainment in the Caliphate

Muslims have enjoyed music for centuries, relishing folk, religious, popular, and foreign songs. But the State outlawed most music. Soon after their conquest, State operatives confiscated or destroyed musical instruments. They also killed musicians. Some musicians have sold or hidden their instruments, too terrified to play them. A celebrated local musician, Ahmad, entertained refugees by pulling his piano in a wagon from refugee camp to refugee camp to deliver his "concerts in the ruins."[62] Some found relief, if only fleeting, in his piano playing and light-hearted singing. But the State set his prized piano on fire. He said, "They burned it on my birthday."[63]

Others pay higher prices for enjoying a song. A fifteen-year-old boy was arrested in central Mosul for listening to "Western music" at his father's grocery store. He was publicly beheaded. There are some exceptions to the ban on music. The music of Cat Stevens, Rock and Roll Hall of Famer, who became Yusuf Islam, is allowed. *Nasheeds* are songs that praise Allah and are sung without instrumental accompaniment.[64] They are allowed, particularly if they promote the Caliphate.

Generation Caliphate—
Child Care and Education in the Islamic State

*They told us we want to make an army to open Rome
and we will control the West and America.*

—Taha Jalo Murada boy in Raqqa[65]

They arrive here as children and quickly turn into killing machines.

—Commentary on boys' education in Raqqa[66]

The State sees today's children as tomorrow's iron-souled leaders. This is another parallel to the Nazi's Hitler Youth and the Soviet's Young Pioneers. The Caliphate grooms Generation Z to be a shock force to conquer the Middle East, North Africa, and parts of Europe. The boys are raised to obey even the harshest and most dangerous orders without hesitation.

Education for boys is very strict, particularly for those abducted from Yazidi or Christian households.[67] They are taught how to behead men by first practicing on dolls. They are deprived of sleep and edible food. A boy explained, "We were given dirty food—rice and beans [and] sometimes soup, but it had worms in it."[68] They have no opportunity to fraternize without supervision.

The slightest infraction—being late for prayers, failing to handle weapons correctly—would result in a beating, as recounted by thirteen-year-old Taha, a boy who was grabbed from his Yazidi family. He was constantly terrified and beaten with sticks. Some boys of Taha's age have been sent on suicide missions with bombs strapped around their waist. Taha explained, "We did not get enough training, but they said in the future you will fight for Jihad."[69]

Primary and secondary education is strikingly different from that in Europe. The State canceled all classes except religious studies. The State decided that basic principles of science are un-Islamic because they declare that there are physical rules of the universe that do not change.[70] This is considered sacrilegious. Any equations that are connected to moneylending are forbidden. The Caliphate promotes works by Islamic scholar Mohammed ibn Abd al-Wahhab, founder of Wahhabism; Muhammad's hadiths and biography; Quranic sciences; Islamic jurisprudence; and the Islamic doctrine. For the more secular-minded parents, home study has become popular.

Death is an ever-present part of daily life in the Islamic State. Many have watched the deaths of family members, friends, neighbors, and work and school mates. It has become part of a common culture, as during Europe's Great Plague and the Thirty-Year War. The Caliphate has captured international headlines for both the frequency and cruelty of its death sentences. They justify the killings by references to Islamic mandates.[71]

Beheadings

In some Western civilizations, beheading was, according to the epoch, a noble way to die. Hanging was reserved for the lowborn.[72] In Britain, bluebloods condemned to die were often, though not always, beheaded. As late as 1977, the guillotine was still being used in France. In America's colonial era, severed heads of criminals were sometimes displayed on Boston Common.[73] Beheading also has a place in Islam's early history. In 680 in Karbala, central Iraq, Muhammad's favorite grandson, Hussein bin Ali, had his head chopped off by the soldiers of the Caliph.[74] In fact, Muslim history is rife with beheadings. Legendary Muslim warrior Saladin ordered the heads removed from 230 Knights Templar in 1187; Turkish invaders beheaded 800 martyrs in Otranto, Italy, in 1480.[75]

Early in the Islamic State, beheading became popular, partially because it is often referenced in Sharia. In the Koran, Allah ordered his followers to smite the infidels' necks. He said, in Koran 47:4, "When you meet those who disbelieve on the battlefield, smite at their necks until you have killed."[76] The Islamic State does this today. It also impales the severed heads of its enemies on spikes.[77]

Stoning

Even the monkeys practiced stoning.

—From the Hadiths

Stoning is part of Sharia. Caliphate leaders endorse this punishment. The caliph Omar, one of Muhammad's closest companions, maintained that the punishment of stoning for adultery was originally in the Koran. He said, "Surely Allah's Apostle carried out the penalty . . . and so did we after him."[78] One hadith discusses a group of monkeys stoning a female monkey to death for adultery.[79] The most accepted hadith, al Bukhari, has four references to death by stoning.[80]

In Sharia, adultery must be proven by four eyewitnesses to the actual act. But in the State, the legal standards are much lower. Sometimes gossip is sufficient evidence for the judges. Males to be stoned are buried to the waist and women to the neck. After this is complete, a crowd pelts the condemned with rocks until the person dies. The condemned are bound tightly, and the soil around the hole in which they are place is well packed. According to Sharia, if the condemned can wrest themselves from the hole, they can live without punishment.[81] Sometimes there are double stonings of unmarried couples found *en flagrante*.[82]

Crucifixion

For Western readers, crucifixions are associated with Romans, Jesus, and Spartacus. Like stoning, crucifixion is a dreadful way to die. The condemned is either tied or nailed to a cross, and death usually comes from suffocation.[83] Emperor Constantine abolished it in the fourth century for being too cruel. The Islamic State brought it back to the Middle East in the twenty-first century.[84]

Sometimes crucifixion can be combined with other tortures. Passions often run high during Ramadan, and, in June 2016, the State reportedly whipped and then crucified three people for eating during the day.[85]

Exotic Torture

The Caliphate experiments with killing. For example, the State murdered five prisoners by locking them in a metal cage and lowering them into a swimming pool. Filmed in Mosul with expensive underwater cameras, a seven-minute-long video captured the terror and agony of the drowning men. The cages were lifted from the pool, revealing dead and nearly dead men foaming at the mouth.[86] Other depraved deaths include bathing the doomed in acid.

FOUR LEVELS OF LIFE IN THE CALIPHATE—ISLAMIC APARTHEID

A person walking the streets of Raqqa or Mosul would notice different standards of living for different social groups. This is not unique in the Islamic world. There is a definite hierarchy of life in the Islamic State that can be divided into four levels: the conquerors, the nonresisting Muslims, the Christians, and the Yazidis.

Level One—Life for the Conquerors in Raqqa

The State's leaders and bureaucratic elites, including those from the West, enjoyed the status of a conquering force in 2014 and 2015. Early in its takeover, well before the Iraqi government's pushback, the State evicted its enemies from upscale homes and expropriated their belongings. Those who resisted were usually shot. The luxury homes of Syrian president Assad's most loyal and now dispossessed bureaucrats and allies were given to State leaders.[87] Men of the new ruling class had new apartments and sex slaves. Fortune had smiled on them.

Beyond that, the State's elite enjoyed a status, if temporary, eerily similar of that of the bureaucratic class of the Soviet Union. They enjoyed special supermarkets, abundant fuel for expropriated luxury vehicles, internet cafés, access to hospitals, and an English-language nursery school for children of the English-speaking cadre.[88]

For the privileged, Raqqa enjoyed a new status as a honeymoon destination for Jihadis.[89] In Mosul, the Caliphate nationalized the 262-room Ninawa International Hotel and flew black flags in front of it to beckon the elite and newlyweds. By Western standards, it was an unconventional and unromantic venue to celebrate nuptials. Women from the al-Khansaa brigade patrolled the grounds, ensuring that there was no dancing, music, snuggling, kissing, smoking, or gambling.[90]

Level Two—Life for the Nonresisting Sunni Muslim

The second level is reserved for less-privileged and less-well-connected Muslims. Some have described this level as having the feel of a very hostile occupation. Women, in particular, face very severe restrictions on behavior. They have been ordered never to walk unaccompanied by a male guardian, and shopkeepers must cover their store mannequins with full-face veils.

Nonresisting Muslim men, too, are regularly harassed and shaken down for what little money they have. If they dress, pray, and behave by the dictates of the State, they can generally survive. However, when towns and cities are contested by the Caliphate's enemies, all residents, Muslim as well as non-Muslim, live in fear. Anyone can be used as a human shield. One example came in late summer 2016, when the Caliphate called on civilians in a northeastern town in Aleppo, promising them freedom from the battle zone. Instead, they forced them at gunpoint to gather in the State's facilities, holding them as hostages to discourage drone attacks.

Level Three—Life for Christians in the Caliphate

The third level is for Christians. There are no known Jews left in the Caliphate. The Christians of Iraq and Syria have an ancient history. They use Syriac in their worship, which is similar to the Aramaic that Jesus spoke.[91] In 638 AD, the second Caliph, Omar, decreed that Christians and Jews could live in peace with Islam as long as they acknowledged the superiority of Islam and paid tribute to Muslims.[92] Under these terms, churches would not be destroyed.[93] But they would live as second-class citizens, or *dhimmis*. As non-Muslims living at the sufferance of their Islamic protectors, they were forced to pay an annual tax, called a *jizya*, in exchange for being allowed to live and practice their faiths.[94] In 1799, a Westerner observing the Ottoman rule noted that Christians who paid the jizya were being permitted to "wear their heads" that year.[95] This ancient practice continues.

Christians have historically been belittled in many ways. They were made to look different through their clothing, hairstyle, and markers worn around their necks to announce their inferior status. Sometimes they were required to post the Arabic letter *nun* (for *Nazrani*, the Arabic word for Christians) to the exterior of their homes. The Caliphate required this of Christians in Mosul.[96] The State also finds Christian symbols to be offensive. They find crosses particularly objectionable and have yanked them from public view.[97]

Christians are also killed for refusing to convert to Islam, for resisting Islamic rule, or for no known reason at all. In June 2016, members of a rival Jihadist organization, Al Nusra, took a Syrian town; they gathered the Christians, pulled one man from the crowd, and slit his throat. The killer then smiled, looked to the man's wife, and said, "Your Jesus did not come to save him from us."[98]

But these deaths do not often make headlines in the West. In some cases, the murders are afforded less media coverage than the killing of wild animals, such as the killing of Cecil the Lion (see Profile Seven) or the point-blank shooting of Harambe, a gorilla living in an American zoo who was shot to protect a toddler who had toppled from a fence into the gorilla's living space. Within one week, the three largest networks gave a coverage of one hour, twenty-eight minutes, seventeen seconds to the "zoo horror." In contrast, the media covered the deaths of twenty-one Christians who were beheaded in just four minutes and thirty seconds.[99]

PROFILE TWENTY: "JESUS WILL ALWAYS LOVE YOU"—
THE GOOD VICAR OF BAGHDAD

The Most Dangerous Parish in the World

A tall, imposing, yet gentle man with a healthy sense of humor and a price on his head, Reverend Andrew White knows Iraq intimately. He was the last vicar of St. George's Church in Baghdad, which may explain the sweatshirt he wore. It read, "Real men become vicars."[100] He demonstrated real and repeated courage as a trusted mediator to the

Archbishop of Canterbury and as his special envoy to the Middle East. Said White, "I've been hijacked, held at gunpoint, beaten up, all sorts of things."[101] He braved death threats and endured the psychological pain of seeing so much suffering of his coreligionists. He carries an AK-47 automatic rifle permit but jokes he never learned to operate the weapon. He made contact with State leaders to ask them to dinner and they said yes, on one proviso. "Yes, we'll come, but we'll chop off your head." Chuckled the reverend, "Rather kind of them to warn me."[102]

"Jesus Will Always Love You"

Reverend White agonizes over what he sees as media disinterest in the erasure of Christianity in Mesopotamia.[103] He spoke of how the State has "hounded" the Christians out of Iraq and how they slaughtered those who remained. He is particularly haunted by the sight of children decapitated because they refused to convert to Islam. Said White, "They chopped all their heads off. How do you respond to that?"[104] On a different occasion, he persuaded a father to allow his children to convert to Islam superficially but hold on to their Christian faith silently. The vicar assured both the father and son, "Yeshua still loves you, he will always love you."[105]

Reverend White is relentlessly stalked by an enemy within—multiple sclerosis. It makes his life and his fight to save Christianity even more difficult.[106] He left the Middle East to return to Britain in 2014 on orders from the Archbishop of Canterbury,[107] but his heart is still in Mesopotamia. "I may no longer be the vicar of Baghdad, but the Middle East is my home."[108]

Neighbors—"Forgive Them"

Let believers not take for friends and allies infidels rather than believers: and whoever does this shall have no relationship left with Allah—unless you but guard yourselves against them, taking precautions.

—Koran 3:28

The Caliphate's conquest of Mesopotamian cities and towns has tested Christian–Muslim relations. Many Christians did not understand how tenuous their peaceful associations were with their Muslim nationals. Families had grown up together, and children studied and played together. They thought they were friends. But soon after the Caliphate took control, some Muslim neighbors very quickly partnered with State operatives to harass Christians and take their property. A Christian man explained that the most vicious of the Jihadis were not the "Bosnians, Arabs, and even Americans and British fighters"; they were their neighbors.[109] Other Muslim neighbors joined the State and killed or chased away Christians from their homes.

Often, Christians have nowhere to go. One explained, "Our neighbors and other people threatened us. But . . . where would we go? Christians have no support in Iraq."[110] A Christian woman from Mosul recalled the murder of her daughter, who died in her arms. According to the mother's account, her girl's dying words were, "Forgive them."[111]

Level Four—Life for Yazidis, a House of Pain

These men are not human. They only think of death, killing.

—Recollections of a Yazidi captive[112]

Of all social and religious cohorts, Yazidis have the worst quality of life. The Caliphate declared this religious minority to be devil worshippers. Yazidis constantly fear for their lives and sometimes pray for death. Men and boys have been randomly killed, taken from their homes, and sometimes impressed to fight for the Caliphate. Women and girls are often sold as slaves, particularly sex slaves. They live in brothels, houses of pain. They hold a status comparable to that held by Slavs in Nazi-occupied Europe. International human rights lawyer Amal Clooney, who defends Yazidi women, said, "We know that systematic rapes have taken place, and that they are still taking place. And yet no one is being held to account."[113] An escaped Yazidi girl said, "Every day I died 100 times over. Not just once. Every hour I died, every hour. . . . From the beating, from the misery, from the torture."[114]

If Yazidi girls are sexual fodder for the Caliphate, the boys have potential as fighters or suicide operators. They drill their dogma into children's minds. One Yazidi mother, whose husband was shot by the State and who later escaped the Caliphate, explained that her nine-year-old son did not want to leave. He wanted to stay in the Caliphate. "My son's brain was changed," said the mother.[115]

By summer 2016, as Iraqi forces dislodged the Caliphate from towns and cities, they sometimes needed to protect the Yazidi dead as well as the living. The Yazidi mass grave sites need to be guarded because they hold evidence for future war-crimes trials.[116] But sometimes there is vengeance. According to one media account, a Caliphate commander was killed by his former Yazidi slave. He had offered her to his friends,[117] and later she shot him. Some Yazidis can fight in military units, as profiled below.

To Abu Bakr—I am the sister of the girls you captured,
the daughter of the mothers you hold.

—A Yazidi fighter in the Sun Brigade, 2015[118]

By 2015, some Yazidi women could mete out justice to their former tormentors. Fighting in a battalion operationally controlled by Kurdish forces, Yazidi women stand proud in the ranks of the "Sun Brigade." It was organized by a Yazidi musician-turned-soldier and staffed with Yazidi women, many of whose friends and relatives were kidnapped by the Caliphate.

Most of the Sun ladies are aged between eighteen and thirty, and many had never held a gun until they joined the brigade. In better, younger years, they were students, teachers, and cooks. Some were wives or sweethearts. Then came the Caliphate and the killing. But by midsummer 2016, Yazidi women and girls were fighting.

A Sun leader said of Yazidis, "Women were throwing their children from the mountains and then jumping themselves because it was a faster way to die. Our hands were all tied. We couldn't do anything about it."[119] Now they can. Today, their hands hold weapons. "We are Yazidi. We are women. You will never be able to take away our honor. . . . We will liberate our homeland."[120] Another said, "We will wipe you out."[121]

Der Untergang—Downfall

In late April and early May 1945, Berlin was a chaotic charnel house. In the Germans' last redoubt, "flying courts-martial" of soldiers and Gestapo shot anyone they suspected of surrendering to the Soviets. Corpses of accused defeatists were roped to lampposts and bedecked with reproving placards to warn others who might flee. Women and children hovered in basements. This was *untergang*, or downfall.

Similar scenes, with different nationalities, were reenacted in Mosul and Fallujah in early summer 2016. Those suspected of trying to flee the advancing anti-State forces were hanged or sometimes burned alive. Roving bands of State soldiers patrol nearly empty streets with orders to kill fleeing civilians.[122] Sometimes entire families are publicly shot.[123] Families are forced to watch as their fathers, brothers, and sons are publicly hanged.[124]

As in Berlin, 1945, most Raqqa residents are hostages, but well-connected families can leave. The families of foreign fighters left, and some inmates were freed of their prisons.[125] In Fallujah, the city forty miles west of Baghdad, roving squads of State soldiers kill anyone who leaves their house or hangs a white flag.[126]

In spring 2016, one resident bewailed, "No one can leave. It's dangerous. There are snipers everywhere along the exit routes."[127] Many jihadists felt particularly trapped when points on the Turkish border were closed. Those who try to leave besieged cities often find themselves in the middle of the desert where they are as "visible as a fly in a bowl of milk."[128] Some State fighters were caught trying to flee dressed as women. They were forced to strip, to the amusement of their captors, and then some were shot.[129]

Fallujah is important to the State and holds a place in Marine Corp tradition. More than a hundred American soldiers died and hundreds more were wounded in intense, house-by-house fighting there in 2004. In June and July 2016, United States–led Coalition forces brought death from above to the fleeing State militants. A Pentagon spokesperson confirmed that air strikes killed hundreds.

Some observers have speculated that as the vise closes around Raqqa, the hardcore will flee to Dabiq for a last stand. Dabiq is a small town in northwest Syria and is the name of the State's Western-oriented publication. It is central to the Caliphate's interpretation of Islam and is surrounded by clouds of apocalyptic prophesies. It is particularly associated with End Times tales of vast slaughter between Muslims and their enemies, often referred to as "Roman" invaders. Some have speculated that it could be a last redoubt, particularly for those cadre eager to become martyrs.[130]

Iraqi and Syrian troops have been on the offensive as of late summer 2016. They are fighting in coordination with their allies, including Western powers. Britain is a leader in the air war, delivering death from above to the Caliphate's gunslingers. The war from the air has been very controversial for many years. Hollywood has made movies about drone warfare, intellectuals have questioned its morality, and military operators praise the strikes as being precise and for reducing unwanted casualties. Bits of the argument are sampled below.

PROFILE TWENTY-TWO: DEATH FROM ABOVE

British defense secretary Michael Fallon had this to say to the men and women of the Royal Air Force about British airpower in the skies of the Middle East:

> Last week we commemorated the Somme.... Back then aviation was almost unimaginable.... By contrast, you enjoy the sort of precision, speed and reach they could only dream of. Yet you, too, continue to protect our freedom ... and nowhere is this truer than our war against

Daesh. . . . Our aircraft have flown more than 2,800 missions in Iraq and Syria. They've conducted 865 airstrikes in Iraq and, since December, 50 in Syria—more than any other except the United States. . . . Our intelligence gathering aircraft, such as Airseeker, are providing a significant amount of the Coalitions' intelligence, reconnaissance, and surveillance. Together they are ensuring our Tornados, Typhoons, and Reapers can clear a path for brave Iraqi troops. . . . Last week saw a significant milestone—the liberation of Fallujah.[131]

Civil rights organizations, including the American Civil Liberties Union and Amnesty International, had this to say to the United Nations about drone killings:[132]

Your excellencies—We are concerned about the lack of transparency in targeted killing operations. Greater disclosure of legal and policy standards, and procedural mechanisms, is a prerequisite to informed assessment and debate. . . . Any measure employed to counter terrorism, including the use of armed drones, comply with states' obligations under international law, including the Charter of the United Nations, international human rights law and international humanitarian law. . . . Ensure transparency on the use of armed drones . . . to ensure compliance with international law, and to conduct prompt, independent and impartial investigations whenever there is credible information of a violation of international law caused by their use. . . . Make public the identity and number of individuals killed or injured in targeted killing operations, and the measures in place to prevent civilian casualties and ensure redress when they occur.[133]

John O. Brennan, then serving as assistant to the president for homeland security and counterterrorism, had this to say about drone warfare in April 2012:

So let me say it as simply as I can. Yes, the United States Government conducts targeted strikes against specific al-Qa'ida terrorists, sometimes using remotely piloted aircraft, often referred to publicly as drones. . . . These targeted strikes are legal. . . the Constitution empowers the President to protect the nation from any imminent threat of attack. . . . There is nothing in international law that bans the use of remotely piloted aircraft for this purpose or that prohibits us from using lethal force against our enemies outside of an active battlefield, at least when the country involved consents or is unable or unwilling to take action against the threat.

Targeted strikes are ethical. . . . We have the authority to target them with lethal force just as we targeted enemy leaders in past conflicts, such as German and Japanese commanders during World

War II. . . . Targeted strikes conform to the principle of proportionality—the notion that the anticipated collateral damage of an action cannot be excessive in relation to the anticipated military advantage.

Targeted strikes are wise. Remotely piloted aircraft in particular can be a wise choice because of geography, with their ability to fly hundreds of miles over the most treacherous terrain, strike their targets with astonishing precision, and then return to base. They dramatically reduce the danger to U.S. personnel, even eliminating the danger altogether. Yet they are also a wise choice because they dramatically reduce the danger to innocent civilians, especially considered against massive ordinance that can cause injury and death far beyond its intended target. . . .

Yes, war is hell. It is awful. It involves human beings killing other human beings, sometimes innocent civilians. I'd hope that the United States would have to rely less on lethal force to keep our country safe. Until that happens, as President Obama said here five years ago, if another nation cannot or will not take action, we will.[134]

Summary

Life in the Caliphate is hazardous, impoverished, and often short. Health care has collapsed, and food and employment are scarce. There is a hierarchy of living standards, from the Caliphate cadre at the top to the Yazidis, who have no human value in the eyes of the State, at the bottom. The Islamic State has lost ground in spring 2016, and roaming firing squads try to keep order. As of summer 2016, there has been a reversal of fortune, as Caliphate fighters, so recently victorious and merciless, are today desperate and scared. Some try to slither out of the combat zones, and others disguise themselves as women and sell eggs, chickens, and anything else of value to survive.[135]

There are stories of hope, even if not all can be confirmed. A Middle Eastern news service posted a video of a young Syrian boy running a gauntlet of Caliphate sniper fire to rescue a small girl. Men cheer "Allahu Akbar" as the boy darts among cars for cover. The young hero scoops up the girl, saving her life.[136] But most stories of resistance do not have happy endings.

1. Camilla Turner, "Fanatics Bent on Creating a 'Fourth Reich,' Says Naipaul," *The Daily Telegraph*, March 23, 2015.

2. Zaid al Fares, "Life Under Isis: Robbery, Sex Slaves, and Headless Bodies in the Street," *International Business Times*, July 31, 2014, http://www.ibtimes.co.uk/life-under-isis-robbery-sex-slaves-headless-bodies-street-1459147.

3. Nadim Roberts, "The Life of a Jihadi Wife: Why One Candaian Woman Joined the ISIS's Islamic State," *CBC News*, July 7, 2014.

4. Noam Raydan and Erika Solomon, "Inside Raqqa: Voices from the Terrified City," *FT Com*, December 4, 2015.

5. Julian Robinson, "Tap Water in Syrian City under ISIS Control Is an Undrinkable Brown Sludge Filled with Worms after Islamic State Engineer in Charge of the Water Plant Steals Its Funds and Goes on the Run," *The Daily Mail*, September 22, 2015.

6. Mary Chastain, "Yazidi MP Vian Dakhil Claims Islamic State Left Due to Stench of Dead Bodies," *Brietbart News*, September 11, 2014.

7. "ISIS Executes More than 4,000 People in under Two Years of the 'Islamic State' in Syria," *Independent* (Ireland), April 30, 2016.

8. Colin Freeman, "ISIL Hires Killer in Wheelchair to Flaunt Equal Opportunities Values," *Daily Telegraph*, May 19, 2016.

9. Robert Spencer, "Reign of Terror: Inside the Islamic State," *Frontpage Magazine*, June 19, 2015.

10. Nick Gutteridge, "ISIS Executioner 'The Bulldozer' Chopped Off Teen's Hand and Foot in Front of Baying Crowd," Expres.com, October 8, 2015, http://www.express.co.uk/news/world/610676/Islamic-State-ISIS-executioner-The-Bulldozer-torture-Free-Syrian-Army-teen.

11. Jay Akbar, "ISIS's Masked Monster: Revealed, the Tubby Jihadi Executioner Dubbed the Bulldozer Who's Part of Terror Group's 'Chopping Committee' Bringing Horror to Captured Iraqi Towns," *Mailonline*, October 9, 2015.

12. Matthew Acton, "ISIS Now Executing Magicians—as Another Gay Man Is Thrown to His Death," *Daily Star (Online)*, April 22, 2016.

13. Simon Tomlinson, "Flattened! Terrifying 20st ISIS Executioner Dubbed the Bulldozer Is 'Captured' by the Syrian Army and Dumped Half-Naked in the Back of a Truck," *Daily Mail*, June 4, 2016.

14. Katie Mansfield, "Notorious ISIS Leader Who Appeared in Sick Execution Videos Killed during Iraq Raid," *Express (Online)*, May 9, 2016.

15. Bel Trew and Graham Keeley, "Bare-Faced ISIS Henchman Dies in Missile Strike," *The Times*, May 10, 2016.

16. Colin Freeman, "Islamic State executioner who devised deadly 'Quranic Quiz' Killed by US Airstrike," *The Telegraph*, May 9, 2015.

17. Luc Mathieu, "Tension, Paranoia Grows in ISIL's Syrian Stronghold of Al-Raqqah," *Paris Liberation Online*, September 17, 2015, 4–5.

18. Pamela Engel, "Syrian Native Describes What Daily Life Is Like in ISIS' de Facto Capital," *Business Insider*, January 16, 2016.

19. Hosam al-Jablawi, "ISIS Math Education Starts with Banning the Plus Sign," *Newsweek*, April 8, 2016.

20. Heather Saul, "Life under ISIS in Raqqa: The City Where Smoking a Cigarette Could See You Publicly Flogged, Imprisoned and Even Decapitated," *The Independent*, February 13, 2015.

21. Ibid.

22. Jerry Lawton, "IS Kills 14 for Seeing Footie," *Daily Star*, May 14, 2016.

23. Gerard Couzens, "Champions League Horror: Vile ISIS Terrorists Slaughter Real Madrid Fans Enjoying Match," *Sunday Express*, May 29, 201.

24. Paul Byrne, "ISIS Extremists Behead Four Footballers after Declaring the Sport Anti-Islamic," *Mirror*, July 8, 2016.

25. "ISIS Financing in 2015," *Paris CAT Online*—website of the Center for the Analysis of Terrorism (CAT), research center chaired by terrorism expert Jean-Charles Brisard, May 2016.

26. "French Jihadism Specialist: Iraqi, Syrian Populations Support ISIL," *Paris Le Point*, May 20, 2016.

27. Elliot Friedland, "Islamic State Charging Enemies 'Repentance Fee,'" *Clarion Foundation*, October 5, 2015.

28. This may not be an authentic posting, though Joby Warrick thinks it probably is. "Another sabiyah [slave], also about $8,000," the posting reads. "'Yay, or nay Joby Warrick,' ISIS Fighters Seem to Be Trying to Sell Sex Slaves Online," *Washington Post*, May 28, 2016.

29. "ISIS Offers Female Slaves as Top Prizes for Koran Competition," *MEMRI*, June 19, 2015.

30. Johnlee Varghese, "Shocking: ISIS Official 'Slave' Price List Shows Yazidi, Christian Girls Aged '1 to 9' Being Sold for $172," *International Business Times*, November 5, 2014.

31. "The Price of Flesh: Selling Women in the Islamic State Caliphate," *The Clarion Project*, July 6, 2015.

32. Nicole Rojas, "ISIS Sex Slaves: UN Official Says Jihadi Group Peddles Girls 'Like Barrels of Petrol,'" *International Business Times*, August 5, 2015.

33. Jay Akbar, "'I Rejoiced When We Had Our First Sex Slave, Forced Sex ISN'T Rape and They Should Be Thankful': Chilling Rant of Twisted ISIS Jihadi Bride Who Justifies Kidnapping and Abusing Yazidi girls," *Mailonline*, May 22, 2015.

34. Under local anesthetic, the hymens were, in the words of a United Nations official, "repaired with stiches, which dissolved. The membrane can then be broken each time the rape victim is married." Louis Dore, "A Woman Was Forced to 'Restore Her Virginity' 20 Times," *The Independent*, May 11, 2015.

35. Sometimes referred to as "mother of the martyrs," she offered her prophet her verses and several of her sons, who died fighting to spread the new faith. The sobriquet of Al Khansaa, means "gazelle" or "snub-nosed" because she was beautiful and had a button nose.

36. Al-Khansaa police auxiliary, often referred to as the "the battalion" or the "brigade."

37. Lydia Smith, "Islamic State's Women Warriors: How Feared Al-Khansa Battalion Was Borne Out of Repression," *International Business Times*, August 13, 2014.

38. John Simpson and James Dean, "Make Babies and Influence People: British Jihadist Brides Sent on Recruitment Drive," *London Times Online*, January 29, 2015.

39. Donna Rachel Edmunds, "ISIS Jihadists Forcing Yazidi Women to Work as Sex Slaves," *Brietbart* (London), September 13, 2014.

40. Sue Reid, "ISIS's Female Gestapo Wreaking Terror on Their Own Sex: They Bite and Whip Any Woman Who Steps Out of Line and Force Girls to Become Sex Slaves. Most Shocking of All? SIXTY of Them Are British," *Daily Mail*, July 10, 2015.

41. "Evil ISIS Forcing Yazidi Sex Slave Women to Have Abortions so They Can Keep Raping Them," *Alalam*, March 13, 2016.

42. Zaid al Fare, "Life under Isis: Robbery, Sex Slaves, and Headless Bodies in the Street," *International Business*, July 31, 2014.

43. Robert Verkaik, "Today's Muslim Women Requesting Caesarean Operations Were Often, in the Words of a British Observer, 'Too Posh to Push.' Now ISIS Clamps Down on Mothers Having 'Un-Islamic' Caesarean Births," *MailOnline*, March 27, 2015.

44. Emily Feldman, "The Woman Who Escaped the Islamic State," *Mashable*, September 10, 2014.

45. Tobias Salinger, "Flesh-Eating Monster! ISIS Fatwa: It's OK to Be a Cannibal," *Daily News*, December 26, 2015.

46. Mary Chastain, "From the Independent, 'The Islamic State (ISIS/ISIL) Is Forcing Residents in Raqqa, Syria, the Capital of Their "Caliphate" in Syria and Iraq, to Donate Blood for Their Injured Fighters,'" *Brietbart News*, February 13, 2015.

47. Hollie McKay, "ISIS Fighters Are Stealing Blood from Civilians," *New York Post*, June 9, 2016.

48. Sam Webb, "ISIS Orders Killing of Kids with Down's Syndrome in Latest Sickening Attack on the Innocent," *Mirror*, December 14, 2015.

49. Oli Smith, "ISIS Terror Doctors Recruited from UK Will Return to Work in NHS," *Express*, January 4, 2016.

50. "Islamic State Group Carries Out Chemical Experiments on Its Detainees in Syria," *BBC Monitoring Middle East*, May 29, 2016.

51. Loaa Adel, "ISIS Uses Lethal Injections to Get Rid of Its Wounded Fighters in Fallujah," *Iraqi News*, May 30, 2016.

52. Brian Ries, "Syrian Woman Wears Hidden Camera to Reveal Life under ISIS Rule," *Mashable*, September 24, 2014.

53. Jean-Marc Mojon, "Men Brace for 'Beard Patrols' in Iraq's IS-Held Mosul," *AFP*, June 1, 2015.

54. Eilish O'Gara, "Happy Days for Barbers as Turkish Men Get Rid of ISIS-Style Beards," *IBT*, August 14, 2015.

55. "Broken Dreams for Woman Forced to Flee IS-Held Syria," *BBC Online*, March 5, 2015.

56. An apologist from Australia wrote, "Nor is it [the niqab] oppressive. I feel liberated by the fact that I choose what you see. We pass judgement on how a person looks before we know them. When you deal with me, you deal with my mind,

my personality, my emotions and what I have to offer as a person—and that's it." Semaa Abdulwali, "The Niqab Makes Me Feel Liberated, and No Law Will Stop Me from Wearing It," *The Guardian*, October 6, 2014.

57. No see-through clothes; only wear loose-fitting clothes; must cover all body parts; no name brands; do not wear masculine clothes or clothes worn by nonbelievers; no clothes with designs that will attract attention; no perfumed clothes. Source: Nick Gutteridge, "Islamic State Fanatics Put Up Billboards Ordering Women to Wear the Burka . . . or Else," *Express*, July 17, 2014.

58. The source of the event was Raqqa Is Being Slaughtered Silently. Samuel Osborne, "ISIS is Putting Girls into Cages with Skeletons for Violating Their Dress Code Say Syrian Activists," *The Independent*, April 29, 2016.

59. Fare, "Life under ISIS."

60. Sara Malm, "The Moment One Woman Ditched the Symbol of ISIS Oppression by Throwing Off Her Niqab after Her Village Is Liberated in Syria," *MailOnline*, June 10, 2016.

61. "Singapore: 'I Felt Liberated'—Life after Islamic State," *Singapore Channel News Asia Online*, June 16, 2016.

62. "Syrian Pianist Tells Stories of War through Music," *Hindustan Times* (New Delhi, India), July 26, 2016.

63. Rana Moussaoui, "His Piano Burned, Musician Joins Migrant Tide," *Agence France Presse*, September 21, 2015.

64. M. Shemesh, "The Songs of the Islamic State—A Major Tool for Reinforcing Its Narrative, Spreading Its Message, Recruiting Supporters," *MEMRI, Inquiry and Analysis*, August 11, 2015.

65. Owen Holdaway, "Exclusive—'I Was Taught How to Cut a Head Off. Where I Should Aim My Knife on the Neck': Yazidi Boy, 13, Relives His Chilling Experience at ISIS Jihad Camp for Lessons in Beheading." *Daily Mail*, August 7, 2015.

66. "Syrian Child Soldier: 'I've Gotten Used to Killing Soldiers,'" MEMRI TV Clip No. 4500.
Following are excerpts from an LDC TV report on a Syrian child soldier, which aired on September 13, 2014.

67. "Mosul: Islamic State Abducts 111 Children," *Asia News*, July 7, 2015.

68. "Syrian Child Soldier: 'I've Gotten Used to Killing Soldiers,'" MEMRI TV Clip No. 4500.
Following are excerpts from an LDC TV report on a Syrian child soldier, which aired on September 13, 2014.

69. Holdaway, "Exclusive—'I Was Taught How to Cut a Head Off.'"

70. Julian Robinson, "ISIS Cancels All Classes Except Religious Studies in Syrian Schools Because 'Even the Two-Times Table Shouldn't Be Taught as All Knowledge Belongs to the Creator," *Daily Mail*, November 7, 2014.

71. Raymond Ibrahim, "Islamic State Fatwa Points to Muhammad to Justify Burning Pilot," *Jihad Watch*, February 6, 2015.

72. Steven Mufson, "A Brutal History of Beheadings Method Is Latest Weapon of Those Sworn to Punish Westerners," *Oakland Tribune*, July 4, 2004.

73. Jeff Jacoby, "Why Beheading?; Theology and History Play into the Use of an Old Horror in Warfare," *The Boston Globe*, September 14, 2014.

74. Mufson, "A Brutal History of Beheadings."

75. "Beheading Shocks Us, But We'll Get Used to It," *Chicago Sun-Times*, September 30, 2014.

76. "Jihadi Cleric Justifies IS Beheadings: 'Islam Is a Religion of Beheading,'" MEMRI Special Dispatch no. 5826, August 25, 2014.

77. "Graphic Video: ISIS Executes 'Spies,' Puts Heads on Spikes," *The Clarion Project*, June 30, 2016.

78. Bukhari, vol. 8, bk. 82, no. 816. Al-Riyadh (Saudi Arabia), July 1, 2014. "The Growing Sunni Opposition to ISIS' Declaration of the Islamic Caliphate," MEMRI, Special Dispatch 5821, August 14, 2014.

79. Bukhari, vol. 5, bk. 58, no. 188.

80. Nadia Shahram, "Quran Does Not Endorse Iran's Stoning of Women," *The Buffalo News*, August 17, 2010.

81. Sonali Salgado, "Iran: In New Film, the Stoning of a Woman Is Deplored," *Inter Press Service English News Wire*, July 15, 2009.

82. Vittorio Hernandez, "IS Stones to Death Man & Woman in Mosul for Adultery," *International Business Times*, March 25, 2015.

83. "The Crucified Man from Giv'at ha-Mivtar: A Reappraisal," *Israel Exploration Journal* 35, no. 1 (1985): 22–27.

84. Ahmed Shiwesh, "ISIS Extremists Execute, Crucify Eight People in Syria's Raqqa," *ARA News*, April 4, 2016,

85. Matt Payton, "ISIS Crucifies Three People 'for Breaking Ramadan Fast,'" *The Independent*, June 16, 2016.

86. John Hall, "Sickening New ISIS Video Shows Caged Prisoners Lowered into a Swimming Pool and Drowned, Shot with an RPG and Blown Up with Explosive-Filled 'Necklaces,'" *MailOnline*, June 23, 2015.

87. Sarah El Deeb, "For an IS Fighter, a Paid Honeymoon in Caliphate's Heart," *Associated Press*, May 26, 2015.

88. Ibid.

89. Ibid.

90. "ISIS Opens Five Star Luxury Hotel in Iraq," *Hotelier Middle East*, May 7, 2015.

91. Christopher Howse, "Christians Driven from the Ruins of Nineveh," *Telegraph*, April 18, 2015.

92. According to the testament: "This is what the slave of God, Omar, the Emir of the Faithful, gave to people of Ailia [Jerusalem] of security and safety for themselves and their money, churches, crosses, patients, and all their denominations." "ISIS Imposes Royalties on Christian Males of Al Qaryatain Town East Homs Doha Zaman al-Wasl," *Syrian Observer*, September 5, 2015.

93. "ISIS Imposes Royalties on Christian Males of Al Qaryatain Town East Homs," *Doha Zaman al-Wasl*, September 5, 2015.

94. Mark Durie, "How Dissimulation about Islam Is Fuelling Genocide in the Middle East," *Lapido Media*, August 12, 2014.

95. Ibid.

96. A gold dinar weighs about 4.5 grams, which at $45 a gram means that a tax regime of one to four dinars equates to US$200 to $800 per non-Muslim adult male. Durie, "How Dissimulation about Islam Is Fueling Genocide in the Middle East."

97. "ISIS Enters Assyrian Town in Syria, Removes Church Cross," *AINA*, January 31, 2015.

98. Madeeha Bakhsh, "Syria: Militants Slit a Christian' Throat, Mock His Wife Saying "Your Jesus Did Not Come to Save Him from Us," *Christians in Pakistan*, June 24, 2016.

99. Katie Yoder, "Nets Cover Gorilla Death 6x More Than ISIS Christian Beheading," *Newsbusters*, June 2, 2016.

100. Mary Wakefield, "God's Man in Baghdad," *The Spectator*, August 29, 2015.

101. Marni Pyke, "'Vicar of Baghdad' Describes Life in Iraq," *Daily Herald* (Arlington Heights, IL), November 21, 2005.

102. Stoyan Zaimov, "Christian Iraqi Population Shrinking; Persecution 'Worse Than Under Saddam Hussein,'" *Christian Post*, June 5, 2016.

103. "'War Junkie' Vicar Brings Saddam Hussein Death Sentence Pen to Dewsbury," *Dewsbury Reporter* (England), February 10, 2012.

104. "British 'Vicar of Baghdad' Claims ISIS Beheaded Four Children for Refusing to Convert to Islam," *The Independent*, December 9, 2014.

105. Ibid.

106. Pyke, "'Vicar of Baghdad' Describes Life in Iraq."

107. John L. Allen Jr., "Grim Toll of Persecution: Thousands Dead, 120,000 More in Exile IRAQ," *The Boston Globe*, December 13, 2015.

108. Mary Wakefield, "I may no longer be the vicar of Baghdad, but the Middle East is my home." *The Spectator*, November 21, 2015.

109. Raymond Ibrahim, "Raymond Ibrahim: When Muslims Betray Non-Muslim Friends and Neighbors," *Jihad Watch*, July 9, 2015.

110. For more on Islamic sanctioned forms of deception, read about *taqiyya*, *tawriya*, and *taysir*. For more on how Muslims are never to befriend non-Muslims—except when in their interest—see Ayman al-Zawahiri's "Loyalty and Enmity," *The Al Qaeda Reader*, 63–115.

111. "ISIS Burns Christian Girl to Death, Her Last Words Were 'Forgive Them,'" *Catholic News Agency, WCBM*, May 10, 2016.

112. Michael Moutot, "'These Men Are Not Human': Teenager Describes IS Slave Market," Your Middle East.Com, September 2, 2015, http://www.your middleeast.com/news/these-men-are-not-human-teenager-describes-is-slave -market_34645.

113. Lin Taylor, "UK: Amal Clooney to Represent IS Slaves," *AAP General News Wire*, June 11, 2016.

114. "Escaped Yazidi Teenager Describes ISIL Slave Market," *Paris AFP*, September 2, 2015.

115. Stephen Kalin, "Scarred Yazidi Boys Escape Islamic State Combat Training," *Reuters*, April 26, 2016.

116. Rikar Hussein, *Animals, Weather, Human Access Endanger Yazidi Mass Graves* (Lanham, MD: Federal Information & News Dispatch, Inc., 2016).

117. Zee Media Bureau, "ISIS Commander Killed by Iraqi Women Forced into Sex Slavery," September 8, 2015.

118. Atika Shubert and Bharati Naik, "From Singer to Soldier: Xate Shingali and Women of The Sun Brigade Take on ISIS," *CNN World*, October 7, 2015.

119. Anugrah Kumar, "Former Yazidi Sex Slaves Form All-Female Battalion to Attack ISIS in Iraq," *Christian Post*, February 13, 2016.

120. Atika Shubert and Bharati Naik, "From Singer to Soldier: Xate Shingali and Women of the Sun Brigade Take On ISIS," *CNN*, October 7, 2015.

121. "Yazidi Female Fighters Tell Daesh They'll 'Wipe Them Out,'" *Sputnik News*, July 12, 2016.

122. Vincent Wood, "ISIS Arms Death Squads to Slay Civilians as Iraqi Army Obliterates Jihadi Stronghold," *Express*, May 25, 2016.

123. "Syria: ISIL Executes Members of a Family for Trying to Flee Manbij, Uses Civilians as Human Shield," *Asia News Monitor*, June 21, 2016.

124. Julian Robinson, "ISIS Hang Four 'Traitors' in Public and Force Their Families to Watch after Accusing the Men of Spying for US," *Daily Mail*, June 27, 2016.

125. "Syria: ISIL Uses Raqqa Residents as Human Shield, Evacuates Own Families," *Asia New Monitor*, May 24, 2016.

126. Sinan Salaheddin and Susannah George, "Iraqi Forces Liberate Fallujah: Islamic State-Held Mosul May Be Next," *South Florida Sun—Sentinel*, June 27, 2016.

127. Lucy Pasha-Robinson, "Fallujah Battle Raging as IS Hide Amid 50,000 Hostages Eire Region," *Sunday Mirror*, May 29, 2016.

128. "Revision: French Intelligence Services on Edge as 'Demotivated' Jihadis Seek to Return to France Paris," *Le Figaro*, June 11, 2016, 3.

129. Joey Millar, "Watch: ISIS Jihadis Humiliated after Captured Dressed as Women While Fleeing Battle," *Express (Online)*, July 24, 2016.

130. Ryan Mauro, "Forces at the Doorstep of ISIS' Apocalyptic Battlefield Dabiq," *The Clarion Project*, June 30, 2016.

131. Michael Fallon, "UK Minister Describes 'New Dawn of Airpower," *Ministry of Defense*, July 7, 2016.

132. The groups were American Civil Liberties Union, Amnesty International Center for Human Rights & Global Justice, and the Global Justice Clinic, NYU School of Law, Center for Civilians in Conflict, Center for Constitutional, Rights, Human Rights Clinic, Columbia Law School, Human Rights First, Human Rights Watch, International Commission of Jurists, Open Society Foundations. Human Rights Watch, "Joint Letter to the UN Human Rights Council on Targeted Killings and the Use of Armed Drones," September 18, 2014, https://www.hrw.org/news/2014/09/18/joint-letter-un-human-rights-council-targeted-killings-and-use-armed-drones.

133. Human Rights Watch, "Joint Letter to the UN Human Rights Council on Targeted Killings and the Use of Armed Drones," September 18, 2014, https://

www.hrw.org/news/2014/09/18/joint-letter-un-human-rights-council-targeted
-killings-and-use-armed-drones.

134. Robert Chesney, "Text of John Brennan's Speech on Drone Strikes Today at the Wilson CenterMonday," April 30, 2012, https://www.lawfareblog.com/text -john-brennans-speech-drone-strikes-today-wilson-center.

135. Jake Davies, "ISIS Militants Sell Chicken Eggs to Make Ends Meet," *Poultry World* (June 3, 2016): 18, accessed June 21, 2016.

136. Mary Chastain, "The Video Is Not Verified, but The Telegraph States Experts Told Them 'They Have No Reason to Doubt Its Authenticity,'" Brietbart .com, November 12, 2014. The Shaam News Network posted a video of a young Syrian boy who ran into sniper fire to rescue a small girl, http://www.breitbart .com/Big-Peace/2014/11/12/Syrian-Boy-Dodges-Sniper-Fire-to-Rescue-a-Young -Girl.

■
7. THE KILLING FLOOR

Killing floor: That part of the slaughterhouse where animals are killed.[1]

I want to do an Islamic Bonnie and Clyde on the kaffir.

—Bridget Namoa, Australian convert to Islam, 2016[2]

INTRODUCTION

The long, lethal arm of the Caliphate had reached well beyond Mesopotamia by 2015. Its cells and lone operatives plotted in European cities and suburbs. A sleepy Southern California town; a Tunisian beach filled with British vacationers; a hip Parisian nightclub; a watering hole for Orlando's gay community; the French Riviera; the squares, streets, and haunts of London town—all these venues, and others, became slaughter pens for the State. The first part of this chapter will discuss the Caliphate's killing in the West and in spots frequented by Westerners. The second part will discuss some Westerners who have gone to the Middle East to fight their enemy—the Islamic State.

KILLING ON THE HOMEFRONT—
WESTERNERS MAKE SENSE OF THE VIOLENCE

From its beginning, the Caliphate encouraged its followers to kill non-Muslim Westerners. Some of its adherents did so, proclaiming their solidarity with the State. The killings became so frequent that the carnage lost its shock effect. The Caliphate innovated and escalated the level of violence. The State's death list is long. Occasionally, Jews were targets, as in Copenhagen and Paris, because Islamists hate Jews in particular. Many killings were random, but some were very personal. A blonde Danish teenager murdered her mother after watching the Caliphate's beheadings of British hostages. Only fifteen years old when she savaged her mom with a large kitchen knife, she was a convert to Islam.[3]

Most of the State's victims had little or no interest in politics and simply wanted to live fulfilling and joyful lives. Many were killed by happenstance. They could not possibly have known that their lives were in danger. One case of hundreds is that of Nohemi Gonzalez. The Mexican American was studying design in Paris, and her boyfriend missed his "little firecracker," as he called her.[4] Dining with friends at a Parisian bistro, she was killed by a bomb blast on November 13, 2015.[5] Dead at age twenty-three, the "little firecracker" was the only known American killed in the Caliphate's Paris attack that day. Like many similar victims, she had fatally bad luck. Had she finished her meal an hour earlier, she would likely be alive today in Los Angeles.

In August 2016, a Norwegian citizen of Somali descent who had moved to Britain went on a stabbing spree in Russell Square, London. One of the victims was a sixty-year-old American woman whose husband was a psychology professor at Florida State University. She and three others—an Israeli woman, an Australian woman, and an American man—were stabbed. Only she died.[6]

Often the killings are directed. In the hills of San Bernardino, a husband-and-wife pair of Caliphate-supporting killers left their baby with family and then went to a well-attended Christmas party to shoot at anything that moved. They killed fourteen fellow workers. The Caliphate was delighted and called the killers, both of whom were slain in a police shootout, "lions [who] made us proud. They are still alive."[7] This is what happened.

PROFILE TWENTY-THREE: SAN BERNARDINO—
"CRY ME A RIVER"

Two-hundred-year-old San Bernardino is a small city located in the hills of Southern California. It is not particularly chic or famous. Gene Hackman, the two-time Oscar-winning actor, was born there.[8] Julie London, whose song "Cry Me a River" made her a famous torch singer in the 1950s, grew up there.[9] San Bernardino is the first important town in California on Route 66, coming from the east.[10] A famous song invited Americans to "get your kicks on Route 66." Many listened. San Bernardino was the gateway for millions of Americans beginning a new life in California, the Golden State.

San Bernardino was also home to Syed Farook and Tashfeen Malik, a married couple with a baby daughter. Syed Farook was born in the United States and turned to Islam with fervor. A county food inspector, he spent much of his free time in the mosque, memorizing the Koran.[11] He described himself on a dating website as enjoying "working on vintage and modern cars, reading and . . . target practice with younger sister and friends."[12] The target practice would prove useful later.

His lonely-hearts ad landed him a wife, Tashfeen Malik.[13] They were married in August 2014, and they had a baby girl. Tashfeen Malik was born in Saudi Arabia to a middle-class Pakistani family. She studied pharmacology, but she was very religious and explored Islam with a passion at night. Most of her neighbors did not know her at all, and she did not mix with males other than those in her family. She was almost always veiled when outside the house.

Few people outside of the family knew the depth of hatred the husband and wife held for the United States.[14] But they made their presence known on December 2, 2015. They dropped off their baby with relatives, explaining that they had a doctor's appointment.[15] They had no such appointment. The couple drove to the San Bernardino County Health Department with heavy firepower. They discharged up to seventy-five assault-rifle rounds into a crowd of workers, some of whom had worked with Farook. They killed fourteen, taking them completely by surprise.

Whose Fault?

The killing ignited the long-familiar debate on gun control. President Obama wanted to tighten gun-control laws to "make it harder for [terrorists] to kill."[16] Omid Safi, director of Duke University's Islamic Studies Center, blamed America's "deadly fetish" with firearms. This claim was rubbished by the National Rifle Association (NRA). The NRA's Chris Cox countered that the weapons used were illegal in California. Laws banning high-capacity magazines in assault weapons were already on the books. A letter to the *Washington Post* opined, "The reason these laws didn't prevent Wednesday's shooting is because gun control does not stop evil."[17] Campaigning for president, Hillary Clinton did not blame the Caliphate; she blamed the NRA.[18]

Others point to a workplace dispute that preceded the shooting. University of Michigan history professor Juan Cole blamed "someone going postal over his work situation."[19] But others rejoined that there are daily, sometimes bitter, disputes at work, almost none of which lead to mass murder.

Professor Steven Salaita blamed American "political violence . . . endemic to the United States."[20] A Columbia University professor underscored the American and Western "Islamophobia and the wanton cruelty of imperialist warfare, [and] the colonial occupation and domination of other people's homeland."[21] This was echoed by Los Angeles executive director of the Council on American-Islamic Relations

San Bernardino

(CAIR) Hussam Ayloush, who added that the United States supports the "dictatorships" and "coups" that "push people over the edge."[22] For this reason, according to the CAIR spokesperson, "We [Americans] are partly responsible."[23]

The argument over gun control would reemerge with vigor after the Florida killing of June 2016. But in winter 2015, residents of San Bernardino tried to heal their community. Several high school girls wore hijabs in solidarity with Islamic students. A seventeen-year-old Muslim girl, Zarifeh Shalabi, was voted prom queen at Summit High School. Her non-Muslim friends passed out colorful scarves and balloons on which were written, "Don't be a baddie, vote for the hijabi."[24] Her friends celebrated: "I feel like we have something to teach the rest of the country. It makes me really proud."[25]

THREE VIEWS OF CALIPHATE-INSPIRED KILLINGS

In response to the multiple murders and the high death count in the name of the Caliphate, Western journalists, politicians, intellectuals, and civil servants often placed the attacks in one of three categories. First, the attacks were not related to Islam; second, the attacks were driven by a distorted view of Islam; third, the attacks were an expression of Islamic mandates. The debate continues.

View One—The Attacks Were Not Islamic

Some in the West hold that political violence perpetrated by Muslims in the name of Islam is not and cannot be authentically Islamic. If Islam is a religion of peace, just as Judaism and Christianity are religions of peace, those who commit violence in its name have warped the religion's meaning. In this view, the perpetrators are fueled with a rage unconnected to any religion. Even when perpetrators roar "Allahu Akbar" or bellow praises for the Caliphate, these proclamations are dismissed as empty or misguided rhetoric.

Those who hold this view underscore the emotional instability or anger of the perpetrator. For example, in Le Mans, France, police arrested a Muslim who was tearing down Christmas decorations from the city center. The perpetrator then tried to grab a police officer's weapon while shouting "Allahu Akbar." Prosecutors declared him mentally ill and had him hospitalized.[26] In Dijon, France, a man yelling "Allahu Akbar" ran over a pedestrian. French prosecutors said, "This is absolutely not an act of terrorism." Rather, it was a "long-lasting and severe psychological disorder."[27] In Bavaria, Germany, a man stabbed four people at a train station while he was yelling "Allahu Akbar." The Bavarian interior minister said the incident was probably not political but an expression of mental illness.[28] There are many similar cases.[29]

This happens in the United States, too. In November 2015, at student at Merced campus of the University of California, Faisal Mohammed, stabbed four of his fellow students and was, in turn, shot dead. Police found a printout of the Caliphate's black flag in his possession.[30] But the county sheriff claimed that Mohammed's religion had nothing to do with his stabbing spree. Rather, he was angry at rejection. The sheriff compared Mohammed's references to Allah to a Christian who comes to Jesus.[31]

View Two—A Twisted View of Islam

The first view is that the attacks were unrelated to Islam and likely driven by mental illness or anger management issues. The second view is that Caliphate-connected violence results from a twisted view of Islam. For example, in Chattanooga, Tennessee, a young and attractive engineer, Mohammad Youssef Abdulazeez, went on a shooting spree, leaving four Marines and a sailor dead.[32] In his words, these were symbols of American power. Before the killing started, he texted a friend: "Whosoever shows enmity to a friend of Mine, then I have declared war against him."[33] Vice President Joe Biden called this the act of a "perverted jihadist."[34]

View Three—The Attacks Are Driven by Islam

The third view of Caliphate-related attacks is that they are a pure expression of Islam. This view takes the killers and the Caliphate at their word. Many of Caliphate-associated killers declared loudly, openly, and repeatedly their allegiance to the Caliphate and their belief in Jihad. In one case, a would-be pro-Caliphate killer repeatedly stated his intentions before and after his failed murder attempt. He was Abdul Shaheed, formerly known as Edward Archer.

Shaheed was well known at the local mosque, had made the pilgrimage to Mecca, and studied Arabic.[35] He pledged his allegiance to the Islamic State and determined to assassinate a police officer in a show of solidarity. But his thirteen-shot blast into officer Jesse Hartnett only wounded his victim, who then returned fire and winged the Jihadi.

Despite Shaheed's declaration of fealty to the State, Philadelphia mayor Jim Kenney said, "This is a criminal with a stolen gun who tried to kill one of our officers. This has nothing to do with being a Muslim or following the Islamic faith."[36] But the perpetrator contradicted the mayor and was emphatic that his motives had everything to do with Islam. Under arrest, he explained to investigating officers, "I follow Allah. I pledge my allegiance to the Islamic State, and that's why I did what I did."[37] Shaheed, in his view, could not have been more clear about his motives.

The most notorious terrorist shooting in American history occurred in June 2016 at the hands of a man who declared his allegiance to the Caliphate as he was shooting. His motives can be examined through three lenses, discussed below.

PROFILE TWENTY-FOUR: ONE SHOOTING
THROUGH THREE VIEWS—OMAR MATEEN

*Let us remember that we have never really blamed all Christians, Republicans,
or Democrats for the violence waged against us [homosexuals].*

—Steven Thrasher, June 12, 2016[38]

*Mommy I love you . . . In club they shootin . . . Trapp in bathroom . . .
He's coming. I'm gonna die.*

—The last texts of Eddie Justice to his mother, Mina, June 13, 2016[39]

It was Gay Pride Week, and homosexuals were celebrating in cities throughout America. They hoped to have fun and find romance. It was also Ramadan, a sacred month for Muslims, and the Islamic State leaders said, "Ramadan, the month of conquest and Jihad. Get prepared, be ready . . . to make it a month of calamity everywhere for the non-believers . . . especially for the fighters and supporters of the Caliphate in Europe and America."[40]

New York–born twenty-nine-year-old Omar Mateen went to the Pulse Orlando, a gay nightclub, and started killing people. In the midst of the attack, he called 911 and pledged his allegiance to the State. Before he was killed by police, he murdered forty-nine people and injured far more. He had made his contempt for non-Muslim Americans well known. Mateen had also told his coworkers that he wanted to become a "martyr" in an operation.[41]

Even in boyhood, he was known for making violent comments and cheering the mass murder of non-Muslims. He was suspended from high school for celebrating the attacks on the American homeland on September 11, 2001. In 2013, he threatened to kill law enforcement personnel and their families.[42] The FBI investigated but terminated the investigations because they thought he was the victim of Islamophobia.[43] Mateen claimed that one of his coworkers had called him a "towel head." But the FBI report concluded that he was not "likely to go postal."[44]

He had visited the gay venue before the day of the shooting. Some have speculated that this was preoperational surveillance. Others offer this as evidence of his conflict with his homosexuality and his inability to cope with it. He laughed as he slaughtered his victims. He disliked Donald Trump, and according to a friend, "he liked Hillary Clinton."[45]

The first lens, which was that the attack was not Islamic, is expressed by left-of-center journalists, gun-control activists, Western Muslim advocacy groups, university professors, and Democratic Party leaders. The British *Guardian* explained, "This is not the typical Muslim experience, but an aberration."[46] The *Boston Globe* opined that it "makes no more sense to blame Islam for the Orlando shooting than it would to blame mental illness for the Sandy Hook massacre."[47]

Chase Strangio of the American Civil Liberties Union (ACLU) put the onus on the Christian right. "You know what is gross—your thoughts and prayers and Islamophobia after you created this anti-queer climate."[48] Ariela Gross of the University of Southern California agreed, stressing what she saw as a legacy of hatred-inspired shooting.[49] Another professor cited "gay panic" and "trans panic," which according to her, is a violent reaction to repressed gayness.[50] The Council on American-Islamic Relations (CAIR) tweeted, "This sick, cowardly act has no justification in any ideology."[51]

In addition to blaming generalized American pathologies, others fault the availability of assault weapons. The front page of one New York daily screamed, "Thanks, NRA 50 dead in Orlando club massacre. Because of your continued opposition to an assault rifle ban, terrorists like this lunatic can legally buy a killing machine and perpetrate the worst mass shooting in U.S. history."[52]

The killer's father opined that his son's witnessing two men kissing warped his mind and that his attack had nothing to do with religion.[53] Nader Hashemi of the University of Denver said Mateen was a "deeply, mentally ill individual—a ticking time bomb that was ready to explode."[54] The head of a Jewish lesbian, gay, bisexual, transexual, and questioning (LGBTQ) group was concerned about the security of Muslims, fearing a backlash of vilification and violence.[55] National Public Radio suggested that Mateen used the Caliphate to gain publicity.[56] Illinois senator Dick Durbin called Mateen's claim to be acting as a Muslim "baloney."[57]

The second view is that Mateen's attack was driven by a twisted view of Islam. The *Orlando Sentinel* talked about "a perverted interpretation of Islam."[58] Thomas Friedman saw the attack as driven from the most reactionary and bitter elements of a generally peaceful Islam. He is sure that the Orlando killing did not express "the essence of Islam." The suicidal violence rests in the sick margins in an otherwise healthy and humane religion.[59] President Obama's comments straddle the first and the second views.[60]

The third view of the Orlando killing is that it was motivated by Islamic mandates and on behalf of the Islamic State. This view is shared by the now-dead killer and the Caliphate. Mateen was loud and clear about his intentions. Former Muslim and cartoonist Bosch Fawstin placed the blame exclusively on Mateen, who was acting on behalf of the Caliphate. America was blameless. Said Fawstin, "I had nothing to do with the atrocity in Orlando. You had nothing to do with it. America had nothing to do with it. Only a devout Muslim did."[61] Philip Haney, a former employee of the Department of Homeland Security, underscored the centrality of the Islamic legal code as motive.[62]

Others are confused about Mateen's motives and cannot be placed in any of these three views. Journalist Peter Bergen speculated that the world will never fully understand Mateen's motives because it is unlikely the world will ever understand the nature of evil.[63] Bernie Sanders speculated on Islamophobia or a hatred of Latinos: "Was he suicidal and wanted to end his life by taking others with him? We may never know the answer to those questions."[64] Mateen was buried in the only fully Muslim cemetery in South Florida. A burial official explained, "Everybody deserves a place [to be buried] and we don't know his side of the story."[65]

This chapter now moves to the Western fight against the Caliphate in the Middle East. Western states and individuals fight the Islamic State with both nonviolent and violent means.

WESTERN-LED NONVIOLENT RESISTANCE

Some Westerners travel to Mesopotamia in the name of humanity. They try to relieve the suffering of refugees. NGOs help feed, shelter, and medically treat the dispossessed. Just as some Westerners are drawn to the Caliphate to serve and kill for Jihad, Western humanitarians are pulled to the Middle East to relieve, to feed, to heal, and to nurture. One of these was Kayla Mueller.

PROFILE TWENTY-FIVE: KAYLA MUELLER— "I FIND GOD IN THE SUFFERING'S EYES"

By all accounts she was a loving, spiritual, and kind woman. She was trusting, perhaps too trusting. Kayla Mueller grew up in Prescott, Arizona, and after college devoted herself to helping the less fortunate. She said she was doing God's work. In a letter to her parents, she wrote, "I find God in the suffering's eyes reflected in mine."[66] She helped HIV/AIDS patients and volunteered at a women's shelter.

Kayla traveled the world trying to relieve the suffering of the downtrodden. This took her to Syrian refugee camps in Turkey. "For as long as I live, I will not let this suffering be normal."[67] She and her boyfriend were kidnapped in August 2013, after leaving a Doctors Without Borders hospital in Aleppo, Syria. Leaders of what would become the Islamic State sentenced her to life in prison in retaliation for the imprisonment of an American of Pakistani descent who had tried to join the Taliban. The United States refused to swap the women.

Kayla became the sex slave of the Caliphate's leader. Abu Bakr announced that he had "married her," and Kayla's parents wept. Her mother countered, "Kayla did not marry this man. He took her to his room and he abused her, and she came back crying."[68] Kayla was allowed to write a few letters to her parents, in which she pleaded for their forgiveness. She begged them to forgive "the suffering I have put you all through . . . in the end, the only one you really have is God."[69]

In February 2015, President Obama announced that Kayla had been murdered.[70] The Islamic State claimed that she was killed by an errant US bomb, but this is almost certainly a lie. Al-Baghdadi may have grown tired of her and had her killed. As of this writing, there are no exact details, but a Yazidi sex slave who later escaped had shared a cell with Kayla and had firsthand knowledge of Kayla's murder. The Yazidi girl also shared another memory of Kayla—that she had eaten very little in her captivity. Instead, she gave what little food she had to the Yazidi girls. Why? "[Kayla] didn't want us to be hungry."[71]

Kinetic Operations—"Harvesting Jihadis"

Several Western countries have made war on the State and continue to do so through drone warfare and elite teams of special operators.[72] There are Western hunter-killer teams that partner with Iraqi forces. One observer quoted a British officer as saying, "It is now time to harvest the Jihadis."[73] Some Western civilians have tried to do so in the service of Kurdish forces. As in the Spanish Civil War, they come from all over the Western world to fight for cause and comrades. The Lions of Rojava, a Kurdish organization, helps foreigners join up with anti-State fighting units.[74]

According to one source, 108 Americans had fought against the State as of summer 2016. "These volunteers paid their own way to the war zone and usually returned home when their funds ran out."[75] They were drawn to fight the State because of the killing of Christians, the general atrocities, and the lure of battle for a good cause. Some veterans had nostalgia for the camaraderie of prior military service.[76]

Canadian Dillon Hillier, a veteran of the Canadian military and son of a politician, became a minor celebrity in his homeland, earning the moniker "Canadian Peshmerga."[77] Reece Harding of Queensland, Australia, nicknamed "Surfie," could not abide what he saw as Western inaction. A fellow surfer described Harding as having a spark of humanity. "Everybody liked him."[78] Leaving his surfing days behind him, the handsome, blond, twenty-three-year-old man told his parents that he needed a short break. In fact, he left to fight with Kurds and was killed by a landmine. His comrades posted a tribute to him on Facebook. The next day, they called his father in Australia to share the tragic news.[79]

A generation older than Surfie, Richard Jansen is a Dutch sniper who, like the Australian, left a comfortable home to fight with the Kurds. In Holland, he worked as a bodyguard for ten years. He wanted to fight Jihadis in Europe but couldn't do so.[80] So he traveled to Turkey to fight with the Kurds. Jansen found Syria to be a target-rich environment and claims to have killed forty State fighters. On Dutch television, he seemed to relish the memories of killing the enemy. "These are not people. It is prize shooting at the carnival."[81] The "carnival" ended for Jansen when he was wounded in combat and sent to a medical clinic in Germany.

The German-born Ivana Hoffmann was the first foreign female to die alongside Kurds. She became a member of a Marxist-Leninist Communist Party at an early age. Her parents were black South Africans and she said she wanted to fight for internationalism.[82] Ivana was killed on the eve of World Women's Day, in March 2015.[83] She was not forgotten in Germany and several thousand friends and supporters carried red banners in Duisburg in her memory. She was nineteen years old.

Thirtysomething Canadian Israeli Gill Rosenberg fought in the ranks of the Peshmerga forces, becoming the first foreign woman to do so. Rosenberg explained, "We Jews always say of the Holocaust—never again. In my opinion that's true not only for the Jews, but for all mankind."[84]

Thirty-six-year-old Keith Broomfield of Massachusetts, like Rosenberg, had a strong religious identity, if a different religion.[85] Keith was a devout Baptist who had had a difficult youth. He heard a calling to fight with the Kurds and stop the State's slaughter.[86] The New Englander had no contacts and knew it was "a crazy thing to do."[87] His father said his son was led by the Lord to go to the battle lines. He did so, where he fought and fell.

An energetic senior citizen, Alan Brooke was desperate to join Kurdish forces, but the sixty-two-year-old retired archaeologist was told to return to his seventy-one-year-old wife in England. Undeterred as of 2016, he said, "I intend to go back. I can't think of a better way to use my pension. My wife is fully supportive."[88]

Some other fighters are highly idiosyncratic, and British character actor Michael Enright is among them. After basic training with the Kurds, he made himself useful as a photographer and documented the brutality of the Caliphate's war. He took risks. His comrades in arms do not doubt his enthusiasm, but some question his stability. Reportedly, he suffers from emotional aberrations, which are sometimes very melodramatic.[89] "It's got to a point where I just want to absolutely annihilate them, and kill them on sight."[90]

Summary

The Caliphate has ordered killings throughout the West. Some of its cadre have traveled from Europe to the Middle East and back to Europe. Others have pledged fealty to the State and killed on its behalf. Westerners have traveled to the Middle East to fight with the Kurds against the State.

In June 2016, an American killed forty-nine victims at a gay nightclub. He paused after a few volleys to pledge allegiance to the Caliphate. He was killed, but other Islamic State operatives plan to attack Westerners. Non-Muslims, particularly those high on the State's enemies list, have taken note. After the Florida attacks, many American gays are worried.[91]

Some public intellectuals and politicians dismiss the charge that the Caliphate-directed or -inspired attacks are driven by Islam. They warn against backlashes against Muslims and the continued need to partner with Muslim leaders to suppress radicalism. A seventeen-year-old New Yorker explained, "Islam is all about peace. In Ramadan, we don't even curse. You're not supposed to do anything bad."[92] But, increasingly, many Westerners see this and similar statements as tortured apologetics. They see the State's attacks as Islam—pure and simple.

NOTES

1. Yahoo Answers, "The 'Killing Floor' Is Mentioned in a Lot of Blues Songs. What Is the Killing Floor?" accessed September 17, 2016, https://answers.yahoo .com/question/index;_ylt=AwrBT9hej91XnL0A10BXNyoA;_ylu=X30DMTEy dmIyN21nBGNvbG8DYmYxBHBvcwM3BHZoaWQDQjE4NzlfMQRzZWMD c3I-?qid=20071225224216AAkSas0&p=%22the%20killing%20floor%22%20and %20definition.

2. "Laura Banks Homegrown Radical: Schoolgirl Alo-Bridget Namoa's Conversion to Islamic Extremism Baffles Friends and Family," *The Daily Telegraph*, February 10, 2016.

3. Alan Hall, "Blonde Danish Teenager, 15, Murdered Her Mother with a Kitchen Knife after Watching ISIS Videos of the Beheading of British Hostages Online," *MailOnline*, September 15, 2015.

4. Daniela Franco, "Nohemi Gonzalez Mourned by Loved Ones as Well as Strangers," *NBC News*, November 16, 2015.

5. Josh Dulaney, "Mourning Cal State Long Beach Students Return to Classes, Build Memorial for Nohemi Gonzalez," *Daily News* (Los Angeles, CA), December 20, 2015.

6. Marint Robinson, "Was 'Devout Muslim' Russell Square Knifeman Radicalised? Police to Trawl 'Impressionable' Attacker's PC for Links to ISIS as Neighbour Claims Mental Illness Is a 'Scapegoat,'" *Mailonline*, August 5, 2016.

7. Nicole Hass, "FBI Expert on CNN Mocks Obama While Covering Shootings; Clearly Not 'Climate Change' Related," *BPR*, December 3, 2015.

8. Harvey M. Kahn, "San Bernardino's Gene Hackman Remains Quiet about Early Life," *El Chicano Weekly*, March 5, 2009.

9. John Weeks, "San Bernardino's Stars of Tomorrow," *San Bernardino County Sun*, July 17, 2010.

10. John Weeks, "San Bernardino-Route 66: Crossroads of History," *San Bernardino County Sun*, September 17, 2010.

11. Robert Spencer, "San Bernardino: Another Jihad Attack, Another Cover-Up," *Frontpage Magazine*, December 4, 2015.

12. Rebecca Kimitch, "What We Know about San Bernardino Mass Shooting Killers Syed Farook and Tashfeen Malik," *Whittier Daily News*, December 20, 2015.

13. Beatriz Valenzuela, "FBI: Syed Farook, Tashfeen Malik Pre-Planned San Bernardino Attack," *Whittier Daily News*, December 7. 2015.

14. Doug Saunders, "San Bernardino Shooter Tashfeen Malik Described as 'Caring, Soft- Spoken,'" *Whittier Daily News*, 2015.

15. "Timeline: How the San Bernardino Shooting Unfolded," *Whittier Daily News*, 2015.

16. Dan Liljenquist, "San Bernardino Terror Attacks and Gun Control," *Desert News* (Salt Lake City, UT), 2015.

17. "The San Bernardino Shooting," *The Washington Post*, 2015.

18. Melanie Mason, "San Bernardino Attack Is Subtle Undercurrent in Clinton Speech," *Los Angeles Times*, June 3, 2016.

19. Cinnamon Stillwell, "Academia on San Bernardino Attack: No Jihad Here," American Thinker, http://www.americanthinker.com/articles/2015/12/academia_on_san_bernardino_attack_no_jihad_here.htm.

20. Ibid.

21. Ibid.

22. "CAIR's Internet Myths and Facts—an IPT Rebuttal," The Investigative Project on Terrorism, Accessed September 17, 2016, http://www.investigativeproject.org/profile/180/cair-internet-myths-and-facts-an-ipt-rebuttal.

23. David M. Swindle, "Three Tricks Islamic Extremists Use to Conceal the Truth about the Orlando Massacre," *Daily Wire*, June 17, 2016.

24. "A Few Miles from San Bernardino, a Muslim Prom Queen Reigns," *Gulf News, USA*, April 30, 2016.

25. Ibid.

26. "Le Mans: A Man Detained after Shouting 'Allah Akbar,'" *Le Maine Libre*, December 23, 2014.

27. Jean-Philippe Ksizek, "French Prosecutor Rules Out Terror Link in Dijon Car Rampage," *AFP*, December 22, 2014.

28. Joern Poltz and Jens Hack, "Knifeman Kills One at Munich Station; No Evidence of Islamist Motive," *Reuters*, May 10, 2016.

29. There are cases in which perpetrators have clear and documented histories of insanity. In June 2016, during Ramadan, a Muslim man stabbed a French nineteen-year-old woman, in Rennes, France, as sacrifice for Ramadan. He explained to the arresting police officer that he heard voices. He had been institutionalized before. "Man Stabs Teenager in France Citing Ramadan 'Sacrifice,'" *The Daily Star* (Lebanon), June 14, 2016.

30. There was also a manifesto that claimed he planned to bind students to their desks, call police to the scene, ambush them with a large hunting knife, take the firearms, and then kill students. Rahul Srivivas, "UC Merced Stabbing Attack

Suspect Faisal Mohammad Was Carrying an ISIS Flag: Reports," *Inquisitor*, November 10, 2015.

31. Oliver Darcy, "Two-Page Handwritten Manifesto Found on Body of UC Merced Attacker—Here's What It Said, and Who He Praised," *The Blaze*, November 5, 2015.

32. Whitlock Craig and Carol D. Leonnig, "Chattanooga Gunman Came from a Middle-Class Muslim Family; Abdulazeez Was a Trained Engineer and a Martial Arts Fighter, with a Prophetic Yearbook Quote," the *Washington Post*, July 17, 2015.

33. Richard Valdmanis, "Tennessee Suspect Texted Friend Link to Islamic Verse before Attack," *Reuters*, July 18, 2015.

34. The vice president's use of the word "Jihadist" surprised some political observers. Since 2008, the executive branch and other high-level federal officials have generally avoided any derogatory use of the word. Some speculated this might indicate an executive-level policy shift. Erik Schelzig, "Biden Calls Chattanooga Shooter a 'Perverted Jihadist,'" *Associated Press*, August 15, 2015.

35. Michael Matza, "Philly Imam Knew Police Shooter, but by Muslim Name," *Jihad Watch*, January 11, 2016, http://www.jihadwatch.org/2016/01/philadelphia-cop-shooter-was-frequent-member-of-local-mosque.

36. Mark Berman, "Police: IS Loyalist Ambushed Pa. Officer," *The Washington Post*, June 15, 2016.

37. "The Man Shot Cop in Islam's Name, Police Say," *Telegraph-Herald* (Dubuque, IA), January 8, 2016.

38. Steven W Thrasher, "Let's Not Give In to Fear after the Orlando Shooting," *Guardian*, June 12, 2016.

39. Marty Clear, Alfred Ng, and Leonard Greene, "'Mommy I Love You . . . He's Coming. I'm Going to Die,'" *New York Daily News*, June 13, 2016.

40. "Omar Mateen, Terrorist Who Attacked Orlando Gay Club, Had Been Investigated by FBI," *The Daily Beast*, June 12, 2016.

41. Michael Isikoff and Jason Sickles, "Orlando Gunman Omar Mateen Watched ISIS Beheading Videos, Sources Say," *Yahoo News*, June 15, 2016.

42. Christian Datoc, "Orlando Terrorist Threatened to Kill Fla. Sheriff and His Family, FBI Dismissed Threat," *Daily Caller*, June 17, 2016.

43. Isikoff and Sickles, "Orlando Gunman Omar Mateen."

44. Daniel Greenfield, "FBI on Orlando Terrorist: I Don't Believe He Will Go Postal," *Frontpage*, July 21, 2016.

45. Bre Payton, "Friend Who Reorted Omar Mateen to FBI: 'He Likes Hillary Clinton,'" *The Federalist*, June 21, 2016.

46. Samra Habib, "Queer Muslim Exist—and We Are in Mourning Too," *The Guardian*, June 12, 2016.

47. "Besides Gun Control, Prevention Must Also Eye Mental Health, Ideological Influences," *The Boston Globe*, 2016.

48. Joel Gehrke, "ACLU Lawyers Blame 'Christian Right,' GOP for Orlando Terrorist Attack," *Washington Examiner*, June 12, 2016.

49. Ariela Gross, "Orlando Mass Shooting Not Deadliest in American History," *Wall Street Journal*, June 14, 2016.

50. Amanda Taub, "Mass Killings and Wife Beatings: A Common Thread," *International New York Times*, June 16, 2016.

51. David Swindle, "Three Tricks Islamic Extremists Use to Conceal the Truth about the Orlando Massacre," *Daily Wire*, June 17, 2016.

52. "Thanks, NRA 50 Dead in Orlando Club Massacre Because of Your Continued Opposition to an Assault Rifle Ban, Terrorists Like This Lunatic Can LEGALLY Buy a Killing Machine and Perpetrate the Worst Mass Shooting in U.S. History," *New York Daily News*, June 13, 2016.

53. Omar Mateen, "Terrorist Who Attacked Orlando Gay Club, Had Been Investigated by FBI," *The Daily Beast*, June 12, 2016.

54. Nader Hashemi, *Campus Watch*, accessed June 17, 2016.

55. Amanda Borschel-Dan Head, "Jewish LGBTQ Group Fears for Muslims after Attack," *Times of Israel*, June 13, 2016.

56. Tim Graham, "NPR: Mateen Only Evoked ISIS as a 'Cover Story' to Gain 'More Publicity' . . . for Shooting 100!" *National Public Radio*, June 18, 2016.

57. Warner Todd Huston, "Dick Durbin Admits He Ordered the FBI to Purge Words Deemed 'Offensive' to Muslims from Manual," *Daily Caller*, June 30, 2016.

58. "Social Plague of Violence: A Battle at Home, Abroad," *The Orlando Sentinel* (Orlando, FL), April 24, 2007.

59. Thomas Friedman, "Lessons of Hiroshima and Orlando," *Seattle Times*, June 15, 2016.

60. Bridge Johnson, "Obama: Orlando Killer Inspired by 'Propaganda and Perversions of Islam' on Internet," *PJ Media*, June 13, 2016.

61. Robert Spencer, "Non-Muslim Utah Lieutenant Governor Spencer Cox Apologizes to LGBTs for Orlando Jihad Massacre," *Jihad Watch*, June 16, 2016.

62. John Haywar, "DHS Whistleblower Philip Haney: Islamist 'Self-Radicalization' Is a 'Surreal' Myth," *Breitbart*, June 15, 2016.

63. Peter Bergen, "Why Do Terrorists Commit Terrorism?" *New York Times*, June 14, 2016.

64. Daniel Greenfield, "Bernie Sanders: We May Never Know Why ISIS Supporter Carried Out Orlando Attack," *Frontpage Magazine*, June 15, 2015.

65. Daniel Greenfield, "'We Don't Know His Side of the Story': All-Muslim Cemetery Buries Orlando Jihadist," *Frontpage Magazine*, June 24, 2016.

66. Jamie Manson, "Kayla Mueller's Encounter with a Suffering God," February 27, 2015.

67. "To Honor Memory of Hostage, Tune in to Pain of Others," *AZ Daily Star*, February 12, 2015.

68. Ken Dilanian, "Islamic State Leader Raped American Hostage, US Find," *Associated Press*, August 14, 2015.

69. Jamie Manson, "Kayla Mueller's Encounter with a Suffering God," February 27, 2015.

70. "US President Confirms Death IS Hostage Kayla Mueller," *Al-Arab* (London), February 11, 2015.

71. "US Hostage Kayla Mueller 'Killed by IS'; Say Ex-Slaves," *BBC*, September 10, 2015.

72. Tom Vanden Brook, "Army to Issue Shoulder Patch for ISIL Fight," *USA TODAY*, September 24, 2015.

73. "Punk Jihadi Sally Jones Heads SAS Top 20 Kill List as Part of 'Jihadi Harvest,'" *Breitbart London*, November 29, 2015.

74. "The Westerners Who Fight against ISIS," *NOW Lebanon*, May 3, 2015.

75. Tim Dyhouse, "'Sending ISIS to Hell': American Volunteers Wage a Lonely War," *VFW Magazine*, June 1, 2016.

76. Ibid.

77. Campbell MacDiarmid, "Kurdish Forces Frown on Foreign Volunteers," *Aina.org*, February 16, 2015.

78. Rory Callinan, "Australia: Queensland Surfie Reece Harding Dies Fighting with Kurds in Syria," *The Sydney Morning Herald Online*, July 1, 2015.

79. Ibid.

80. "The Westerners Who Fight against ISIS.".

81. "Dutch National Claims to Have Killed Dozens of ISIL Fighters," *de Volkskrant Online*, June 25, 2015.

82. Ryan Lucas, "News Guide: Latest Developments on Islamic State Group," *AP Online*, 2015.

83. Louise Osborne, "First Female Western Fighter Dies Fighting the Islamic State," *The Guardian*, March 9, 2015.

84. Oliver Lane, "Israeli-Canadian Woman Who Went to Fight ISIS to Prevent 'Another Holocaust' Flies Home," *Brietbart*, July 13, 2015.

85. Thomas Gibbons-Neff, "Americans Fighting with Kurds Is Killed in Syria," *The Washington Post*, June 11, 2015.

86. Jonathan Spyer, "RIP Keith Broomfield, Killed in a Firefight with ISIS," *Rubin Center IDC* (Herzliya, Israel), June 19, 2015.

87. Zeina Karam. "Body of American Killed Fighting IS Handed Over to Family." AP Online, Press Association, June 11, 2015.

88. "Brit, 62, Sent Back from Iraq as 'Too Old' to Battle ISIS; Quest to Fight Militants Is Shattered," *The Mirror* (London), March 16, 2015.

89. Jordan Matson, "Attention to Whomever Is in Charge of Monitoring My Account for the State Department," *Facebook*, June 4, 2015, https://www.facebook.com/jordan.matson.3/posts/863151780439578.

90. John Hall, "'Mentally Unstable' British Actor Fighting ISIS in Syria Should Be Removed before He Is Abandoned or Murdered, Says Ex-US Marine," *Daily Mail*, June 4, 2015.

91. Emily Thode and Melissa Mecija, "Craigslist Ad Threatens Orlando-Style Massacre in San Diego," *KGTV*, June 14, 2016.

92. Liz Robbins, "New York Muslims of a Cherished Holiday Respite," *New York Times*, June 18, 2016.

8. THE CALIPHATE ABROAD, PART ONE: THE ANGLO-SAXONS

INTRODUCTION

Earlier chapters explored why Westerners are drawn to and sometimes repulsed by life in the Caliphate. Chapters 8 and 9 will return to Europe to give more detail about Muslim–non-Muslim relations in select countries. These chapters will expand on the Caliphate-related themes presented earlier, such as social divisions, recruitment, support bases, cell formation, and the political environment in selected European countries and in the United States. The Anglo-Saxon countries are Britain, Germany, and the United States. The French-speaking countries are France and Belgium.

The Deluge

The influx of migrants and refugees into Europe and the United States presented opportunities for the Caliphate. In the West, reports of the Caliphate's troops disguising themselves as refugees and migrants became central national security concerns in 2015 and 2016. Thousands of migrants filtered up the continent and encamped in the "jungle refugee centers" in Calais and other French coastal cities. Many hoped to brave the choppy English Channel for a new home in Britain. After the Florida, Istanbul, and Nice attacks, the great migration became a dominant issue in Europe and in the American presidential election year of 2016.

In April 2016, soon after the Brussels attack, a survey revealed that respondents in nine out of ten European countries described the Caliphate as a "major threat."[1] At the time, migrants were streaming from the Middle East, North Africa, and Eurasia by the hundreds of thousands. Many Europeans saw this as the gravest threat to European harmony since the Cold War and the greatest menace to social cohesion since the ethnic shifts and cleansing in the post–World War II period.

Some Europeans used biblical metaphors, including the "great flood," to describe the current migration. British commentators looked to history, citing the French invasion of England 1,000 years earlier. Continentals drew imagery of the Visigoths, Vandals, and Huns, vastly exaggerated and alarmist historical analogies but ones that depict the unease with which some Europeans live with their new nationals.

Social services throughout Europe were inundated with demands that could not be met. Federal and local authorities needed to innovate to provide shelter for individuals, families, and chunks of Middle Eastern neighborhoods now transported to Europe. Police forces were strained, and some felt hampered by the inability to communicate in a common language or wrangle with customs that were distinctly non-European. There were simply not enough officers, prosecutors, prison guards, or prison space to cope. As an example, police in the German city of Keil allegedly collectively stopped pursuing cases where refugees were caught shoplifting because it was too much work to prosecute them.[2]

Greece, the entry point for many migrants, faced daunting and morbid problems in 2015, as nearly 90 percent of the migrants arrived on Greek soil as their point of entry to Europe. Pope Francis praised the Greek people for their kindness to "the cradle of civilization, the heart of humanity."[3] But many Greeks found it hard to cope. The island of Lesbos, of Greek myth, was inundated with migrants, some of whom died there. Its mayor explained that there was no room left in the main cemetery to bury anyone.[4]

Bodies that washed up on Greek shores were referred to by "cadaver number." On the small island of Samos, the body of a short-haired boy in a black shirt and jeans was tagged as "Cadaver #4" in January 2016. It belonged to a young Syrian named Yamen, who had, like so many others, drowned at sea. His cousins and aunts and uncles made it alive to Europe and Canada, and they searched for Yamen's whereabouts. His uncle flew from Montreal to bring the boy to Canada for burial in a family plot.

Northern Bound—Destination Unknown

Northern Bound—"Just Wait"

It's our dream that there should be a caliphate not only in Syria but in all the world, and we will have it soon, inshallah.

—A Caliphate leader in reference to the migration to Europe, 2015[5]

The route through the Greek islands was the most frequented entry point for the million-plus migrants of 2015 and 2016. Passage through the Balkans were called "Jihadist highways." The head of France's internal intelligence service confirmed that the Islamic State was using migrant routes through the Balkans to infiltrate Europe.[6] European security services became strained trying to monitor migrants and migratory patterns.[7] From Greece, migrants often headed north, hoping to reach the wealthier states, primarily Germany, France, and Britain. Some had immigrated because they were destitute and desperate.[8] Others came to better their lives for themselves and their families. Others came to emulate Muhammad's *hijrah*, the journey from Mecca to Medina. Some came to infiltrate, plan attacks, and kill. Greek officials uncovered places in Athens where Caliphate cadre would stay before they scattered to France, Belgium, Denmark, Spain, and Germany.[9] They would be provisioned in these safe houses and given contact information for their destination.

In February 2015, the Caliphate boasted that it would infiltrate thousands of its followers among the migrants. According to one source, in September 2015, 4,000 Islamic State Jihadis had already entered Europe. A Caliphate leader said, "These Muslims were going to Europe in the service of that caliphate, They are going like refugees. Just wait."[10]

Several European Union countries, particularly those in Eastern Europe, built temporary fences. Hungary, Serbia, Slovakia, Romania, and Croatia erected barriers. But once migrants entered Europe, it was very unlikely that they would be deported; at one point in 2016, the European Union deported only seven migrants a day.[11] Many deportation-bound migrants claimed sudden, unrecognizable diseases that prevented them from flying on aircraft. They could stay. The EU counterterrorism chief conceded that it was "relatively easy" to enter the European Union with the sea of refugees.[12] Enter they did.

In the Name of Humanity

*This is the Syria of 2015, where anyone who is upwardly mobile
is now also westwardly mobile.[13]*

Many Westerners were moved by the human dimension of the migration crisis. Commercial and social media captured some of the pain. A Swedish journalist found a love poem, protected in a plastic bag and washed up on the shore of a Greek island. Many rickety boats coming from the Middle East capsized, and the poem may have been part of the flotsam. Translated from Arabic, some lines read, "My Rose, I promise you, I will love you till the last minute of my life . . . will not let anything separate us . . . I promise you."[14] The fates of the author and his beloved Rose are unknown as of this writing.

Particularly stirring was a photograph of a drowned little boy washed up on a Turkish shore in September 2014. This image touched the heartstrings of the world. Alan (sometimes spelled Ayan) Kurdi was three years old and dressed in Western clothing. Some of the boy's family drowned with him. His father, Abdullah, pleaded to the world, "My message is I'd like the whole world to open its doors to Syrians."[15] His voice opened the doors of Europe.

European celebrities and intellectuals tended to be more sympathetic to the migrants than others. Academy Award-winning actress Emma Thompson blamed racism, claiming that if the refugees were white, the British would feel "quite differently about it."[16] In London, after the curtain went down on a performance of *Hamlet*, Benedict Cumberbatch, who played the Dane, made an impassioned soliloquy against the "utter disgrace of the British government!"[17]

Festung Europa

*The Belgians believed, as the British security services did before 7/7,
that if they allowed Islamism to gestate at home, the terrorists would spare
the country that had given them sanctuary. That fallacy now lies
on the scrapheap of ideas where it always belonged.*

—Editorial from the *Spectator*[18]

Attitudinal surveys expose the increasing panic Europeans have about the Islamic State and concern about the increasing tide of migration. By June 2016, three out of four respondents to a survey saw migrants as a "significant" threat.[19] Self-identified conservatives tended to see the migration as a greater crisis than self-identified liberals.[20]

While many in Europe's chattering classes have welcomed Middle Easterners to their continent, others are not as hospitable. Tabloid journalists and European common men and women are not persuaded that there is a human right to move to a certain country and to become one of its citizens.[21] This was, in part, reflected in the British vote to leave the European Union.

Many Europeans do not want any more Middle Eastern refugees at all. Katie Hopkins, of the *British Daily Mail*, proposed launching a fleet of "gun ships" to stop the armada of refugees from reaching British shores.[22] In that spirit, Rod Liddie, of the *Sun*, mocks "lefties" who bleat, "They [the migrants] are human beings! Let them in." But Liddie rejoins that there are "7 billion people in the world. They would not all fit in Britain."[23]

With resignation, Hungarian Nobel laureate Imre Kertész, a survivor of Auschwitz, predicted the end of Europe because of liberalism, which is "childish and suicidal." Having lived through the Nazi epoch, he lamented and feared the end of democracy. He bemoaned the idea that "the doors are wide open for Islam."[24] Former Briton Niall Ferguson, professor at Harvard, said Europe had "opened its gates to outsiders who have coveted its wealth without renouncing their ancestral faith" and whose views are "not easily reconciled with the principles of our liberal democracies."[25] Former prime minister David Cameron claimed that British voters backed a vote to leave the European Union because people believe the country has "no control" of its borders. The concern about Islamic extremism is shown in Tables 8.1 and 8.2.

France, home to persistent and spectacular attacks, saw national concern about Islamic extremism more than double in the ten years between 2005 and 2015. There was a surge in concern in the other Western countries, probably reflecting the increase of Islamist-driven attacks.

Table 8.1. Public Opinion—Response to the Question "Are You Very Concerned about Islamic Extremism in Our Country?"

	2005 (%)	2006 (%)	2011 (%)	2015 (%)	Change from 2011 to 2015 (%)
France	32	30	29	67	+38
Spain	43	35	32	61	+29
United Kingdom	34	42	31	52	+21
Germany	35	40	26	46	+20
United States	31	38	36	53	+17
Italy	—	—	—	53	—
Australia	—	—	—	48	—
Canada	22	—	—	33	—
Poland	7	—	—	22	—
Russia	52	40	35	23	−12

Source: Nicolai Sennels, "Concern about Extremism Rising in West, but Falling in Russia," Spring 2015 Global Attitudes Survey, Q23, Pew Research Center, "Sharp Increase in Concern about Islamic Violence," August 1, 2015.

Interestingly, Russia saw a significant decline in concern about Islamic extremism.[26]

According to a different poll, conducted by Pew Polling in spring 2016, there was a significant increase in "unfavorable views of Muslims."[27]

Washington-based Pew Research Center found the share of people believing that "refugees will increase the likelihood of terrorism in our country" was 46 percent in France, 52 percent in Britain, 61 percent in Germany, 71 percent in Poland, and 76 percent in Hungary.[28]

"Raqqa Scatter," Refugees, and Infiltrators

Many European security and intelligence personnel agree that it is easy for the State to infiltrate their forces into Europe. As elements of the State are driven from large towns and cities, such as Raqqa, its soldiers scatter and, often, desperately look to leave the Middle East. They are able to buy Syrian identity documents that allow them to hide among refugees.[29] Anecdotes highlight the dangers of accommodating those crawling ashore, one of whom was Ahmad al Mohammad. He was fed and clothed by French volunteers of Médecins Sans Frontières, who wished him *bon voyage* on his trip to Paris.[30] In November 2015, al Mohammad detonated himself as a suicide bomber in that city as his co-conspirators killed targets in a nightclub and in the streets.

Table 8.2. Percentage of Those Who Held an "Unfavorable" Opinion of Muslims from 2015 to 2016

Country	2015 (%)	2016 (%)	% Change
Hungary	NA	72	NA
Italy	61	69	+8
Poland	56	66	+10
Greece	53	65	+12
Spain	42	50	+8
Netherlands	35	35	0
Sweden	35	35	0
France	24	29	+5
Germany	24	29	+5
United Kingdom	19	28	+9

Source: Adam Taylor, "Anti-Muslim Views Rise across Europe," *Washington Post,* July 11, 2016.

European leaders have tightened security at transportation and public venues. However, determined Caliphate militants are still effective, as demonstrated by the June 2016 attack on Istanbul. By international standards, that airport was well protected. However, there were glaring vulnerabilities in both physical protective measures—such as barriers, gates, and fences—and in the human security element. Vetting guards, many of whom are foreign born and most of whom earn meager wages, has proved very difficult. In France, eighty-two of the people hired for security posts on the soccer championship were on French terror watch lists.[31, 32] One of the men responsible for beheading a French priest in 2016 had worked at a French airport as a luggage handler. He "easily" passed employment security checks.[33]

In spring and summer 2016, the Caliphate struck around the world at venues frequented by Westerners. Three American college students were killed at a siege in an upscale Dhaka, Bangladesh, restaurant, which was a favorite haunt for Westerners.[34] The ringleader was young, university educated, and raised in a well-to-do home. Caliphate operatives demanded captives recite verses from the Koran to save their lives. This was a pass/fail test. Those who failed were stabbed or shot and lay dead or dying on the floor of the Holey Artisan Bakery in the diplomatic zone. The ringleader's father wept, "That's not my son, that's not my son. He was full of humanity."[35] There is overwhelming rejection of suicide killing in Western Muslim communities. But more than a few support it.

Table 8.3. Support among American, British, German, and French Muslims for Suicide Bombers

	Always Justified(%)	Often/ Sometimes Justified (%)	Rarely Justified (%)	Never Justified (%)
All US Muslims	13	8	5	78
18–29	26	15	11	69
30 or older	9	6	3	82
All UK Muslims	24	15	9	70
18–29	35	19	16	59
30 or older	17	13	4	77
All German Muslims	35	16	19	64
18–29	42	19	23	57
30 or older	31	15	16	69
All French Muslims	25	16	0	69
18–29	29	17	9	65
30 or older	22	14	5	71

Source: "42% of French Muslim Youth Support Suicide Bombing, Young US Muslims Not Far Behind," *JNI.Media*, July 15, 2016.

In many Muslim countries recently seen as embracing modernity, there is growing support for the Caliphate and suicide operations. Tunisia is one such country, and it is profiled below.

PROFILE TWENTY-SIX: TUNISIA—ON THE BEACH

If the mountain won't come to Muhammad,
Muhammad must go to the mountain.

—Islamic proverb

How could a place of such beauty, of relaxation and happiness
be turned into such a scene of brutality and destruction?

Tunisia is a popular vacation spot for Europeans. Only 600 miles from Italy, it has an educated, though highly unemployed, workforce. For Britons, there is sun, gardens, birds, flowers, and turquoise water.[37] For the culturally minded, there are historic sites and ancient Roman treasures.[38] But Tunisia has also produced over 3,000 volunteers for the

Islamic State. The country has been transformed from a model of progressive secularism into a center of radicalism.[39] Cities swarm with unemployed or semiemployed youth. Some work in the tourist trade, and some are students with free time. One was Seifeddine Rezgui.

The Shooting Starts

Seifeddine Rezgui was a twenty-three-year-old student who pledged allegiance to the State. In younger years, he enjoyed break dancing and later switched to kung fu, which he often practiced.[40] To those who knew him, he seemed content and smiled a lot. For this reason, he went unnoticed as he rented a lair where he could plan a killing spree. From his safe house near popular resorts, Rezgui could walk near the Marhaba Hotel and mix and mingle among European guests to plan his attack.[41] He would later return, this time with an assault weapon, to walk along the shoreline of a Tunisian resort and kill Westerners. Ambling from the beach, to the pool, to the lobby, he sprayed fire at anyone who looked European. He did so as an operative for the State and with apparent merriment. By the end of his spree, he had shot dead thirty-eight foreigners, thirty of whom were British.

Rezgui decided who would live and who would die. One young woman spoke Arabic to him and convinced him that she was a fellow Muslim.[42] The killer chuckled, "You go away."[43] A Briton remembered, "He was laughing and joking around, like a normal guy."[44] Rezgui walked up to a local mechanic and said, with a smile, "I don't want to kill you, I want to hit tourists."[45] The survivors recounted the panic, the running, and the gunshots. Some people went to their rooms to barricade themselves.[46] As with the Florida killer one year later, his Tunisian counterpart laughed and smiled as he shot his victims.

There were heroes on the beach that day. A sixty-one-year-old man pounded the beach looking for survivors and rendering aid as he heard periodic gunfire. He used towels to bandage those with gunshot wounds. A British nurse wanted to help, but she couldn't. She had been shot in both legs.[47] Sarah Wilson recounts how her fiancé, Matthew, took bullets for her: "Matthew put himself in front of me then he was hit, he moved and the man shot him again."[48] Matthew lived, but not Rezgui, the killer.[49] A police officer shot the murderer while he was on his knees praying. Rezgui then stumbled, and a shop owner threw terracotta tiles on his head.[50] A police officer blasted a *coupe de grace* into his skull.

The Caliphate claimed the massacre was an "attack upon the nests of fornication, vice and disbelief in God . . . worse is to follow."[51] The State's supporters chuckled about the butchery and made morbidly sarcastic comments in their tweets.[52] But most Britons were somber. There was a national moment of silence held in the House of Commons, and royalty and commoners alike took part.[53]

GREAT BRITAIN

Many people born in Britain have little attachment to the country and that makes them vulnerable to radicalization.

—UK prime minister David Cameron, referring to some Muslims[54]

Muslim–Non-Muslim Relations

The Muslim population of Britain surpassed 3.5 million in 2015, to become approximately 5.5 percent of the overall population of sixty-four million. Britain has the third-largest Muslim population in the European Union, after France and Germany.[55] As the number of Muslims in Britain swells, so do concerns about their influence in society. Many Britons, particularly the less educated, are concerned about a social transformation they cannot prevent.[56]

As discussed in chapter 4, this tension is reflected in the media, particularly in the tabloids, and in radio and television talk shows. The year 2016 marked the tenth-year anniversary of the publication of Melanie Phillips's *Londonistan*. Her disquieting neologism "Londonistan" resonated with many public intellectuals and became a buzzword in debates about Islamic influence.[57] Non-elites organized among themselves.

Largely as a reaction to expanding Islam populations, the English Defense League was launched, in May 2009, among the working class.[58] It was largely loathed by the intelligentsia but struck a chord in many rough-and-tumble neighborhoods. Its creator, Tommy Robinson, has been physically assaulted, on video, by Islamists in his hometown of Luton. Britons increasingly share his concerns about the march of Islam. A survey in 2010 revealed that 63 percent of Britons did not disagree with the statement "Muslims are terrorists," and 94 percent agreed that "Islam oppresses women."[59] Three-quarters of those interviewed believe that Islam is bad for Britain. The numbers are higher today.

In cities, many working-class parents fear that their daughters will become prey to Pakistani child-rape gangs and prostitution rings and that municipal officials will be hampered by fear of being charged with anti-Muslim animus.[60] The autobiography *Girl for Sale* described the sexual exploitation of Lara McDonnell, who was victimized by a Muslim pedophile gang when she was only thirteen years old.[61] Some youths fear their nation's future. A 2015 survey of ten-to-sixteen-year-old British children revealed that 35 percent agreed that "Muslims are taking over England."[62]

Police and security forces find themselves hindered in conducting antiterrorism planning. From patrolling the streets, to entering homes, to interviewing suspects, to conducting training exercises, all activity must be conducted with religious sensitivity. In an antiterrorist exercise conducted to test emergency response capabilities in 2016, a participant pretending to be a Caliphate operative yelled "Allahu Akbar." The chief constable who ran the exercise was forced to ask forgiveness from the Muslim community. He apologized, "On reflection we acknowledge that it was unacceptable to use this religious phrase immediately before the mock suicide bombing, which so vocally linked this exercise to Islam."[63]

Other Britons are less contrite than confused. Many cannot understand why some of the brightest and most ambitious and high-achieving young British Muslims support the Caliphate. They do not understand why a prestigious, left-oriented school would produce suicide bombers, as described in the following profile.

Twenty-Seven: The Old School Tie—The Holland Park Martyrs and the "Socialist Eton"

If there is any British secondary school that could lay claim to the title of alma mater for Caliphate Britons, it would probably be London's Holland Park School, which is also a good example of the red-green partnership in schools and on campuses discussed in chapter 3. Dubbed the "Socialist Eton," Holland Park embodies multicultural London. In the words of the academy, "Latin mottos gave way to egalitarian ideals."[64] It has attracted the children of the trendy rich, such as Anthony "Wedgie" Benn; powerful socialist politicians, such as Prime Minister Tony Blair and Roy Jenkins; as well as the progeny of left-oriented public intellectuals, particularly those connected with the newspaper *The Guardian*.[65] The school calls them "socialist grandees and a smattering of literati and glitterati of West London."[66]

Holland Park boasts some impressive educational statistics. Many of its graduates, from all ethnic backgrounds, perform well on standard testing and university admission. Some continue on to Oxford or Cambridge. But by May 2015, what set Holland Park apart from other schools was its five alumni who had died fighting for the Islamic State.[67] At least six former pupils from Holland Park School left Britain to become Islamic fighters or have been linked to terrorism.[68] Former female students have also been arrested for supporting the Caliphate.

This is confusing for most of the academy's graduates. They remember a Holland Park that promoted poetry, multiculturalism, and inclusion. Many warmly reminisce about their old school. Their salad days bring memories of long hair, rock and rock, stealing a smoke, and making out. One graduate stated, "Contrary to popular opinion, we didn't have bomb-making classes at Holland Park Comprehensive."[69]

Militant Islam

Britain, like the United States, France, and Belgium, has been victimized by Islamic terror for years. The government has tried to fight, as Prime Minister Cameron called it, the "poisonous Islamist ideology," while being respectful to Islam.[70] Nonetheless, four out of ten British Muslims want Sharia law introduced into parts of the country.[71] A fifth of the Muslims surveyed expressed sympathy with the "feelings and motives" of the suicide bombers who attacked London.[72] In 2006, then Labour MP Sadiq Khan bewailed how many Muslims "feel disengaged and alienated."[73] Less than one decade later, there would be twice as many British Muslims fighting for the Caliphate as there would be British Muslims serving in the British armed forces, and Mr. Khan would be Lord Mayor of London.[74]

By fall 2015, British security forces were busy monitoring more than 3,000 homegrown Islamic extremists. Half of the Islamists on terrorist watch lists live in London, especially in the capital's east and west, and most others live in West Midlands and Manchester.[75] Despite efforts to assimilate Muslims into the main of British society, the number of violent suspects being monitored has risen by more than 50 percent since 2007.[76] Only one in three British Muslims would inform the police if they believed that a fellow Muslim was connected to a terrorist organization.[77] British Muslim organizations are, at best, ambivalent about cooperating with police and security forces. Some leaders have disparaged the Prevent Strategy, which was a national program created to reduce radicalism.[78] Prevent was based on four pillars: stopping terrorist attacks, preventing people from becoming terrorists, protecting Britons against terror, and mitigating the impacts of terrorist attacks.[79]

Daily trials, arrests, convictions, sentencing, incarceration, and parole of Islamic extremists are part of the British justice system. But there is angst about where to incarcerate the incorrigibly radical, particularly those who are Caliphate supporters. Some criminologists recommend housing them collectively to isolate the contagion or militancy. Others are concerned about the optics of a British Guantanamo Bay or "The British Alcatraz."

Profile Twenty-Eight: Banned in Britain

The Home Secretary will seek to exclude an individual if she considers that his or her presence in the UK is not conducive to the public good.[80]

—Statement from the British Home Office, BBC News, 2012

What do Americans Pamela Geller, Robert Spencer, and Michael Savage have in common? Beyond despising Islam, they share the dubious distinction of being banned from Britain. And they are not alone. Duane "Dog" Chapman, a husky, roughly hewn American celebrity bounty hunter, who used the "N" word once too often; Albert Speer, the Nazi war criminal; L. Ron Hubbard, the founder of Scientology; Pablo Neruda, a Nobel laureate in literature; and Fred Phelps Sr., who founded the antihomosexual Westboro Baptist Church, were all on the eclectic banned-persons list, though at different times. Menachem Begin was on it and then off it and then back on it and then off it when he died. The list keeps American klansmen and neo-Nazis from British shores.[81] Many Muslims and leftists petitioned then secretary May to keep Republican candidate Donald Trump out of Britain. As prime minister, her decision is pending.

Nation of Islam leader Louis Farrakhan was banned. Over the years, Farrakhan has applauded Sharia-driven violence and poured scorn over whites and Jews. But in 2001, then attorney and now mayor Sadiq Khan had the decision overturned.[82] Khan described the judge's decision as "brave and sensible."[83]

But Geller, Spencer, and Savage do not understand why Louis Farrakhan is permitted to visit Britain while they cannot. They claim that they never advocated violence. In fact, Spencer and Geller planned to lay a wreath at a memorial to British soldier Lee Rigby, who was beheaded by Islamic jihadists in spring 2013.[84] But the British government wrote them, "Your presence here is not conducive to the public good." The government called their rhetoric "Islamophobic." All are still fighting the ban, and Geller said, "the Magna Carta is dead."[85] As for the petition to ban Republican nominee Donald Trump from British shores, Geert Wilders said, "Welcome, Donald Trump, to the company of Pamela Geller, Robert Spencer and myself."[86]

Radicals in the Ranks

Many elements in Muslim civil society partner with British authorities. But some who advise the British government are, themselves, radicalized. Some Islamists enter the British civil service intending to promote their agenda, while others are radicalized while in service. Others are not employed by the government but serve as advisers. Some are unmasked by their own sloppiness and others through investigations.[87]

The Caliphate likely has other activists working in the government. Caliphate-supporting accounts can be traced back to the offices of national civil service.[88] Far more alarming is Caliphate penetration into the military. A navy officer who trained at one of Britain's most prestigious maritime colleges joined the State and brought with him an exhaustive knowledge of Britain's navy and commercial fleet. "This suddenly raises the spectre of IS damaging shipping," said former Royal Navy chief admiral Lord West.[89] Veterans of other services have also shown sympathy for the State.[90] Two radicals, neither of whom served in the military, one still emboldened and one repentant, are profiled below.

PROFILE TWENTY-NINE: A TALE OF TWO BRITONS

Anjem Choudary—Black Flag over Downing Street

British activist and lawyer Anjem Choudary was arrested in August 2015, and many Britons do not understand why it took so long to incarcerate him. Britain's most notorious radical Muslim preacher was formally charged with enlisting British citizens to support the Caliphate.[91]

For years prominent on the radical Islamist scene, Anjem Choudary promised, "One day, the black flag of Islam will be flying over Downing Street." He is very vocal about this goal. Though a practicing lawyer, he despises any man-made laws, particularly those of his own country. "Who said that you own Britain anyway? You belong to Allah. Britain belongs to Allah, the whole world belongs to Allah. There isn't anywhere on the earth that I won't propagate God's law."[92]

He has no time for individual countries, which he considers man-made, and therefore inauthentic, political constructs. Countries will "not be liberated by individuals, but by an army. Eventually there'll have to be a Muslim army. It's just a matter of time before it happens."[93] He has many followers.

He promises that the Islamic State offers a delightful lifestyle. "Close your eyes and imagine a society in which everybody has free food, clothing, and shelter. You haven't got a house? Here is your house. You don't have to go live in a cardboard box outside the council for a few weeks before they give you a house. You don't have electricity? Here is free electricity. Here is free water. What else do you want? Do you want a salary? Here, take some money. There is no society like that."[94]

He hates the Pope, who, in his words, should be killed for criticizing Muhammad.[95] He seemed very pleased with drummer Lee Rigby's killing. Choudary told his votaries that Rigby is being tortured in hell.[96] He said, "If an adult non-Muslim dies in a state of disbelief then he is going to the hellfire."[97] He proclaimed, "It's Cameron who's guilty, not me."[98]

In September 2016, in Old Bailey, Choudary was convicted of "inviting support for a proscribed organization."[99] The proscribed organization was the Islamic State. He was given a five-and-one-half-year sentence.

Abu Muntasir—"I Am Sorry"

The "godfather" of the British Jihadis has openly wept in regret for brainwashing young British Muslims to kill in the name of Islam. In the 1980s and 1990s, Abu Muntasir recruited scores of young men to fight in Afghanistan, Kashmir, Burma, Bosnia, Chechnya, and in other distant wars in the name of Jihad. "For me, I always had an inner voice telling me that a lot of this is not right."[100] He grew to hate himself for promoting Jihad. In recent years, he has partnered with other ex-radical recruiters, including ex-skinheads, gang leaders, and Islamists to halt the spread of radicalism.[101]

Emmy-winning filmmaker Deeyah Khan made a video about Muntasir and several former extremists. In the film, Muntasir admitted that he encouraged British Muslims to fight abroad and die for Islam. But his conscience began to haunt him when he imagined those whom he recruited as mangled corpses and amputees. Muntasir was convinced that killing or hurting people was contrary to his nature. He had to stop, and he did.

Today, he warns the West of radical Islam. "There is grooming [referring to the radicalization process]. . . . So the parents need to have more communication with their children, they need to have more of an overseeing aspect of how to be a good parent."[102] As for his past, Muntasir sighed, "Why I have never been arrested, I don't know."[103]

The Caliphate

As mentioned in chapters 5 and 6, British subjects are well represented in the ranks of the Caliphate. At home, British police and security forces try to balance civil liberties with public security. The Caliphate can fly its black banner in London because, as its former mayor said, "Britain is a free country."[104] Sir Bernard Hogan-Howe, the commissioner of the Metropolitan Police in London, opined that carrying the flag was "not necessarily the worst thing in the world."[105] But some Londoners see this as cavalier and have pressed the police to be more aggressive. London police failed to arrest a man who draped himself in an Islamic State flag and strolled past Big Ben and the Houses of Parliament. On his shoulders was a small child waving a smaller State flag.[106] Some Britons saw this as trespassing the bounds of free speech and wading into the danger zone of incitement. They ask themselves, "What will come next?" Germans ask the same questions.

GERMANY

Muslim–Non-Muslim Relations

*Of course there are Muslims in Germany. But Islam
is not part of the German mainstream culture.*

—Alexander Dobrindt, the general secretary
of the Christian Social Union, 2011[107]

History follows Germany, and many Germans are sensitive about their global image. Germany never had the colonial associations Britain or France had with the Middle East, although there were some connections in the twentieth century to Muslim states and people. The Ottomans were allied with Germany as one of the central powers in World War I, and the Grand Mufti of Jerusalem was a guest and very minor, though enthusiastic, partner of Hitler in World War II. But Germany's connection to the Muslim world began to develop in earnest during the economic boom of the post-war period when Turks were invited to live there as guest workers.

For reasons that will be long debated, Chancellor Merkel invited over one million refugees to migrate to Germany and put down roots there. She called this influx "an opportunity for tomorrow" and cheered her fellow Germans on to be "self-confident and free, humanitarian and open to the world."[108] Amid the world's greatest refugee wave since World War II, some Germans took hope from history.[109] In the wake of World War II, there were twelve million refugees in Germany who had fled the onslaught of the Russian army.[110] They were absorbed and helped build the German Economic Miracle of the 1950s and early 1960s. Many Germans were confident that their model could be replicated with their new Muslim neighbors.

But many Germans were unprepared for the current human infusion and are bewildered by Chancellor Merkel's decision-making. Some provide an economic explanation, citing the fact that Germany's birth rate is well below replacement, which may lead to an insufficient domestic workforce.[111] Others have suggested that the chancellor wants

Migrant Art in Berlin

to purge any lingering traces of German war guilt. There are other, less conventional explanations. Some have turned to psychology, suggesting the chancellor has no children of her own and, as leader of a country, she has adopted millions of children.

Kultur Kampf

Many Germans openly welcomed their new neighbors. Germans gave migrant children teddy bears and candies and offered parents help with housing and directions.[112] Some German families took refugee families into their homes and gave their own possessions to donation centers. In November 2015, an Ernst and Young study concluded that Germany would not be able to provide shelter for a projected 370,000 migrants fleeing Middle Eastern misery.[113] The migrant population has soared to many times that figure less than one year later.

But there were problems that became increasingly noticeable. Initially, the press ran stories on cultural idiosyncrasies and clever anecdotes. For example, German nudists were forced to clothe themselves when a refugee shelter was built next door.[114] Public swimming pools in Germany struggled with some Muslim swimming customs; some pools banned the burka-bikini or "burkini" as potentially unhygienic.[115] But soon serious problems developed between the cultures. Germans could establish different swimming times for the sexes, but there were thousands of reports of mass groping by those with "migrant backgrounds."[116] In Munich, public pools, for instance, published cartoons warning migrants not to grope women in bikinis. The sex-pest dust-ups flared in summer 2016. Sharia patrols yelled at women and children in a nudist swimming pool that they were "sluts" and "infidels" and should be "exterminated."[117]

Other anecdotes are ominous. A Muslim set a German woman's hair on fire at a train platform in summer 2016. Why? According to the Muslim, "She wasn't wearing a hijab."[118] Earlier, a Jewish man wearing a *kippah*, a traditional Jewish head covering, was beaten and kicked by Middle Eastern–appearing men. The victim volunteered at a refugee center in Cologne welcoming Middle Eastern immigrants.[119]

If any single event focused public attention on the cultural clash, it was the New Year's Eve celebration of 2016 in Cologne that resulted in over 1,000 complaints of molestation. Women and girls recounted thefts, molestation, and harassment by Middle Eastern–appearing men. Cologne's mayor brushed the assaults away as cultural misunderstandings and poor policing.[120]

One of the molested was sixteen-year-old Bibi Wilhailm, a German girl, who had her *cri de coeur* censored by Facebook under the charge of hate speech. Bibi recounted being harassed by Muslim men. "You [Muslim men] have no right to attack us because we are wearing T-shirts . . . why should we, children, have to grow up in such fear?"[121] She continued, "The politicians live alone in their villas, drink their cocktails, and do nothing . . . Please, do something."[122] In England, another girl, far more violated than was Bibi, pleaded that her voice be heard. Below are their words.

PROFILE TWENTY-NINE: TWO ANGLO-SAXON TEENAGE GIRLS

Bibi's Plea to Germany and Its Men

You have killed Germany.

—Bibi, 2016[123]

I am almost 16. I would like everyone to know what is going on, what I am authentically feeling at this moment . . . And I am so scared everywhere. . . . It is just very hard to live day-to-day life as a woman. I just want to say that I am not a racist. But one day, a terrible thing happened at the supermarket. I ran all the way home. I was so frightened for my life. There's no other way to describe it.

But more importantly, I cannot understand why Germany is doing nothing! . . . Men of Germany, these people are killing your children, they are killing your women. We need your protection. We are

Migrants in a Hungarian Shelter Hoping to Go to Germany

so scared, we don't want to be frightened to go to the grocery store alone after sunset. One day, my friend and I were walking down the street, and a group of Arabs were protesting and demonstrating. They shouted, 'Allah! Allah! Allah is the one God! Kill those infidels! Allah Allah!' What should I do? Should I wear a burka? Why should I have to convert to Islam. . . .

The life of Germany has changed because these people cannot integrate. We give them so much help. We support them financially and they do not have to work. But they only want more babies and more welfare and more money. Men of Germany, please, patrol the streets and protect us. Do this for your women and your children. If you do that, I believe that we will have a chance. Thank you, Angela Merkel, for killing Germany! I have no more respect for you, Merkel. . . . You have killed Germany!

Emily's Letter—"This Is England, 2015"

Is there such a thing as a child prostitute?

—Emily, 2015[124]

In October 2015, "Emily" of Rotherham, England, wrote an open letter to social services. She, like Bibi, weeps with the frustration, anger, and fatalism of a girl who feels powerless and is convinced that the civil service and civil society have abandoned her.[125]

To the medical professionals who did nothing—Were you blind to my bruises, multiple sexually transmitted infections . . . You gave me treatment, I took the medication but how could it work when I was being raped by the same men every day . . . Were you deaf to my pleas for help? Did you even listen when I told you what was happening? No. You had me down as a sex worker.

To the school as a whole—Did you never wonder why I missed so much school? While you were teaching students math, science, and English. I was in a cold room of a half-renovated flat. Lying naked on a bed while approximately eight men were taking turns raping me.

To the policeman who told my mother I was a known prostitute when she came to you for help—I was a child. Is there such thing a child prostitute? You were the most insensitive officer I ever met, and the only reason I can think of for you being how you were, is that maybe you were covering up out of fear of causing racial tension?

To the politically correct government who refuses to see that Muslims are a problem, the idiots that think Islam is compatible with our ways—Think again. Open your eyes to the million girls already raped and trafficked by Pakistani Muslim gangs. I wait and I wait. I wait for justice, it's never served.[126]

From Willkommenskultur to Pegida

By summer 2016, polling revealed that, in the view of many Germans, Muslim migrants were no longer very welcome. The era of Willkommenskultur, or Welcome Culture, quickly faded. By then, less than a third of native Germans, or 32.3 percent, still wanted more immigrants, and half strongly associated the migration with terrorism.[127] Some Germans saw the million-migrant inflow as the latest twist in a continuing cultural death spiral, reflecting a deep national self-loathing. Importing Muslims to serve as a vast labor pool for menial jobs was, in this view, shortsighted and, ultimately, self-destructive.[128] For them, Eurabia is a teeming Muslim ghetto within Germany. It is poor, unassimilated, angry, and religiously supremacist.[129] They fear Yugoslavian-style balkanization and, then, disintegration.[130]

Fearing Islamic swamping of German society and anger at censored dissenting voices, antimigrant activists established Pegida, short for Patriotic Europeans against the Islamization of the Occident. Some called it blatant racism, and its controversial leader did not help his cause by calling foreigners "cattle" and "trash."[131] Some intellectuals opined that

Pegida has become a catch-all movement for frustrated Europeans who are turning to nationalism to cope with social trends they do not understand and do not welcome.[132] Others do not see an alternative.

Militant Islam

The number of Caliphate supporters in Germany continues to grow. Germany's domestic security services set the number of radical Salafists at over 8,000 in September 2015, and it could be over 10,000 by summer 2016. By summer 2016, 60 percent of the new arrivals had no documentation, making it difficult and sometimes impossible to verify their claims of nationality and age.[133] The radical element in Germany is growing. Some of the Islamist groups have canvassed the refugee centers for those who share their radical views or those who look like easy marks for conversion to the cause. Under the flag of humanitarian assistance, radicals recruit for the Caliphate and the police are challenged to stop it or even fully understand it.[134] Guarding against the Caliphate or other Islamists is fraught with problems.

First, German police, like other European police and security forces, often cannot verify the identity of migrants. In 2015, the German border police were only able to obtain 10 percent of the migrants' fingerprints. Hundreds of thousands of migrants could not be identified by their travel documents, many of which were forged.[135]

Second, it is difficult to monitor and penetrate domestic Islamist cells, some of which recruit for the Islamic State. There are civil liberties that hamper investigations.[136] There are well-known personalities in the German Islamist movement, but many take care to avoid language that might be threatening. But by late July 2016, many Germans were anticipating a mass killing, like those suffered by Britain, France, Spain, and Belgium. According to a poll released on July 22, 2016, 69 percent of Germans believed that a terrorist attack would hit Germany "soon."[137] They were right. Later that day in Munich, an Iranian-German, previously unknown to German security professionals, killed nine victims and then himself. Germany had joined the killing club.

PROFILE THIRTY: A LONG, HOT SUMMER

Munich had not seen anything like this since the 1972 Munich Olympics. Ali Sonboly, eighteen years old, lured children to a McDonald's by offering free food. Perhaps the tactic worked; most of his victims were in their teens. He killed nine and then killed himself. Sonboly was an Iranian German, which didn't precisely fit the mold of Caliphate killers. Most Iranians are Shia, and the Islamic State is Sunni. After an investigation, the Munich chief of police said, "There is absolutely no link to the

Islamic State." It was a "classic act by a deranged person" and described an individual "obsessed" with mass shootings.[138] When the shooting started, CNN's Wolf Blitzer initially speculated that a "right-wing" antirefugee shooting was taking place.[139] At MSNBC, Chris Matthews explained that Germany was undergoing a "nativist attack."[140] But why, then, did Sonboly yell "Allahu Akbar"?[141]

Two days after the McDonald's attack, a twenty-one-year-old Syrian refugee killed a forty-five-year-old Polish woman with a machete and injured two other people before being arrested in the southern German city of Reutlinge. Authorities said the assailant and victim knew each other from working in the same restaurant, and the incident was not related to terrorism.[142] Others are not sure.

One day after that, a Syrian man, whose asylum bid had been rejected in Germany, pledged allegiance to the Islamic State on his cell phone. He then tried to get into an outdoor music festival so he could explode his bomb-laden backpack. Having been turned away, he blew himself up outside a wine bar instead, injuring fifteen people.[143] The perpetrator was identified as Mohammad D. The Bavarian interior minister said that he didn't know if this man "planned suicide or if he had the intention of killing others."[144] The BBC headlines ran, "Syrian Migrant Dies in German Blast."[145] The BBC changed the headlines after being mocked on social media. Readers snickered at what they saw as the anodyne and empty wording of the headline. The revised column read, "Syrian Asylum Seeker Blows Himself Up in Germany." The Caliphate attacker explained his motive. He did it so "Germans won't be able to sleep peacefully."[146] Many don't.

July 2016 ended in an explosion near a migrant processing center near Munich. At first, the police suspected that right-wing extremists had detonated the bombs. But witnesses described several "Arab-looking men" seen fleeing from the scene. By the end of the month, the motive was still unknown.[147] The summer of 2016 rocked Germany as few summers since unification. Rage at the chancellor spewed across the social networks, coining a new hashtag of contempt—"#Merkelsommer."

The Caliphate

Before 2016, some of the Caliphate's recruiting was loud, open, and unmasked. There was unfettered street proselytizing, and when young men traveled in packs, they were sometimes emboldened. For example, a group of seven men sang a war chant favored by the Islamic State and tried to recruit fellow passengers while riding on the Berlin U-Bahn railway. They were singing one of the Jihad nashids, mentioned in chapter 6.[148] Some of this was caught on video and posted on social media. This further tarnishes the image of the migrants, but it draws some troubled young German men to the ranks of Islamists, where they find comradery. According to the German military security service, twenty-nine former German soldiers have traveled to Syria and Iraq, and twenty-two soldiers were classified as Islamists, as of spring 2016.[149]

In 2015 and 2016, German police arrested many suspects for terrorist-related activities. They expect more.[150] Some security officials speculate that the Caliphate will plan a sustained attack using the Mumbai model. This was a sophisticated three-day attack, in Mumbai, India, in which simultaneous sites were struck, including a railway station, a Jewish institution, two hotels, and a restaurant. It garnered world media attention, and the Indian military and paramilitary forces appeared unprepared and incompetent. Some killers acted independently; others were more coordinated.[151] German security are also concerned about Istanbul-style attacks, and so is the German public. One survey found that almost two-thirds of Germans expect an attack like those in Istanbul or Brussels to happen at a German airport.[152]

Returning in Singles and Doubles

The Caliphate ordered its support base to kill at will and with fury. Its tactics of choice were shooting, stabbing or gutting with a knife, running over, hurling victims from a building, choking, or poisoning Western symbols of authority. Their followers responded with random, unexpected, and lethal attacks. This has caused great social anxiety, particularly for police officers who want to patrol the street but often cannot do so for fear of their safety.

German police force units are facing something very new. There are stabbing sprees of random pedestrians, similar to those committed by Palestinians in Israel. For example, in Hanover, a fifteen-year-old girl with a German passport and Moroccan ancestor, as well as suspected ties to the Caliphate, stabbed a police officer in the neck. The stab came as a bolt from the blue.[153]

The Islamic State claimed responsibility for an attack on board a train in Germany in mid-July 2016 that left three people seriously injured, according to the terrorist group's news agency. The announcement came hours after an axe-wielding teenage Afghan refugee attacked passengers on a train. He was shot and killed by police. During an investigation, officials said they found a hand-painted flag of the Islamic State group in the attacker's room. During the attack he yelled "Allahu Akbar."[154]

German courts are ramping up to handle cases of residents and nationals returned from Middle East fighting. Germans are trickling home in singles and in pairs, hoping to reintegrate into the society they left. The Federal Criminal Police Office estimates that 820 people with

German passports have left Europe to fight in Syria and Iraq with Islamic State and, by January 2016, an estimated 250 fighters had returned.[155] According to a former Jihadi who served the Caliphate, those who return are "treated like heroes" in the Muslim areas of Germany.[156]

When German fighters return, they sometimes face the justice system. Referred to as "Jihadi tourists" by the German press, they chose to come back to Germany because they were "disappointed" with Islamic State.[157] In 2014, a court sentenced a twenty-year-old man who traveled to Syria to fight alongside a group associated with the Islamic State to three years and nine months in juvenile detention, the country's first conviction of a returned Jihadist.[158] Another Caliphate fighter who returned to Germany was sentenced to four and one-half years in prison for belonging to a terrorist organization. The twenty-five-year-old German national had traveled to Syria in October 2013 and later pledged his oath to the Caliphate. He took part in interrogations and prison guard duty. He may have killed people, and German authorities are determined to find out. He is Harry S., profiled below.

Profile Thirty-One: Harry S.—When They Return

The case of Harry S. illustrates the challenge Western societies face when Western Caliphate fighters return home. Harry S. was put on trial in Germany for belonging to a terrorist organization. Baptized as a Catholic, he grew up in a poor part of Bremen. His parents emigrated from Ghana to Germany and then London to build a better life. Harry S. certainly had above-average intelligence and studied engineering, for a while, at university. Something happened to him emotionally, he converted to Islam, and his religious Christian mother threw him out of her house. But London's mosques welcomed him, and so, too, did minor criminal syndicates. Serving as a lookout for a robbery, he was arrested and imprisoned, where he was radicalized. Upon release, he returned to Bremen, got married, and then determined to go to Syria and fight the Jihad, which he did.

Harry said he went through several phases of commando training, which were arduous. There were a total of ten different training levels. "Hardly anyone reaches the last; most die before that." But he wanted out because of the suffering he saw and the lack of compassion. "Humanity—that is of interest to nobody."[159] In Palmyra, his nerves were shattered and conscience jolted when he witnessed blindfolded prisoners standing in rows and being riddled with bullets. A few weeks later, he fled to Turkey and then to Germany, where he was arrested at Bremen Airport.

German prosecutors are not convinced that Harry's stories are truthful. His version of events has changed, and his sudden pangs of morality are dubious. Did he voluntarily exit the commando school, or did he wash out? In Palmyra, did he just witness the killings or did he take part? Is there evidence to support his claims? Certainly, other Westerners who return home will face similar questioning. Harry could face up to ten years in prison for belonging to a terrorist organization. As for the foreign fighters still with the Caliphate, Harry has more respect for the French than for the Germans. The French rushed enemies and blasted their weapons into their battle lines. The French had élan. The Germans were more reluctant. In Harry's words, when it came to fighting, "the Germans always got cold feet."[160]

THE UNITED STATES

The Ikhwan must understand that their work in America is a kind of grand jihad in eliminating and destroying the Western civilization from within and sabotaging its miserable house by their hands.

—From the *Holy Land Foundation* trial[161]

Muslim–Non-Muslim Relations

ISIS is little more than a criminal gang that attaches itself like a leech to revered symbols of Islam.

—Nihad Awad, Council on American Islamic Relations[162]

Concern about Islam and the Caliphate proliferates across the Atlantic. In the United States, American popular culture and politics grapple with the Caliphate's imagery and ambitions. Since the attacks on the American homeland, common and elite opinion has wrestled with the role of Islam in American society.[163]

Organized Islamism in the United States came into focus in the high-profile *Holy Land* trial that exposed a network of Islamic Brotherhood operations in the United States. The trial centered on a 1991 strategy paper and associated documents that laid a blueprint for a "civilization Jihad."[164] The Brotherhood planned to infiltrate American civil society by building coalitions, casting Muslims in the light of discriminated minority, adopting civil-rights-sounding rhetoric, demanding special protections, and attacking those who impede its agenda.[165] The most controversial Islamist organization is the Council on American Islamic Relations (CAIR).

Muslims counter that memos and audiotapes used in the *Holy Land* trial were poorly translated and represent the intentions of only a small minority of Muslims. They add that the Muslim Brotherhood

Table 8.4. Percentage Who Say the Next President Should _____ When Talking about Islamic Extremists

	be careful not to criticize Islam as a whole (%)	speak bluntly even if critical of Islam (%)	other/ don't know (%)
Postgraduate	65	30	5
College Graduate	51	44	5
Some College	53	39	8
High School or Less	45	41	14
Republican/Republican Leaning	29	65	6
Conservative	26	70	4
Democratic/Democratic Leaning	70	22	8
Liberal	80	13	7

Source: "Republicans Prefer Blunt Talk about Islamic Extremism, Democrats Favor Caution," Pew Research Center, February 3, 2016.

has almost no influence in the United States.[166] According to CAIR and the Center for Race and Gender at the University of California, Berkeley, Islamophobia is well funded; they claim that over $200 million was spent between 2008 and 2013 to malign Muslims.[167]

James Zogby, longtime Arab-American activist, was emphatic that "Islamophobia and those who promote it are a greater threat to the United States of America than Anwar al-Awlaqi and his ragtag team of terrorists."[168] He reasoned that the demonization of Muslims in America leads to their alienation, which, in turn, closes avenues of cooperation with law enforcement.

Whatever the stronger argument, the results of a July 2016 Opinion Savvy poll show that Americans are not comfortable with bringing Sharia-supporting Muslims to the country. Seventy-one percent wanted supporters of Sharia to be identified before they are admitted into the United States, and 80 percent did not want those who support Sharia to be admitted.[169] Thirty-four governors are refusing to take in any more, in case Jihadi fighters slip into their states and repeat the carnage of Paris.[170]

Republicans, significantly more than Democrats, tend to identify Muslims and Islam as a risk. As Tables 8.4 and 8.5 indicate, Trump-supporting Republicans are more heavily inclined to criticize Islam than are Democrats. The more educated respondents are significantly more reluctant to criticize Islam than the less educated.

Table 8.5. Non-Trump Republicans Favor Greater Scrutiny for Muslims Living in the United States, as of March 2016

As part of the government's efforts to prevent terrorism, Muslims living in the United States should . . .	Overall Republican and Republican Leaning (%)	Trump-Supporting Republican and Republican Leaning (%)	Non-Trump Republican and Republican Leaning (%)	Trump Non-Trump Difference (%)
be subject to more scrutiny than people in other religious groups	53	64	45	+21
not be subject to additional scrutiny solely because of religion	41	28	50	−22
Don't know	6	8	5	NA

Source: Samantha Smith, "Trump Supporters Differ from Other GOP Voters on Foreign Policy, Immigration Issues," Pew Research Center, May 11, 2016.

Militant Islam

"101 Mohammads"

—With the arrest of Mohamed Bailor Jalloh, in July 2016,
101 persons with the name Mohammad, or a variant of that spelling,
have been arrested in the United States on terrorism-related charges.[171]

How come we don't have an intifada in this country?[172]

—Berkeley lecturer Hatem Bazian at a peace rally in San Francisco, 2004

The attacks of the twenty-first century gave American intelligence and security forces a robust mandate to identify and neutralize threats from Islamic violence. National security agencies built training programs to help professionals identify signs of Muslim radicalism. These were revised when advocacy groups advised the FBI to purge some training materials deemed offensive by Muslims.[173] Earlier FBI training material, from 2006, drew a profile of "homegrown Islamic extremists." Five years later, the term "Islamic extremist" would be purged from the training material of many federal agencies.[174]

Government leaders determined that using words such as "Jihad," "Sharia," and "Islamist" would alienate moderate Islamists.[175] Instead, leaders promoted value-neutral terms to describe violence committed by Muslims in the name of their religion. One young woman who is part of the government's efforts is Laila Alawa, discussed below.

Profile Thirty-Two: Laila Alawa—"Not on My Watch!"

*The US has never been a utopia unless you were a straight white male
that owned land. straight up period go home shut up.*

—Laila Alawa[176]

9/11 changed the world for good, and there's no other way to say it.

—Laila Alawa[177]

The US Department of Homeland Security (DHS) invited experts on terrorism to pool their intellects and efforts to combat violent extremism. Secretary Jeh Johnson said it is "critical" not to use the word "Islamic" when referring to the Caliphate's attacks.[178] He created the Subcommittee on Combatting Violent Extremism, and one of the sitting members on its advisory council is the twenty-five-year-old Laila Alawa. Though an American citizen, she stated, "I will always be Syrian. I will always be from Syria. I will always be of Syria." The DHS thought this might be valuable. "Laila Alawa was selected as a subcommittee member because of her perspective as a Syrian American woman of the millennial generation," said J. Todd Breasseale, assistant secretary for public affairs at DHS.[179]

Alawa strongly identifies as a Muslim and wears a hijab. She is also a very outspoken woman who uses social media to disparage America, free speech, and white people. She sees America as very Islamophobic and tweeted that only "idiots" believe that "America is the best nation in the world. After September 11, 2001. Being American meant you were white."[180]

Alawa is outspoken in her belief that "Islamophobic" rhetoric shouldn't be allowed. "We are living in a country that deems it 'freedom of speech' to spew absolutely hateful speech about Muslims. That's not freedom of speech," she tweeted. Less than two weeks after the Boston bombings, Alawa tweeted, "You can't say something intolerant and not expect consequences. Not on my watch."[181]

On her watch, the lexicon and focus of "countering violent extremism" changed. Alawa and her fellow subcommittee members recommended that the DHS devote more attention to "anarchists, sovereign citizens, white-supremacists, and others."[182] The subcommittee urged DHS to avoid using the words "Sharia" and "Jihad" because they might offend Muslims.[183] For all her anger, Laila is optimistic about America's destiny. As she tweeted, "Ya know . . . white people in America? They're not gonna be dominant majority for much longer."[184]

The Caliphate

Thousands of people inside the United States are consuming online "poison" from ISIS alone.

—FBI director James Comey, May 2015[185]

The debate about the Caliphate's Islamic component continues, as the Caliphate orders killings worldwide. Democratic and Republican candidates sparred in 2016, a presidential election year. As mentioned earlier, public intellectuals have taken sides. Ayaan Hirsi Ali, a well-known critic of Islam who has been invited to and disinvited from campuses across the United States, disagreed with Vice President Joe Biden's assertion that "ISIS had nothing to do with Islam."[186] In a debate with him, she "begged to differ."[187] She and an increasing numbers of Ameri-

Table 8.6. How Americans See the Islamic States Threat 2015–2016

	Very Serious Threat (%)	Moderately Serious Threat (%)	Just a Slight Threat (%)	No Threat at All (%)	No Opinion (%)
May 2016	73	17	5	5	0
October 2015	70	19	6	3	3
April 2015	68	19	6	6	1

Source: CNN/ORC Poll. April 28–May 1, 2016. N=1,001 adults nationwide. Margin of error ± 3. http://www.pollingreport.com/isis.htm.

cans see the Caliphate as strongly connected to Islam. President Obama will not use the term "radical Islam" because, in the words of Deputy National Security Advisor Ben Rhodes, "we will be more effective in combating that ideology of ISIS if we don't describe them as a religious organization."[188]

When former speaker of the house Newt Gingrich advised that American Muslims who follow Sharia should be investigated and, perhaps, deported, President Obama responded, "The very suggestion is repugnant and an affront to everything we stand for as Americans."[189] There is ongoing debate about how to deal with Caliphate supporters when they return. "But I can't see any reason why we should lock up ISIS members when they can instead be spending time around impressionable young people while in a position of authority," said Rep. Keith Ellison, himself a Muslim, spoke in favor of such a design. "If you integrate them back into their family relationships and you have responsible faith leaders, then that's going to be the check on them that they need."[190]

But many returned fighters are not likely to completely renounce their affiliation with the Caliphate. Instead, the Islamic State has likely radicalized thousands of people in the United States, according to two scholars, Sebastian and Katharine Gorka. They compiled a list of eighty-two individuals in the United States who were identified by law enforcement as being affiliated with the Islamic State.[191] As of summer 2016, the FBI has conducted investigations into Caliphate-related threats in all of its fifty-six offices.

Caliphate propaganda promises more attacks like the one in Orlando and boasts that it will attack cities such as San Francisco and Las Vegas. Pictures on its website include landmarks like San Francisco's Golden Gate Bridge and the Financial District. FBI director James Comey recently warned that his caseload of Caliphate suspects has exploded to more than 900 in all fifty states, with hotspots in the New

York–New Jersey area, as well as Chicago, Detroit, Cleveland, and Minneapolis.[192]

Americans certainly see the Islamic State as threatening. A CNN/ORC International poll asked, "Would you say that the Islamic State represents a very serious threat to the United States, a moderately serious threat, just a slight threat, or no threat at all?" The percentage of Americans who see the Islamic State as a threat has grown.[193]

Caliphate killings often come as a shock to the neighbors of the perpetrators. Sometimes neighbors had clues about impending violence, but usually they were unaware. The Boston marathon bombers, Chattanooga shooter, San Bernardino husband-and-wife team, and the Orlando shooter were not seen as unusual. Often, neighbors are shocked when their fellow citizens are unmasked as belonging to or sympathizing with the Caliphate. Often, people with concerns are reluctant to discuss them for fear of being seen as intolerant.[194] In 2015 and 2016, some of these quiet neighbors were exposed as Islamists.

In Tennessee, twenty-four-year-old Muhammad Youssef Abdulazeez shot four marines dead. In the shaded, quiet neighborhood where Abdulazeez lived with his family, about seven miles from the Naval Reserve Center where the killings occurred, neighbors were stunned by the developments. "I didn't find anything wrong with the kid," a neighbor said. "He just intermingled with the kids in the neighborhood." He had earned an electrical engineering degree at the University of Tennessee at Chattanooga, according to an online résumé. Abdulazeez worked out three to five days a week but would often interrupt his workout and unfurl his prayer rug in the gym's offices to conduct evening prayers.[195]

In Mississippi, Jaelyn Young and Muhammad Dakhlalla, Syria-bound Mississippi newlyweds, were arrested in transit before they could honeymoon with the Caliphate. Muhammad's father, a longtime imam of the Islamic Center of Mississippi, initially claimed to be "absolutely shocked."[196] Their neighbors in Starksville, Mississippi, appeared equally stunned. Mohammad's mother, a convert to Islam, was known locally as the "hummus lady" for her delicious Mediterranean specialties. The father was praised for his lamb dishes. When a neighbor saw police cars in front of the Dakhlallas' home, he immediately guessed that "some idiot redneck did something to the mosque."[197] In San Bernardino, neighbors were also surprised by the hate.

In Alabama, Hoda Muthana determined to join the Caliphate, which she did. In fact, she may have inspired the Nice, France, killer when she tweeted, "Go on drive-bys and spill all of their [nonbelievers] blood, or rent a big truck and drive all over them. Veterans, Patriot, Memorial Day parades . . . rent a big truck n drive all over them. Kill them."[198]

In the Great Lake state of Minnesota, ten men were convicted on a series of charges relating to the Caliphate. They have much in common. They are all first- or second-generation Somalis in their early twenties who freely took advantage of educational and employment opportunities in the Twin Cities. They all appeared to be talented and resourceful. They had social lives centered on local mosques and supplemented their education with Islamic studies. Above all, they wanted to follow Jihad and die as martyrs. One of these, Abdirizak Mohamed Warsame, wanted to die because of, in his words, "the reward you would get and the fact that this life is temporary."[199]

PROFILE THIRTY-THREE: TWO MEN FROM MINNESOTA

Douglas McAuthur McCain—"I'm with the Brothers Now"

"Islam over everything," wrote Douglas McAuthur McCain shortly before his self-proclaimed martyrdom in Syria for Al Nusra. His passport was found on his corpse. He was also identified by a distinct neck tattoo.[200] By the time of his death, the thirty-three-year-old McCain had called himself "Duale, The Slave of Allah" on Facebook. During the course of his life, he had changed. Born in Illinois in 1981, he later moved with his family to Minnesota's Twin Cities area, where he grew up black in a heavily white neighborhood. He was described as a "goofball" and a basketball rat. Classmates in his overwhelmingly white high school recalled an "always smiling" joker. He spent some time in Sweden rapping and playing basketball, and he made friends of some young Swedes, who described him as a genuine American performing artist. A Swede recalled, "He's a good dribbler, passer and . . . a really nice guy. He smiles a lot and brings a lot of good energy."[201]

But the smiling joker was spiritually unfulfilled and unfocused, and he had had a few run-ins with the law. He was charged with disorderly conduct and obstruction. His mugshot revealed the neck tattoo. Around 2004, McCain "reverted" to Islam, according to his Twitter feed, and moved to California, where he indulged his passion for basketball. But his devotion to Islam grew in San Diego, and he earned enough money working at a Somali restaurant there to move to Syria to take up Jihad. His rapping and basketball days were put on hold.

He headed to Raqqa. Judging by the tone of his tweets, he was happy in "R Town." He found the brotherhood that had eluded him in America. He wanted to be killed as a martyr alongside his fellow Muslims, and he was. His last recorded tweet was "I'm with the brothers now."[202]

The Poet and His Mother

Like McCain, Abdirizak Mohamed Warsame had been raised for many years in Minnesota. If McCain found expression and relief in basketball, Warsame turned to verse. As a teenager, this boy, who had immigrated with his family to the United States at age ten, became an artistic fixture in the "Little Mogadishu" neighborhood. He was popular in the youth arts scene and made some videos about teenage life.[203] He hoped to inspire his generation of local Somali Americans. He wrote, "You guys are tomorrow." He wrote that there were no limits to his generation's achievements. "All you have to have is determination."[204] Warsame was the local teenage bard of Little Mogadishu.

His mother and cousin helped organize Somali youth to assimilate and stay away from radicalism. His mother tried to intervene against extremism and pled to the Somali community, "We have to stop the denial thing that we have and we need to work with the FBI."[205] She was unaware how close radicalism was to home.

After high school, Warsame attended community college and worked part time to support his family. Soon, he turned to videos to fill a spiritual void, and he found Anwar al-Awlaki, the bin Laden of the internet. A community activist explained, "I think he found himself surrounded by very angry young people." In 2014, he and some friends planned to travel to the Islamic State and fight for it, but he never made it out of the country. He faces fifteen years in prison. As for his mother, the community anti-Jihad activist, after her son's guilty plea she said, "I didn't know. It hurts me even hearing it now."[206]

Summary

By summer 2016, of the British who served with the State in the Middle East, one in six had been killed. An estimated 400 have returned to the United Kingdom. This caused much concern for British security personnel and the common Briton. A British colonel who headed efforts in Afghanistan said, "We have seen what the Islamic State can do in Brussels, in Paris, in the US and most recently in Turkey. They can, and will, try to do the same thing here."[207]

German security officials estimate that over 800 men and women have left the country to join the Jihadis in Syria and Iraq. Well over 200 have returned.[208] In April 2016, most Europeans polled, 86 percent, feared another terrorist attack in Europe, and 70 percent thought that immigration was a driver for that terror.[209] It became common for many Germans to refer to Angela Merkel as the worst chancellor since Hitler.

Americans, too, fear the Caliphate. President Obama and Secretary of State John Kerry claim that its indiscriminate killing in the West reflects its desperation. These death pangs are driven by the coming defeat in Mesopotamia. But many Americans are skeptical. They do not believe that the Caliphate is on the run. They see a muscular and militant Islam threatening their country.

NOTES

1. "Singapore: Europeans View Islamic State as Top Threat—Survey," *Singapore Channel NewsAsia Online*, June 13, 2016.

2. Lydia Willgress, "EU Leaders Insist There Is 'No Link' between the Migrant Crisis and New Year Sex Attacks in Cologne—and Vow to Bring about an End to 'False Accusations,'" *MailOnline*, January 30, 2016.

3. Gerard O'Connell, "Francis in Greece: Words and Actions on Refugee Crisis," *America* 214, no. 15 (2016): 8–9.

4. David Carter Berlin, "Greeks Run Out of Burial Plots for Drowned Migrants," *The Times* (London), November 3, 2015.

5. Robert Spencer, "'A Lot of Those People Are ISIS': Trump on Hillary's Plan to Take 65,000 Muslim Migrants Yearly," *Daily Mail*, July 1, 2016.

6. Ibid.

7. "'Staggering Number' of Europeans Embraced Jihad, Many Returning Home, EU Claims," *FoxNews.com*, April 6, 2016.

8. "Could This Lead to War in Europe?" *Daily Mail*, March 19, 2016.

9. Vasilis G. Lampropoulos, "Searching for 10 Jihadists in Greece," *Vima*, June 5, 2016.

10. Robert Spencer, "'A Lot of Those People Are ISIS'" *Jihad Watch*, July 1, 2016.

11. Nick Gutteridge, "EU Deport Only Seven Migrants a Day," *Express*, December 26, 2015.

12. "Analysts See Jihadists Hiding among Refugees as Highly Unlikely Despite Growing Warnings," *Paris AFP (North European Service)*, September 16, 2015.

13. Colin Freeman, "UK Commentary Warns UK Taking in Syrian Refugees May Deprive Syria of People It Needs to Rebuild," *London Telegraph.co.uk*, September 14, 2015.

14. Alexandra Sim, "Refugee's Love Letter Found Washed Up on Greek Beach Sparks Search for the Writer," *The Independent*, November 17, 2015.

15. "Heartfelt Pleas of Drowned Boy's Dad," *Daily Record* (Glasgow, Scotland), December 24, 2015.

16. Tom McTague, "Britain Is Racist for Not Taking in More Refugees, Claims Hollywood Star Emma Thompson," *MailOnline*, September 3, 2015.

17. Neil Johnston, "He Concluded His Performance by Shouting to the Audience, 'F*** the Politicians'; Neil Johnston, "Cumberbatch Curses MPs' Failures on Refugee Aid," *The Times*, October 31, 2015.

18. Leah McLaren, "Europe's Jihadi HQ," *Maclean's*, April 11, 2016.

19. According to a wide-ranging US-based Pew Research Center survey carried out across Europe, 76 percent of respondents are seen as a significant threat. In spring 2016, the pollsters surveyed over 11,000 Europeans in France,

the Netherlands, the United Kingdom, Germany, Italy, Spain, Sweden, Greece, Poland, and Hungary. This selection of countries represents 80 percent of the EU population and 82 percent of the bloc's economic output. In Spain, 93 percent considered IS to be their biggest threat, followed by France (91 percent), Italy (87 percent), and Germany (85 percent). The Netherlands, Hungary, and Sweden polled at around 70 percent. "Europeans Fear ISIS and Refugees, Oppose Increased Military Budgets," *Brussels EurActiv.com*, June 15, 2016.

20. Ibid.

21. Pamela Geller, "What Are Muslims Fleeing? Shariah Law? Good Question. The Invasion of Europe and America," *WND*, August 23, 2015.

22. Chris Mandle, "Katie Hopkins Sets New Record after Making Racist Remark Just 47 Words into Debut Mail Online," *The Independent*, November 2, 2015.

23. Rod Liddle, "Cyprus Migrants Prove They Want Dosh, Not Safety," *The Sun*, November 5, 2015.

24. "Europe will soon go under because of its previous liberalism which has proven childish and suicidal. Europe produced Hitler, and after Hitler there stands a continent with no arguments: the doors are wide open for Islam," *Gates of Vienna*, accessed September 4, 2015, http://gatesofvienna.net/2016/08/the-looming-crisis-in-europe/.

25. Niall Ferguson, "As Europe's Wealth Has Grown, It's Military Power Has Shrunk," *The Wall Street Journal*, November 16, 2015.

26. Adam Taylor, "Anti-Muslim views rise across Europe," *Washington Post*, July 11, 2016.

27. Ibid.

28. It is difficult to explain the anomaly of Russian opinion. "Half Europeans Fear, Resent Refugees: Survey," *Reuters*, July 11, 2016.

29. Nick Fagge, "UK Journalist Buys Syrian Papers Reportedly Used for ISIL Fighters Entering Europe Among Refugees," *London Mail Online*, September 17, 2015.

30. "Paris Attacker Welcomed Ashore in Greece and Given Help and Clothes by French Volunteers," *The Sun* (UK), November 23, 2015.

31. "Euro 2016: 82 Security Staff Revealed to Be on Terror Watch List—French Intelligence," *RT*, June 5, 2016.

32. Fiona Hamilton, "ISIS Recruiting Refugees in European Training Camps," *The Times* (London), January 26, 2016.

33. Peter Allen and John Ingham, "ISIS Priest Killer 'Easily' Passed Checks to Work as Airport Baggage Handler," *Express*, July 29, 2016.

34. An update on this story: "20 Hostages Killed, 13 Saved in Bangladesh Jihad Attack," *Associated Press*, July 2, 2016.

35. Alexandra Field, "Dhaka Attack: 'That Is Not My Son,' Killer's Horrified Father Cries," *CNN Wire Service*, July 4, 2016.

36. "UK Daily+ Finds Link between Tunisia Beach Massacre, Islamist Extremism in Britain," *Daily Mail Online*, June 30, 2015.

37. Lara Marlowe, "Beneath Idyllic Surface, All Is Too Quiet for Comfort; Locals Are Contemplating the Effect of the Attack on Their Own Future," *The Irish Times*, June 5, 2015.

38. Janine Di Giovanni, "Tunisia's ISIS Connection; This Tiny Nation Sends More Foreign Jihadist Fighters to Syria Than Any Other Country," *Newsweek*, June 16, 2015.

39. "Tunisia—from Arab Spring to the Cradle of Terror," *Daily Mail*, July 16, 2016.

40. "The Laughing Assassin; Break-Dancing Student Who Was Turned into a Ruthless Killer by IS Masters," *Sunday Mail* (Glasgow, Scotland), June 28, 2015.

41. "Lair of Assassin; Slaughter on the Beach Murderer's HQ Gunman Rented Flat on This Street to Plot Attack He Made Three Recces," *The People* (London), 2015.

42. "Hotel Worker Spared by Gunman for Speaking Arabic," *Hotelier Middle East*, June 30, 2015.

43. Craig McDonald, "The Laughing Assassin; Break-Dancing Student Who Was Turned into a Ruthless Killer by IS Masters," *Sunday Mail* (Glasgow, Scotland), June 28, 2015.

44. "My Brave Fiancé Took 3 Bullets for Me and Shouted: Run for Your Life, Tell the Kids Daddy Loves Them; Slaughter on the Sunbeds: Hero Dad Saves Girlfriend," *The Mirror* (London), June 27, 2015.

45. Craig McDonald, "The Laughing Assassin; Break-Dancing Student Who Was Turned into a Ruthless Killer by IS Masters," *Sunday Mail* (Glasgow, Scotland), June 28, 2015.

46. Ian Lewis, "Terrified Couple Run for Their Lives from Tunisian Gunman; 'We Heard People Screaming and Running, We Had to Get Inside, We Just Ran,'" *Carmarthen Journal*, July 1, 2015.

47. Harriet Sinclair, "Allen Braved the Bullets to Save Life of a Tourist; Heroism in Tunisia: Holiday-Maker from Chelmsford Escorted His Wife to Safety Then Returned to Beach to Help Those Trapped or Wounded in Killing Zone," *Essex Chronicle*, July 2, 2015.

48. My Brave Fiancé Took 3 Bullets for Me and Shouted: Run for Your Life, Tell the Kids Daddy Loves Them; Slaughter on the Sunbeds: Hero Dad Saves Girlfriend," *The Mirror* (London), June 27, 2015.

49. Ibid.

50. Lydia Willgress, Thomas Burrows, and Jennifer Smith, "Filmed from a Hotel Balcony, the Chilling Moment ISIS Gunman Is Seen Sprinting across Tunisian Beach after Killing 38 Innocent Tourists," *MailOnline*, June 28, 2015.

51. Flora Drury, "'An Attack upon the Nests of Fornication, Vice and Disbelief in God': ISIS's Chilling Words after Tunisian Massacre Which Killed 38 as They Warn 'Worse Is to Follow,'" *Mailonline*, June 27, 2015.

52. Loulla-Mae Eleftheriou-Smith, "ISIS Schoolgirl Amira Abase Who Fled London to Join Terrorists in Syria Mocks Victims of Tunisia Massacre," *Independent*, July 5, 2015.

53. "Heartfelt Messages for Sue," *The Tamworth Herald*, July 2, 2015.

54. William Kilpatrick, "Multiculturalism and the Rise of Domestic Terrorism," *Crisis Magazine*, August 18, 2015.

55. Soeren Kern, "The Islamization of Britain in 2015, Sex Crimes, Jihadimania and 'Protection Tax,'" *The Islamization of Britain in 2015*, December 31, 2015, http://www.gatestoneinstitute.org/7151/britain-islamization.

56. "In the UK, the survey found that people who have been educated to a higher level believe the refugee issue to be less of a threat, only 30 percent said they were concerned. This compares to 62 percent of people that have received less education. This represents a difference of 32 percent." "Europeans Fear ISIS and Refugees, Increased Military Oppose Budgets," *Brussels EurActiv.com*, June 15, 2016.

57. Graham Smith, "A Review from 'Goodreads,'" accessed January 3, 2016.

58. John Gee, "The Political Uses of Islamophobia in Europe," *Washington Report on Middle East Affairs*, December 1, 2011.

59. Haroon Siddique, "Three-Quarters of Non-Muslims Believe Islam Negative for Britain: Muslim Organisation Calls for Efforts to Improve Awareness as Four-Fifths of Those Polled Admit to Little Knowledge of the Faith," *The Guardian*, August 2, 2016.

60. Ian Tuttle, "'The Rotherham Rapes' Muslim Connection," *National Review*, August 27, 2014.

61. "Mohammed was selling me for £250 to paedophiles from all over the country. They came in, sat down and started touching me. If I recoiled, Mohammed would feed me more crack so I could close my eyes and drift away. I was a husk, dead on the inside." Lara McDonnell, "Groomed to Be a Sex Slave and Branded a Racist for Bringing My Sex Abusers to Justice: One Woman Reveals Her Horrific Ordeal in a Tell-All Book," *Daily Mail*, April 22, 2015.

62. "1-in-3 Children Think Muslims 'Taking Over,'" *The Mirror* (London), May 20, 2015.

63. Surrender of Britain update: "Police Chief Apologises after Fake Muslim Shouts 'Allahu Akbar' in Simulated Suicide Bomb Attack at Manchester's Trafford Centre," *Telegraph*, May 10, 2016.

64. Holland Park School homepage, accessed July 3, 2016, http://www.hollandparkschool.co.uk/school/history.

65. Melissa Benn, "School for Scamps," *New Statesman*, March 6, 1998.

66. Holland Park School homepage, accessed July 3, 2016, http://www.hollandparkschool.co.uk/school.history.

67. Dipesh Gadher and Richard Kerbaj, "Five from the Same School Die in Jihad," *Sunday Times Online*, May 23, 2015.

68. "2,000 Brits Now Fight for ISIS; UK Jihadists Soar as Government Fails to Stop Menace," *Sunday Mirror* (London), October 12, 2014.

69. Lamiat Sabi, "I Went to the UK's School of Jihadis and I Can't Believe How It Has Been Treated by the Press," *The Independent*, November 4, 2014.

70. "Cameron Declares War on 'Poisonous Narrative' of IS." Western Mail (Cardiff, Wales): MGN, January 2, 2016.

71. Patrick Hennessy and Melissa Kite, "Poll Reveals 40pc of Muslims Want Sharia Law in UK," *The Telegraph*, February 19, 2006.

72. Ibid.

73. Ibid.

74. Madeline Grant and Damien Sharkov, "'Twice as Many' British Muslims Fighting for ISIS Than in UK Armed Forces," August 20, 2014, http://europe .newsweek.com/twice-many-british-muslims-fighting-isis-armed-forces-265865.

75. Sean O'Neill, "Three Thousands Terror Suspects Plotting to Attack UK," *The Times*, September 18, 2015.

76. Ibid.

77. James Dean, "Survey Reveals Chasm between Muslim Values and Rest of UK," *The Times*, April 11, 2016.

78. Jane Miller, "Jihadis in London," *In These Times*, May 1, 2015.

79. "2010 to 2015 Government Policy: Counter-Terrorism," Policy Paper of United Kingdom, May 8, 2015, https://www.gov.uk/government/publications /2010-to-2015-government-policy-counter-terrorism/2010-to-2015-government -policy-counter-terrorism.

80. "US Self-Defense Expert Banned from Entering UK," *BBC* News, May 9, 2012.

81. "Home Office 'Names and Shames' 16 People Banned from UK," *The Guardian*, May 5, 2009.

82. Donna Rachel Edmunds, "Labour's Muslim Mayoral Candidate: 'I Am the West,'" *Breitbart*, January 2, 2016.

83. "Farrakhan UK Ban Overturned," *BBC News*, July 31, 2016, http://news .bbc.co.uk/2/hi/uk_news/1467587.stm.

84. James Brooks, "US Anti-Islam Activists Banned from Entering UK," *AP Online*, June 26, 2013.

85. "US Anti-Mosque Campaigners in Brum EDL Ban; May Stops Far-Right Authors from Entering Britain," *Sunday Mercury* (Birmingham, England), June 30, 2013.

86. Geert Wilders, "Delusional Britain Would Rather Ban Donald Trump Than Confront Unpleasant Facts," *Breitbart*, January 19, 2016.

87. An example is Mouloud Farid who was privy to "highly sensitive and clas-sified police and intelligence information." He was vetted, despite his connection to Hizb ut-Tahrir, a global Islamist movement. Samuel Westrop, "UK: Extremists in the Heart of Government," *Gatestone Institute*, August 14, 2015, http://www .gatestoneinstitute.org/6307/uk-extremists-government.

88. Jasper Hamill, "Trace ISIS Twitter Accounts Back to Internet Addresses Linked to Department of Work and Pensions," *Mirror*, December 14, 2015.

89. Omar Wahid, Mark Nicol, and Tahira Yaqoob, "Navy Officer Joins ISIS: Defence Experts Warn of Terror Attacks on Ships as Highly Skilled Sailor Turns from Playboy into Jihadi after Watching Videos of Assad's Atrocities in Syria," *Mail On Sunday*, May 8, 2016.

90. "RAF Gunner and Paraplegic Man Jailed for Terrorism Offences," *BBC*, July 15, 2016.

91. Maajid Nawaz, "As a Former Extremist Who Knew Anjem Choudary, I Fear for the Mentality of British Muslims," *The Independent*, August 7, 2014.

92. "Britain Belongs to Allah, Claims Radical Cleric!" *Hindustan Times* (New Delhi, India), February 9, 2006.

93. "The Flag of Islam Should Be Flown," United Ireland, October 19, 2006, http://unitedirelander.blogspot.com/2006_10_01_archive.html.

94. "British Islamists: The Caliphate Will Expand to Europe and the U.S." MEMRI, clip no. 4562, September 16, 2014, http://www.memritv.org/clip_transcript/en/4562.htm.

95. "Muslim Repeats His Demand for the Pope to Be Killed," *Daily Mail* (London), October 20, 2006.

96. "Met Probes Cleric's Rant about Rigby; Terrorism," *The Mirror* (London), June 5, 2013.

97. "Of Skinheads and Jihadists; Violent Extremists. (How Violent Extremists Come to Hate) (Conference Notes)," *The Economist* (US), July 2, 2011.

98. "Radical Cleric Charged with Supporting ISIS; It's Cameron Who's Guilty, Not Me, Pleads Choudary," *The Mirror* (London), August 6, 2015.

99. Bryony Jones, "Britain's 'Most Hated Man' Anjem Choudary Jailed for ISIS Support," *CNN*, September 6, 2016.

100. Tracy McVeigh, "'Recruiter' of UK Jihadis: I Regret Opening the Way to ISIS," *The Guardian*, June 13, 2015.

101. "Of Skinheads and Jihadists; Violent Extremists. (How Violent Extremists Come to Hate) (Conference Notes)," *The Economist* (US), July 2, 2011.

102. Donna Rachel Edmunds, "'British Muslims Have Nothing to Apologise for When It Comes to Islamic Terrorism,' says Labour MP," *Breitbart* (London), June 26, 2015.

103. "Youngest UK Suicide Bomber, 17, in IS Attack," *The Mirror* (London), June 15, 2015.

104. Michael Wilkinson, "'Extremists Are "Free" to Fly ISIL Flags in London,' Says Boris Johnson," *The Telegraph*, July 8, 2015.

105. Ibid.

106. "London Police Slammed for Not Arresting Man Draped in IS flag," *Times of Israel*, July 6, 2015, http://www.jihadwatch.org/2015/07/uk-man-carries-islamic-state-flag-by-big-ben-and-the-houses-of-parliament-police-refuse-to-arrest-him.

107. Soeren Kern, "Does Islam Belong to Germany? Islam Is a Political Ideology That Is Not Compatible with the German Constitution," *Gatestone Institute*, July 5, 2016, http://www.gatestoneinstitute.org/8392/islam-belongs-to-germany.

108. "Chancellor Angela Merkel Tells Germany that Refugee Influx Is an Opportunity," *The Straits Times*, December 31, 2015.

109. "Chancellor Angela Merkel Tells Germany that Refugee Influx Is an Opportunity," *The Straits Times*, December 31, 2015.

110. Rachel Martin, "In Germany, Migrants Find Footing but also Some Resistance," *NPR Weekend Edition*, September 20, 2015.

111. Chris Tomlinson, "German Migration Boss Claims Germany Needs More Migrants," *Breitbart*, June 12, 2016.

112. "Germany's Nervous Mainstream Shifts Rightward," *DW*, January 2, 2016.

113. "Germany Unable to House 300,000 Refugees," *The Local* (Germany), November 9, 2015.

114. Allan Hall and Euan McLelland, "Members of 111-Year-Old German Naturist Club Have Been Banned from Skinny Dipping in Lake in Case They Offend Residents of New Refugee Centre," *Daily Mail*, June 25, 2016.

115. Ishaan Tharoor, "Europeans Are Now Fretting about Muslim Girls in Swimming Pools," *Washington Post*, July 1, 2016.

116. "Police Report Increase Sex Crimes at Swimming Pools," *The Local* (Germany), July 8, 2016.

117. Chris Tomlinson, "Young Muslims Threaten Nudist Bathers with 'Extermination,'" *Breitbart*, July 26, 2016.

118. "Muslim Sets Fire to German Woman's Hair Whilst She Is Waiting for a Train on the Platform," *Liveleak*, July 11, 2016.

119. Arutz Sheva, "Jewish Man Wearing Kippah Beaten in Berlin," *JTA*, June 23, 2016.

120. "'German State See Turbo-Radicalization' of Far-Right, Islamic Extremists," *DW*, July 4, 2016.

121. Raheem Kassam and Chris Tomlinson, "'Angela Merkel You Have Killed Germany!'—16 Year Old Girl's Migrant Fears Video That Some Claim Facebook Are 'Censoring,'" *Breitbart* (London), January 22, 2016.

122. Ibid.

123. "WATCH: German Girl's Migrant Fears Claim Facebook Is 'Censoring'" *Heavy*, January 22, 2016, http://heavy.com/news/2016/01/bibi-wilhailm -european-migrant-crisis-facebook-youtube-full-uncensored-english-translation -isis-islamic-state-syria-iraq/.

124. "This is England, 2015," *Examine Islam*, Posted on October 2, 2015 http:// examine-islam.org/2015/10/this-is-england-2015/.

125. Lucy Thornton, "Child Sex Abuse Gangs Could Have Assaulted One Million Youngsters in the UK," *Mirror*, February 5, 2015.

126. The letter was posted on *Examine Islam*, a website that is hostile to the Muslim presence in Europe. Dr. Silinsky has verified the authenticity of the letter and has corresponded directly with "Emily." For more information, please visit "This is England, 2015," posted on October 2, 2015, by *Examine Islam*.

127. Chris Tomlinson, "German Public Say 'Auf Wiedersehen' to 'Refugees Welcome'" *Breitbart*, July 8, 2016.

128. "Thwarting 'Eurabia'; Save Europe from Itself," *The Washington Times*, September 27, 2005.

129. "Tales from Eurabia; The West and Islam. (An Unhelpful Way to Look at Islam in Europe)," *The Economist* (US), June 24, 2006.

130. Ross Douthat, "Germany on the Brink," *International New York Times*, January 11, 2016.

131. "PEGIDA Leader Goes on Trial in Germany for Incitement," *AP Worldstream*, April 19, 2016.

132. Derek Scally, "Germany's 'Anti-Islamisation' Group and the 'New Nationalistic Normality'; Protests by Pegida, a Group Focused on European Patriotism, Are Drawing More Followers Each Week," *The Irish Times*, January 10, 2015.

133. Tomlinson, "German Migration Boss."

134. Dubbed the "No Means No" law by the media, it explicitly covers cases in which a victim withheld consent but did not physically fight back. It also lowers the bar for deporting sexual offenders, classifies groping as a sex crime and targets assaults committed by large groups. "German Intelligence 'Concerned' Islamists Recruiting Refugees," *AFP (North European Service)*, September 22, 2015.

135. Nicolai Sennels, "German Police: Only 10% of Migrants Are Checked with Terror Databases," *Jihad Watch* (Berlingske), December 25, 2015.

136. For this reason, in spring 2016, the German Ministry of the Interior wanted greater license to monitor the more radical mosques. "We Have to Know What Happens There': German Govt Wants to Watch Mosques & Imams," *RT*, May 20, 2016.

137. "Three Quarters of Germans Fear Terror Attack 'Soon,'" *The Local* (Germany), July 22, 2016.

138. Simon Morgan and Valerie Leroux, "Munich Gunman's Spree Linked to Breivik Not IS Group," *AFP*, July 23, 2016, https://www.yahoo.com/news/lone -munich-shooter-kills-nine-commits-suicide-002815425.html?ref=gs.

139. A. J. Caschetta, "Munich Jihad Shooting Exposes Media Double Standard," *Jihad Watch*, July 23, 2016.

140. Ibid.

141. "Munich Gunman Obsessed with Mass Shootings," *BBC*, July 24, 2016.

142. "Warsaw Confirms Polish Citizen Killed in Reutlingen Machete Attack," *Sputnik*, July 25, 2016.

143. Tomislav Skaro and Kirsten Grieshaber, "Germany: IS Claims Responsibility for Attack in Bavaria," *Associated Press*, July 25, 2016.

144. Dean Schabner, "Syrian Denied Asylum Injures 12, Kills Self in Explosion, German Official Says," *ABC News*, July 24, 2016.

145. Trey Sanchez, "MSM Paints Muslim Suicide Bomber as 'Syrian Migrant Killed in German Blast,'" *Truth Revolt*, July 25, 2016.

146. David Rising, Kirsten Grieshaber, and Tomislav Saro, "IS Attacker: Germans 'Won't Be Able to Sleep Peacefully,'" *Phill.com*, July 25, 2016.

147. "'Violent Explosion' Outside German Office for Migration—'Arab Men' Fled Scene," *Breitbart* (London), July 27, 2016.

148. Oliver Lane, "Muslim Gang Chanted Islamic State War Song, Handed Recruiting Leaflets on Train," *Breitbart*, December 18, 2015.

149. Michael Fischer and Susann Prautsch, "Are Islamists Using the German Military as Training Ground?" *DPA*, April 12, 2016.

150. "Germany Arrests Syrian IS Suspects over DUSSELDORF Plot," *BBC*, June 2, 2016.

151. V. Duemer, D. Ruch, and F. Schneider: "Does ISIL Have Plans to Attack the European Championship?" *Hamburg Bild.de*, June 17, 2016.

152. Michelle Martin, "German Spy Chief Says Can't Rule Out Istanbul-Style Attacks at Home," *Reuters*, July 3, 2016.

153. "Germany Probing Islamic State Link to Policeman's Stabbing," *Reuters*, March 3, 2016.

154. Michael Edison Hayden and Brian McBride, "ISIS Claims Responsibility for Attack on Train by Ax-Wielding Teen Refugee," *ABC News*, July 19, 2016.

155. Virginia Hale, "'Deradicalised' Islamic State Fighters Producing Terror Propaganda Videos in Germany," *Breitbart*, July 19, 2016.

156. Ibid.

157. Ibid.

158. Melissa Eddy, "Germany, in a First, Convicts a Returned Jihadist," *New York Times*, December 5, 2014.

159. "Germany: Trial Against Suspected 'Islamic State' Member Harry S. Begins in Hamburg," *Bonn DW*, June 22, 2016.

160. Ibid.

161. Jason Trahan, "Group's Takeover Plot Emerges in Holy Land Case," *The Dallas Morning News*, September 18, 2007.

162. Nihad Awad, "ISIS Is Not Just Un-Islamic, It Is Anti-Islamic," *Time*, September 5, 2014.

163. Tom Gjelten, "Some American Muslims Irritated by Obama's Call for Them to 'Root Out' Extremism," *NPR*, December 9, 2015.

164. Trahan, "Group's Takeover Plot Emerges in Holy Land Case."

165. Jason Trahan, "Holy Land Foundation Defendants Guilty on All Counts," *Dallas Morning News*, November 24, 2008.

166. He said, "Fox News continues to utilize the nation's most notorious Islamophobes and Islamophobia enablers, like Robert Spencer, Pamela Geller, Ayaan Hirsi Ali, Brigitte Gabriel, and Zuhdi Jasser, as regular commentators on issues related to Islam and Muslims." Robert Spencer, "Hamas-Linked Terror Org CAIR Demands That Fox Drop Those Who Speak the Truth about the Jihad Threat," *Jihad Watch*, January 12, 2015.

167. "Confronting Fear: Islamophobia and Its Impact in the U.S. 2013–2015" documents the ways this and other funding has made Islamophobia manifest in America, as well as a new national strategy to improve American understanding and acceptance of Islam. The report also found that mosque attacks had reached an all-time high in 2015. Frances Kai-Hwa Wang, "Mosque Attacks, Apparent Anti-Islam Spending Up: Report," *NBC News*, June 20, 2016.

168. James Zogdy, "Islamophobia Can Create Radicalisation," *The Nation* (Pakistan), March 7, 2011.

169. Andrew Bostom, "Shocking Polls Show What U.S. Muslims Think of U.S Laws," *PJ Media*, July 2, 2016.

170. Ben Ashford, "America's Enemies Within: How Nearly Seventy Have Been Arrested in America over ISIS Plots in the Last 18 Months—Including Refugees Who Had Been Given Safe Haven but 'Turned to Terror,'" *Dailymail.com*, November 18, 2015.

171. Neil Munro, "101 Muhammads Jailed by U.S. Anti-Terror Agencies Since 9/11." *Breitbart*, July 15, 2016.

172. Roz Rothstein, "The War against Israel and its Supporters on Campus." Jewish Policy Center, Summer 2016, https://www.jewishpolicycenter .org/2016/06/20/the-war-against-israel-and-its-supporters-on-campus/.

173. The letter was signed by the leaders of virtually all significant Islamic groups in the United States: fifty-seven Muslim, Arab, and South Asian organizations, many with ties to Hamas and the Muslim Brotherhood, including the Council on American-Islamic Relations (CAIR), the Islamic Society of North America (ISNA), the Muslim American Society (MAS), the Islamic Circle of North America (ICNA), Islamic Relief USA, and the Muslim Public Affairs Council (MPAC).

174. Sam Stein, "Witness at Ted Cruz Hearing Accuses Congress' Two Muslim Members of Muslim Brotherhood Ties," *Huffington Post*, June 28, 2016.

175. Daniel Halper, "WH: America Needs to 'Redouble' Effort to Explain True 'Tenets' of Islam," *The Weekly Standard*, January 7, 2015.

176. Peter Hasson, "Syrian Immigrant Who Said 9/11 'Changed the World for Good' Is a Homeland Security Adviser," *Daily Caller*, June 13, 2016.

177. Peter Hasson, "Syrian Immigrant Who Said 9/11 'Changed the World for Good' Is a Homeland Security Adviser," *Daily Caller*, June 13, 2016.

178. Mike Levine, "DHS Secretary Won't Describe ISIS as 'Islamic' Terrorists," *ABC News*, July 23, 2015.

179. Peter Hasson, "Syrian Immigrant Who Said 9/11 'Changed the World for Good' Is a Homeland Security Adviser," *Daily Caller*, June 13, 2016.

180. Ibid.

181. Ibid.

182. Pamela Geller, "Obama's Homeland Security Advisor Is Syrian Migrant Who Cheers 9/11, It 'Changed the World for the Good,'" *Atlas Shrugs*, June 16, 2016, http://pamelageller.com/2016/06/obamas-homeland-security-advisor-is-syrian-immigrant-who-cheers-911-it-changed-the-world-for-the-good.html/#sthash.AHKDwFlq.dpuf.

183. Peter Hasson, "DHS Secretary: Right-Wingers Pose Same Threat as Islamic Extremists," *Daily Caller*, June 14, 2016.

184. Hasson, "Syrian Immigrant."

185. "FBI Chief: Potentially 'Thousands' of Online ISIS Followers in US," *ABC News*, May 7, 2015.

186. Bradford Thomas, "Biden Lectured Ayaan Hirsi Ali on Islam," *Truth Revolt*, October 12, 2014.

187. Ayaan Hirsi Ali, "Wall Street Journal: Notable and Quotable: Ayaan Hirsi Ali," *IWF*, November 21, 2014, http://www.iwf.org/media/2795654/Wall-Street-Journal:-Notable-&-Quotable:-Ayaan-Hirsi-Ali.

188. Bridget Johnson, "Rhodes: ISIS Fight 'Will Be More Effective' Not Calling Them 'Religious Organization,'" *PJ Media*, June 15, 2016.

189. Jordan Fabian, "Obama Blasts Gingrich's Muslim Test as 'Repugnant,'" *The Hill*, July 15, 2016.

190. Daniel Greenfield, "Keith X. Ellison: Set My ISIS Jihadists Free There's Going to Be People Watching Them, Encouraging Them," *Frontpage Magazine*, July 10, 2015.

191. Daniel Wiser, "Islamic State Radicalizes 'Thousands' in United States," *Daily Caller*, November 25, 2015.

192. Paul Sperry, "Obama's ISIS Strategy Only Increases Risk of a US Attack," *New York Post*, November 22, 2015.

193. "CNN/ORC Poll ISIS," Polling Report, accessed September 18, 2016, http://www.pollingreport.com/isis.htm.

194. "Developing: 2 Suspects Named in Mass Killings," *CBSLA.com*, December 2, 2015.

195. Rick Jervis, "Chattanooga Shooter Straddled Worlds," *USA TODAY*, July 17, 2015.

196. Daniel Greenfield, "Media Cover Up Mississippi Mosque Imam's Role in ISIS Case," *Frontpage Magazine*, August 12, 2015.

197. Richard Faussetaug, "Young Mississippi Couple Linked to ISIS, Perplexing All," *New York Times*, August 14, 2015.

198. PJ Carroll, "Alabama ISIS Member Pitched Idea to Ram People with a Truck a Year before Nice," *The Daily Caller*, July 15, 2016.

199. Scott W. Johnson, "'Minnesota Men' on Trial," *The Weekly Standard* 21, no. 39 (June 20, 2016): 12–14.

200. Cassandra Vinograd and Ammar Cheikh Omar, "American Douglas McAuthur McCain Dies Fighting for ISIS in Syria," *NBC News*, August 26, 2014.

201. Ibid.

202. Ibid.

203. Meira Svirsky, "From Poet to Jihadi: The Story of a Somali American in Minnesota," *The Clarion Project*, April 10, 2016.

204. "Abdirizak Mohamed Warsame and ISIS: A Cautionary Tale," *CBS Minnesota*, April 9, 2016.

205. Svirsky, "From Poet to Jihadi."

206. "Abdirizak Mohamed Warsame and ISIS."

207. Dan Warburton, "Sixth of ISIS Brits Killed in Fighting," *The People*, July 3, 2016.

208. "Germany: Trial against Suspected 'Islamic State.'"

209. Virginia Hale, "Study: Majority of EU Citizens Fear Muslim Migration," *Breitbart London*, July 4, 2016.

9. THE CALIPHATE ABROAD, PART TWO: THE FRENCH SPEAKERS

It took Hitler 10 years to control France. But our state shook France in an hour from the north to south. May Allah bless you O soldiers of the Caliphate.

—A Caliphate supporter's tweet after
a French priest was beheaded, July 2016[1]

INTRODUCTION

France and Belgium have proportionately large Muslim populations. They are also venues for Caliphate attacks and breeding grounds for Islamism. The Islamic State struck both countries in 2015 and 2016 and changed the lives of their citizens.

FRANCE

Muslim–Non-Muslim Tensions

In France, relations between Muslims and non-Muslims have long been strained. The French absorbed many French nationals who fled Algeria in the 1960s. Then came waves of North Africans in the succeeding decades. Elites predicted assimilation because of earlier successes.[2] But relations, always tenuous, became tense by the twenty-first century, as discussed in chapter 2.

By the new millennium, many leaders and opinion makers in Europe were nervous about growing Islamic communities. French intellectual Alain Finkielkraut coined the term "homesick at home."[3] He and his compatriot Eric Zemmour, sometimes called the "Rush Lim-

"I Would Rather Die Standing on My Feet." A Memorial for *Charlie Hebdo* Victims

baugh of France," write wistfully of "*les Trente Glorieuses*," which were the thirty years after liberation from the Nazis until the leftist cultural ascent of the mid-1970s. In 1965, few Europeans could have imagined that their fellow citizens would be too scared to sketch religious cartoons a half a century later. Fewer still could imagine that groups such as the Islamic State would hold an appeal for European Muslims who were raised on the Continent and were often well educated.

Today, French intellectuals still speak in hushed tones about Islam, lest they offend the sensitivities of a watchful and politically active Islamic constituency. As mentioned in chapter 3, some critics are scared they could be harmed, fired, or taken to civil or criminal courts for making the wrong comment about Islam in France.[4] Bridget Bardot was threatened with prison and fined for opining that France was "being invaded by sheep-slaughtering Muslims."[5] Michel Houellebecq was tried for defaming Islam in 2001, when he called it "the most stupid religion."[6] These high-profile cases serve as warnings to critics of radical Islam.

In Britain, Germany, and the United States, common people have become more alarmed by Islam than the politicians or intellectuals. After two deadly attacks, the *Charlie Hebdo* and the Bataclan killings in 2015, the Muslim image plummeted in French eyes, even among socialists.[7] The image would dive even more after the truck attack on the Riviera. By spring 2016, 47 percent of the French saw Islam as a threat to French identity, and many wanted to halt mosque construction.[8] This has spurred the fortunes of right-oriented politicians in France, particularly Marine Le Pen of the right-oriented National Front (FN), who is expected to run for president in 2017.[9]

Patrick Calvar, the head of France's general directorate for internal security, warned that his country was "on the verge of civil war" between Muslim communities and French nationalists.[10] Gilles Kepel, a political scientist and specialist in Islam, also claimed that France is on the verge of a major social explosion because of the failure of Muslims to integrate into French society.[11] Social liberalism and sexual license are despised by Islamic fundamentalists, which helps explain honor killings and Sharia patrols. The Islamic State has called for attacks on symbols of Western sexual decadence, such as swinger clubs,[12] but even more offensive is any criticism of Muhammad.

The killing in Nice was particularly explosive. Unlike the more cosmopolitan Paris, Nice is politically and culturally conservative. Many of the non-Muslims are descended from the white Algerian population, called "*pied noirs*." Nice also has a large Muslim population. Said one observer, "If you wanted to light the fuse of race war in France, Nice would be a clever choice."[13]

The statistics are stomach-churning: almost 250 innocents have been murdered in France in 2015 and 2016—more than the total number of French nationals killed by them in the entire twentieth century.[14]

While police, military, and paramilitary personnel are prepared and alert for attack, many French engaged in civil society are not. Many attacks come without warning and are directed against persons completely unconnected with national security. Some Islamist attacks are difficult to explain. A man-and-woman couple armed with a knife and an axe and shouting "Allahu Akbar" attacked a charity leader at a soup kitchen near Paris. The attackers allegedly called him an "infidel dog,"[15] but the charity leader fed Muslims out of compassion.

The look of Paris changed after the 2015 attacks, with more dog patrols, random checks at gates and in terminals, video surveillance cameras, and "profilers"—police officers, sometimes in plain clothes—around public transportation venues.[16] Steps may go further; right-wing politicians reiterated calls for preventive detention or electronic bracelets for suspected Islamists, longer prison sentences, shutting down mosques, and deporting radical imams.[17]

The Caliphate

Pro-Caliphate activists have partnered with French Islamist organizations from the State's beginning. They have shouted support for the Caliphate at demonstrations and waved the "black flag of Jihad," which quotes the Shahada—"There is no god but Allah, Muhammad is the messenger of Allah."[18] By January 2016, France was host to 8,250 radical Islamists, a 50 percent increase over the previous year. As in Britain and France, Islamists have infiltrated the civil services, police forces, and armed forces. According to one report, police officers broadcast Muslim chants while on patrol.[19] France is between 9 and 11 percent Muslim, and 16 percent of French citizens have a positive opinion of the Caliphate. This percentage increases among younger respondents, spiking at 27 percent for those aged eighteen to twenty-four.[20]

PROFILE THIRTY-FOUR: A FRENCH GIRL AND A FRENCH WOMAN

In France, more teenage girls than boys joined the Caliphate in 2016. Among all recruits, females began to edge out French male residents who are preparing to travel to the Caliphate or did so.[21]

"The Story of A"

It is sometimes difficult to determine what factors trigger the transformation from conventional politics and normal lifestyle to a full embrace of the Caliphate's beliefs, values, and aspirations. Some teenagers who live uneventful, seemingly normal lifestyles have become Caliphate propagandists or killers. But the full-turn conversions and blood lust of some converts beggar the imagination. This is the story of "A." Because A is not an adult, her full name was not released, but authorities did reveal that she was Jewish, one of two known French Jews to join the State, and she had been raised in a religious home. Her parents were described as "loving and open," and she was an outstanding student, until she found Islam online.[22] She began to wear a veil, but this did not mask her increasing hatred of the West, France, and Jews. She has said repeatedly that she wants to kill her parents.

A is certainly an anomaly in the spiritual ranks of the Islamic State. According to a French anthropologist who extensively studied French women in the State, most converts to Islam come from atheistic homes with spiritual voids. But A was raised in a religious home and her parents don't know what happened to her. Many people convert to Islam, very few of whom feel compelled to kill their parents.

A's mother and father moved to a new apartment because of their daughter's Jihadi ties, and they keep their address a secret. They are worried about their daughter attacking them, as she has repeatedly sworn to do. Perhaps some Friday, as they are lighting candles, breaking bread, and saying prayers over their Sabbath meal, their daughter will storm into their home brandishing a butcher knife and lunge at them, shouting, "Allahu Akbar."[23]

Emilie's Manhunt

Emilie converted to Islam at age seventeen and changed her name to Samra. She began to wear a niqab because this, she predicted, would help her reach the highest level of paradise. But she only started to wear it after the French government banned it in 2012. A female journalist remarked that without her heavy clothing, Emilie/Samra is strikingly pretty. She takes Islam very seriously, and when Emilie thought her son was possessed by a demon, she shook her boy, yelling, "Jinn [a jinn is a spirit], leave my son!" According to Emilie's account, the jinn quickly left her son.[24]

As with many European converts to Islam, Emilie had a tough childhood. She lamented, "My father has erased me from his heart."[25] He left the family when Emilie was two years old, and her experiences with men never got much better. She described her life as "a series of failures."[26] She dropped out of school and became both a Muslim and a barmaid. She married an Islamic man who impregnated her, but he beat her, sold drugs, and went off to prison.

She looked for a new man and advertised for a "virile and pious Muslim."[27] One suitor claimed to be a former friend of bin Laden, which initially impressed Emilie because she admired bin Laden and mourned his death. But Emilie later became convinced that this man had never met bin Laden and had made up the story to get her into bed. After he published a selfie with a naked Emilie, she broke off the relationship.

Emilie hoped to travel to the Islamic State to find the right kind of man. But police were on to her, froze her bank account, and kept an eye on her. She supports violence against nonbelievers, including those killed in Paris. Nonetheless, she insists, "I am French, born French. I consider myself a human being. I am no monster."[28]

Attacks

The Islamic State has vigorously targeted France. In 2015, Islamic State spokesperson Abu Muhammad al-Adnani demanded, "If you can, kill a disbelieving American or European—especially the spiteful and filthy French—or a Canadian."[29] Why were the French singled out as being particularly "filthy"? According to the Clarion Foundation, there are several reasons. First, France fights. Its soldiers have been battling Jihadis around the world, from Syria to Timbuktu. The French approve of French armed forces intervention in Iraq, and 70 percent back the air strikes in Syria.[30]

The Caliphate sees France as a leading infidel state and one committed to the destruction of its organization and similar Islamist organizations around the world. Further, French leaders, unlike many other Western leaders, have asserted that their country is at war with a variant of Islam. The French ambassador to America clarified afterward, saying, "We are at war with radical Islam. It means that right now . . . Islam is breeding radicalism which is quite dangerous for everybody."[31] This language is much sharper than most rhetoric of other Western leaders.

Further, the Caliphate and other Islamists despise French civilization, which is centered on and helped to create the Western canon. France is the home of the Enlightenment and promotes those liberal values. France held the thin line of European civilization in 732 at the Battle of Tours. Later, its nobility and commoners fought in the Crusades.[32] Some symbols are unendurable for the Caliphate. The acerbic and antireligious *Charlie Hebdo* weekly; the Bataclan theater, home to Western music; police and military personnel; and Bastille Day are hateful signs for Islamists.

In July 2016, a Tunisian Jihadist plowed a rented eighteen-ton truck through a crowd celebrating Bastille Day in Nice, France. At full throttle, the driver zig-zagged through spectators who had come to enjoy the fireworks and patriotism.[33] The driver, Mohamed Lahouaiej-Bouhlel, was shot dead while yelling "Allahu Akbar," but not before killing eighty-four people, including ten children, and injuring over a hundred more. Babies lay dead in the street, having been jolted from their buggies, which were crushed during the mile-long killing spree. There were twenty-seven nationalities among the dead. Before the blood was cleaned from the pavement, the Caliphate's fans flooded social media with posts celebrating the event.

The Caliphate claimed responsibility. Donald Trump and Hillary Clinton, who agree on very little, saw the carnage through the same lens. Secretary Clinton said, "I'd even call this World War III. It's a very different kind of war." Her rival, Trump, used the same words: "This is war."[34]

PROFILE THIRTY-FIVE: "KISS THE DEVIL"

Some survived the rampage in the Bataclan by pure chance. "I was supposed to be there on Friday night," said a twenty-eight-year-old journalist of the web magazine *French Metal* who struggles with survivor's guilt. "I had a ticket but couldn't find anyone who wanted to go. It was pure chance."[35] She lived, but several of her friends died, and she wept in front of a makeshift memorial at the Bataclan theater in Paris. Others wept, too, for the eighty-eight people who were killed and the scores more who were wounded.

The theater was one of six attack sites where coordinated shootings and suicide bombings killed at least 129 people. The Islamic State claimed responsibility for the attacks.[36] The terrorists shot anything that moved in the theater, which has hosted artists from Edith Piaf to Prince. Elsewhere in Paris, on November 13, 2015, their Caliphate-connected associates killed without mercy anyone they believed to be non-Muslim. They struck cultural targets in Paris's vibrant east end, which teems with nightlife. A local woman explained, "They were attacking culture—music, celebrations, everything fanatics don't like."[37] The group performing that night was a Southern California band. It was a heavy metal group whose signature song was, "Kiss the Devil."[38]

As they shot into the audience, the killers laughed, played with some musical instruments, and asked, "Where's the singer? Where are the Yanks?"[39] Some of the doomed were shot while huddling in dressing rooms. Some of the survivors played dead.[40] Others threw their bodies on the injured, young, or female to save them.[41] Some of the victims died quickly and others slowly, having bled out on the floor.[42] For some it was a family catastrophe. A thirty-five-year-old mother clutched her son against her, probably saving his life. But her mother, the boy's grandmother, was killed.[43] The killers kicked the fallen victims to check for signs of life. One man lived thanks to his artificial leg.[44]

Very quickly after the attack, Western leaders assured the world that the attack had nothing to do with Islam. Others said they refused

Bataclan Café after the Shooting

to fight hate with hate, words that would presage US attorney general Lynch's sentiments after the Orlando killing, less than one year later. One Frenchman said to the Caliphate, "I will not give you the gift of hating you." His wife, Helen, had been murdered with the rest. Said the widower, "I do not know who you are, and I do not want to know. You are dead souls."[45]

Foreign Fighters

French foreign fighters, as well as other Westerners, are reeling from the series of military setbacks in Syria and Iraq and have been battered by multiple airstrikes. The Caliphate is seeing a hemorrhaging of its foreign volunteer fighters, which keep the intelligence services on edge. By June 2016, at least 248 French Jihadis had returned to France, while 666 were still in the Middle East. Other fighters, seasoned and dedicated, have returned.[46]

The proportion of French women who are part of the State has increased to 35 percent of the French serving. Observers speculate that women in the Caliphate are being groomed for more violent activities in the Middle East and in France. Already active in domestic activities, logistics, and recruiting, they are likely to become more violent.

Patrick Calvar anticipates more attacks by individuals exploding powerful bombs fabricated as vests. Individuals would go to crowded events and shopping areas and detonate the charges. The goal is to im-

Marion Le Pen, "A Combination of Joan of Arc and Bridget Bardot"

mobilize France.[47] Islamic State is likely to use car bombs and other explosive devices as it seeks to carry out more atrocities in France.[48]

Profile Thirty-Six: French-Speaking Political Leaders

Marion Maréchal-Le Pen—
"Either We Kill Islamism or It Will Kill Us"

She has been called a combination of Joan of Arc and Bridget Bardot.
French member of Parliament Marion Maréchal-Le Pen took national
office at twenty-two years old, the youngest parliamentarian since 1791.[49]
Four years later, she is one of the NF's most promising politicians. Heir
to a two-generation conservative family tradition, she is the niece of NF
leader Marine Le Pen and shares many of her aunt's views—respect for
Western, particularly French, civilization; a strong Catholic identity;
and a conviction that France is in a life-and-death struggle with political
Islam. "Either we kill Islamism or it will kill us again and again. You are
with us and against Islamism, or you are against us and for Islamism."[50]
Her fan base is largely traditional young Catholic men.

Tall, blonde, and attractive, she is more popular than ever, and, like
Aunt Marine, she has distanced herself from her grandfather's anti-Semitic barbs. After a French priest was murdered in his Norman church,
she joined the army reserves of her constituency and invited her fellow

citizens to join her. She enlisted to take the war to the Islamic State and intends to do so in a military uniform and, if need be, with arms.

Some Europeans are concerned about an emergent dynasty. One writer spoke of the "Poison le Pens." "Maréchal-Le Pen, like many in the far-right, slipped in under the radar. Would it be enough to hope the voters will swiftly push her back again at the next available opportunity?"[51] Perhaps she will be voted out, but it is not likely anytime soon. Too many of her constituents and fans look to the "golden girl of the right" for national leadership.

Belgium's Yves Goldstein—
No Chagalls, Dalis, Warhols, or Dreams

Yves Goldstein is a council member from the Belgian town of Schaerbeek and chief of staff for the minister president of the Brussels Capital Region. He does not share the political pedigree of Le Pen, but he faces very similar problems. Belgium and France face unprecedented and increasingly frequent outbursts of Islamic radicalism and violence. But, unlike Le Pen, he largely blames Europeans and not Muslims for the tinderbox. If Marion Le Pen embodies an invigorated push-back against mounting Islamic presence in Europe, Goldstein exemplifies the multicultural bridge builder.

The council member insists his country's young Muslim rage is driven by ethnic alienation and poverty. The attacks have little to do with true Islam. Radicals cherry-pick violent verses to militarize the unemployed young.

The youth have no connection to the larger society because that society has excluded them and encouraged them to ghettoize. "We failed!" he said. "We failed in Molenbeek and Schaerbeek, too, to ensure the mixing of populations."[52] This failure, in turn, bred anger, crime, and radicalization. "We have neighborhoods where people only see the same people, go to school with the same people." The youth of Molenbeek, he said, live "in a little box" that needs to be opened up.[53]

This, he explains, is why there is such support for the Caliphate in the Muslim pockets of Belgian cities. According to his estimates, 90 percent of the high school seniors in Molenbeek and Schaerbeek described the Brussels attackers as "heroes."[54] Goldstein's parents were Holocaust survivors who found refuge in Belgium, but all the Jews have now left Schaerbeek, and the last two synagogues are being sold and may be converted into mosques. In his 2012 election campaign to Schaerbeek, the Socialist Goldstein was accused of "stabbing Palestinians in the back."[55]

But Goldstein wants, above all, to integrate Muslims. The most powerful antidote to narrowness and intolerance, for Goldstein, is liberalism. Western literature and art can draw the alienated Muslims out of their cultural islands. He further reasons that just as the West can draw inspiration from the classics of Islam's Golden Age, so can Belgium's Muslims find cultural enrichment in the West. Goldstein laments, "These young people will never go to museums until 18 or 20—they never saw Chagall, they never saw Dalí, they never saw Warhol, they don't know what it is to dream."[56]

BELGIUM

A recent cover [of a British satirical magazine] proclaimed, "Cameron to bomb ISIS heartland," with a fighter pilot saying, "Belgium, here we come!"

—*Private Eye* magazine, 2016[57]

A ghost town, a mummy of a town, it smells of death,
the Middle Ages, and tombs.

—Charles Baudelaire's description of Brussels, circa 1860

Small Belgium, located in the heart of Western Europe and home to the headquarters of the North Atlantic Treaty Organization (NATO) and the European Union, has more Caliphate foreign fighters per capita than any other Western country. It contains many symbols of Western military, cultural, political, and social power. It also contains more Muslims per capita than any other country in Europe. Half of the country's Muslims live in Brussels. Most of the Muslims in Brussels are from Morocco (70 percent).

As in the other European countries, the Muslim population in Belgium is young. Nearly 35 percent of the Moroccans and Turks in the country are below eighteen years of age, compared to 18 percent of the native Belgians. Since 2008, the most popular name in Brussels for baby boys has been Mohammed. It is also the most popular name for baby boys in Belgium's second-largest city, Antwerp, where an estimated 40 percent of elementary school children are Muslim.[58] If there is any Western country that exemplifies the Great Replacement, the transition from a secular to a Muslim Europe, it is Belgium. By early 2016, Belgium's intelligence services identified 451 Jihadists.[59] They were, largely, not poor. Only one in six Jihadists comes from an impoverished background.[60]

Muslim–Non-Muslim Relations

Belgium was never an imperial power, other than its holdings in the Congo, nor was it associated with militarism.[61] Nonetheless, Brussels was targeted because, in the words of the State, "Crusader Belgium has not ceased to wage war on Islam."[62] Most Belgians were unaware of this image, and many Europeans asked how a country known for its beer, chocolate, and bureaucracy could end up being the European hotbed of radicalization and extremism. In many ways, Muslims and non-Muslims live very separate lives in the country.

To the tourist, the Molenbeek area of Brussels feels like a South Asian or modern Northern African city. It is spread across six square kilometers, and with a population of close to 100,000, it is nearly twice as dense as the average Brussels neighborhood. The Bataclan murders in Paris were plotted there, and approximately a hundred men and women left Molenbeek to fight in the Middle East.[63]

Belgium has been a hotbed of radical Islam for more than a decade, breeding organizations like Sharia4Belgium, which want, as their name proclaims, to have Sharia introduced in Belgium. They are loud, intimidating, and belligerent. When the Bataclan murders occurred, one leader of the group said, "We couldn't hold our joy."[64] That November 2015 attack in neighboring France panicked Belgium as well. The metro was closed down. Prime Minister Charles Michel said authorities feared a "Paris-style" attack "with explosives and weapons at several locations" despite the hundreds of soldiers patrolling the city, home to the EU and NATO.[65]

But Belgians are concerned about the many attacks that receive little or no media attention. For example, youths threw a petrol bomb under a Christmas tree, setting it aflame. As they ran away, the teens could be heard yelling "Allahu Akbar." "Today they will set fire to a Christmas tree, tomorrow they will behead a Christian," wrote one man.[66]

The Caliphate

The Caliphate used Brussels as its center of planning and operations for two mass murders—the Paris killing of November 2015 and the Brussels attack of March 2016. In the Brussels attack, one of the three chief perpetrators, known as the "man in the hat," was born in Syria and came to Europe as a refugee in 2015. The Islamic State bragged that it was sending cadre disguised as refugees to Europe to conduct operations.[67]

Belgian security officials are worried that the State is planning a primitive biological attack. Security officials found rotting animal testicles in a terror suspect's backpack. Such material can be used to poison food supplies or to create a deadly concoction aimed at spreading fatal diseases. The Brussels prosecutor issued a statement saying, "The rucksack contents . . . could at no time have been used to make a biological weapon."[68]

Memorial for the Brussels Attack

Profile Thirty-Seven: Brussels Is on Fire

I will tell you, I've been talking about this a long time, and look at Brussels. Brussels was a beautiful city, a beautiful place with zero crime. And now it's a disaster city. It's a total disaster, and we have to be very careful in the United States.

—Donald Trump in reference to the Brussels attack of 2016[69]

It was an apocalyptic scene with blood and dismembered body parts scattered. Witnesses heard some men yelling in Arabic before the nail-filled bombs rocked the Brussels airport and the subway system, killing dozens. Witnesses described the ceiling caving in and blood everywhere after two explosions in the departure hall at the Brussels airport.[70] The Islamic State struck with suicide bombers, and the entire country went into lockdown. All flights were canceled, arriving planes and trains were diverted, and Belgium's terror alert level was raised to maximum. Authorities told people in Brussels to stay where they were, bringing the city to a standstill. Security was also tightened at all Paris airports.[71]

"Brussels is on fire," is a hashtag to express the Islamist sense of triumph. The most common remark under the hashtag was "You declared war against us and bombed us, and we attack you inside your homeland."[72] After each additional attack, ISIS supporters celebrated, writing "Allahu Akbar." The popular hashtag was inspired by a similar hashtag created by Caliphate supporters after the November 13 Paris terror attacks: "Paris is on fire."[73]

In a British prison, terrorist convicts shouted "Allahu Akbar" after learning of the attack. Some burst into song and dance to celebrate the slaughter.[74] According to one source, the council of Belgian imams rejected a recent initiative to pray for the souls of the victims of the Brussels terror attacks on the grounds that praying for non-Muslims ran counter to Islamic law.[75] Several days after the attack, Belgians organized a "March against Fear." But it was canceled out of security concerns.[76]

SUMMARY

For the French, 2015 and 2016 were years of terror. There were shootings, bombings, beheadings, stabbings, and a spectacular vehicular murder. After the murder of Father Hamel, one of his parishioners, a middle-aged woman, expressed the anxiety of many of her country: "Nowhere in France is safe anymore."[77]

In April 2016, Belgian security services conceded that there were probably dozens more Caliphate supporters in the country. European intellectuals asked themselves and their audiences what the small Central European country had done to deserve the attacks and the hatred of their Muslim compatriots.[78] When the killings came, Belgium went into shock. But some Muslim leaders refused to offer a prayer for the dead because it was counter to Islamic law.[79] Others celebrated the slaughter. According to Belgian interior minister Jan Jambon, "a significant section of the Muslim community danced" when attacks took place.[80] Belgians who were fighting for the Caliphate in the Middle East tweeted their joy to former neighbors. From Syria, one said, "We will drink your blood to the last drop."[81]

NOTES

1. Michael S. Smith II, "'ISIS' Says 'It Took Less Time to Shake France Than Hitler' *Heavy Magazine*, July 26, 2016, http://heavy.com/news/2016/07/isis -islamic-state-nashir-amaq-news-nazi-germany-comparison-telegram-channel -chatjacques-hamel-saint-etienne-du-rouvray-normandy-france-murder-hostage -taking-killing-terrorist-attack/.

2. Michel Gurfinkel, "Latest Survey Finds 25% of French Teenagers Are Muslims," *PJ Media*, March 14, 2016.

3. Rachel Donadio, "Before Paris Shooting, Authors Tapped Into Mood of a France 'Homesick at Home.'" *New York Times*, January 8, 2015.

4. As an example of the fear of offending Muslims and broaching the issue of Islam in Germany, a clothing firm refused to print for PEGIDA, an anti-Islamist, grassroots German organization, but had no apparent hesitation about selling T-shirts with Osama bin Laden's smiling face on them. Raheem Kassam, "Printing Firm Refuses to Make Anti-Islamism T-Shirt Still Sells Che, Bin Laden Gear," *Brietbart.com*, July 14, 2015.

5. Name calling and fines did not silence the megastar of *And God Created Woman*. By 2008, she had been fined four times for inciting racial hatred. "Bridget Bardot on Trial for Muslim Slurs," *Reuters*, April 15, 2008.

6. Donadio, "Before Paris Shooting, Authors Tapped Into Mood of a France 'Homesick at Home.'"

7. In 2010, 39 percent of Socialist Party voters felt Islam was too prominent within French society—a majority of 52 percent feel this to be the case six years on. Virginia Hale, "Total Rejection of Islam in France from All Across the Political Spectrum," *Breitbart*, May 1, 2016.

8. Ibid.

9. Elsa Keslassy, "Gunmen Kill 12 at French Satirical Magazine Charlie Hebdo," *Variety*, January 7, 2015.

10. Leo McKinstry, "How I've Seen the France I Love Torn Apart by Hatred," *Daily Mail*, July 16, 2016.

11. Soeren Kern, "European 'No-Go' Zones: Fact or Fiction? Part 1: France," *Gatestone Institute*, January 20, 2015, http://www.gatestoneinstitute.org/5128/france-no-go-zones.

12. There are an estimated 500 sex clubs in France. Liam Deacon, "Arrested: Suspected Islamic State Terror Cell Plotting Attacks on Swingers Clubs," *Breitbart.com*, February 2, 2016.

13. John Lichfield, "If You Wanted to Light the Fuse of a Gallic Race War, This City on Riviera Would Be Clever Choice," *Belfast Telegraph*, July 16, 2016.

14. John R. Bradley, "Jihadi France," *Daily Mail*, July 28, 2016.

15. Stephen Jones, "Charity Boss Stabbed by Couple Shouting 'Allahu Akbar' Armed with Axe and Knife," *Mirror*, July 1, 2016.

16. "French Airport Security Staff Worried about Terrorist Threat," *Paris L'Express.fr*, June 29, 2016.

17. Lara Marlowe, "France and US Face Complex Question about What to Do with Known Jihadists; Liberal Democracy Status Is Challenged by Calls for Authority and Repression," *The Irish Times*, June 16, 2016.

18. Jamie Weinstein, "Black Terror Flag Flies over Paris Anti-Israel Rally [VIDEO]," *Daily Caller*, August 25, 2014.

19. Yves Mamou, "France: Jihad Infecting Army, Police," *Gatestone Institute*, March 16, 2016, http://www.gatestoneinstitute.org/7624/france-jihad-contaminating-army-police.

20. Madeline Grant, "16% of French Citizens Support ISIS, Poll Finds," *Newsweek*, August 26, 2014.

21. "Why Are Young French Girls Flocking to ISIS?" *Virtual Jerusalem*, March 11, 2016.

22. Ari Yashar, "How a Jewish French Girl Joined ISIS, Tried to Blow Up Parents," *Israel National News*, October 15, 2014.

23. Ibid.

24. Agnes De Feo and Marie Lemonnier, "French Journalist Recounts Meeting with ISIL Recruiter on US Terror Blacklist, L'Obs," *Business Insider*, May 12, 2016, http://www.businessinsider.com/isis-al-qaeda-car-attacks-nice-france -2016-7.

25. Ibid.

26. Ibid.

27. Ibid.

28. De Feo and Lemonnier, "French Journalist Recounts Meeting with ISIL Recruiter."

29. "ISIS and Al Qaeda Have Specifically Called for the Type of Attack That Just Happened in France," *Business Insider*, July 14, 2016.

30. "France: Opinion Polls Find French People Take Positive View of Armed Forces, Back Their Operations," *Paris Ministry of Defense*, July 7, 2016.

31. Ian Schwartz, "French Ambassador: France Is At War With Radical Islam," *Real Clear Politics*, January 14, 2015.

32. Clarion Project Staff, "Why France Again," *The Clarion Project*, July 15, 2016, https://www.clarionproject.org/analysis/why-france-again.

33. Tess de la Mare, Ellie Flynn, Jonathan Reilly, Tom Michael, and Peter Allen, "Bastille Day Massacre at Least Ten Children among 84 Slaughtered by Truck Driver Who Ploughed through Nice Crowd 'Like a Bowling Ball While Shouting Allahu Akbar,'" *The Sun*, July 14, 2016.

34. Daniel Halper, "Clinton, Trump Agree the World Is at War," *New York Post*, July 15, 2015.

35. Ruadhan Mac Cormaic, "Paris Aftermath: They Attacked Culture—Music and Revelry," *The Irish Times*, November 17, 2015.

36. Jared T. Miller, "Friday the 13th," *Newsweek*, November 27, 2015.

37. "ISIS Video Features Posthumous Message from Paris Attackers; Shows Attackers Prior to the Operation, Executing Prisoners," *MEMRI, Special Dispatch*, January 25, 2016.

38. David Browne, Jonathan K. Dick, Patrick Doyle, Romain Flon, and Kory Grow, "After the Nightmare," *Rolling Stone* no. 1250/1251 (2015): 13–14.

39. "Bataclan Terrorist 'Played Xylophone' During Attack," *The Mirror* (London), December 29, 2015.

40. "Death Metal Singer: Gunmen Killed Fans in Dressing Room," *The Mirror* (London), November 23, 2015.

41. David Maher, "We Can't Return for Memorial of ISIS Gun Massacre in Paris," *The Daily Mirror*, February 15, 2016.

42. "'Heroic Nick Died Silently, Saving Others in Bataclan," *The Mirror* (London), November 27, 2015.

43. "Mum and Gran Die Protecting Louis, 5 from Gig Massacre," *Daily Record* (Glasgow, Scotland), November 19, 2015.

44. "Fake Leg Saved Me," *The Mirror* (London), November 17, 2015.

45. "We Fled Hell. Then Went Back in to Save Our Pal; War on Terror British Wife Reveals Horror Inside the Bataclan," *Daily Record* (Glasgow, Scotland), November 19, 2015.

46. "Revision: French Intelligence Services on Edge as 'Demotivated' Jihadis Seek to Return to France," *Paris Le Figaro* (electronic edition), June 11, 2016, 3.

47. John Irish, "French Security Chief Warns Islamic State Plans Wave of Attacks in France," *Reuters*, May 19, 2016.

48. "ISIS to Unleash Car Bombs in France, Warns Spy Chief," *The Times*, July 13, 2016.

49. "Beware the Poison le Pens," *Daily Mail* (London), June 21, 2012.

50. Donna Rachel Edmunds, "Marion Marechal-Le Pen: 'Either We Kill Islamism or it will Kill Us." Breitbart.com, July 23, 2016.

51. "Beware the Poison le Pens."

52. Steven Erlanger, "Blaming Policy, Not Islam, for Belgium's Radicalized Youth," *New York Times*, April 7, 2016.

53. Ibid.

54. Ibid.

55. "Belgian Election Campaign Marred by Anti-Semitic Outbursts, Says Jewish Leader," *States News Service*, October 22, 2012.

56. Erlanger, "Blaming Policy, Not Islam."

57. Steven Erlanger, "An Enduring and Erudite Court Jester in Britain," *New York Times*. December 11, 2015.

58. Soeren Kern, "Belgium Will Become an Islamic State," *Gatestone Institute*, November 9, 2012, https://www.gatestoneinstitute.org/3442/belgium-islamic -state.

59. "Belgian Vice PM Acknowledges Street Celebrations Following Brussels Attacks," *JTA*, March 30, 2016.

60. Ibid.

61. Natalie Nougayrede, "The Lesson of Brussels: Jihadi Terrorism Crosses Borders, and so Must Solutions," *The Guardian*, June 3, 2016.

62. "ISIS Claims Credit for Belgium Attacks, Promises More Killing," *IPT News*, March 22, 2016, http://www.investigativeproject.org/5222/isis-claims -credit-for-belgium-attacks-promises.

63. Ian Buruma, "In the Capital of Europe," *The New York Review of Books* 63, no. 6 (April 7, 2016): 36.

64. Abigal Esman, "Belgian Breeding Ground Fuels New Terror Wave, Special to IPT News," *Investigative Project*, November 23, 2015, http://www.investigative project.org/5046/belgian-breeding-ground-fuels-new-terror-wave.

65. Alexadre Hielard, "Empty Streets and Shuttered Shops in Tense Brussels," *AFP*, November 21, 2015.

66. Frank Chung, "Teenagers Set Christmas Tree on Fire in New Year's Eve Rampage," *News.com.au*, January 3, 2016.

67. David Wright, "Donald Trump: Brussels 'Just the Beginning,'" *CNN*, March 22, 2016.

68. Peter Allen, "Brussels Terror Suspect Who Was Shot by Police at Tram Stop Had Rucksack Containing Animal Testicles and Faeces, Prompting Fears

ISIS Is Planning Crude Biological Attack on Food Supplies," *MailOnline*, April 8, 2016.

69. Wright, "Donald Trump."

70. Raymond Ibrahim, "An Islamic Apocalypse in Brussels," *Jihad Watch*, March 23, 2016.

71. "Brussels in Lockdown: Deadly Blasts Confirmed as Suicide Attacks," *TVNZ*, March 22, 2016.

72. John Hayward, "Islamic State Supporters Celebrate Brussels Attack on Twitter: Expect More Bombs, More Death!" *Breitbart London*, March 23, 2016.

73. Maayan Groisman, "ISIS Supporters on Social Media Celebrate Lethal Brussels Bombings," *Jerusalem Post*, March 22, 2016.

74. Patrick William, "Jailed Jihadis Cheer Bombs: Belmarsh Inmates Rejoice after Brussels Attacks," *Daily Star Sunday*, March 27, 2016.

75. "Belgian Imams Refuse to Pray for Souls of Non-Muslim Victims of Brussels Attacks," *MEMRI*, March 26, 2016, http://www.memri.org/clip/en/0/0/0/0/0/0/5418.htm.

76. "Brussels 'March against Fear' Cancelled over Security Concerns," *DW*, March 26, 2016.

77. Ofeibea Quist-Arcton, "Al-Qaida Militants Target Westerners In West Africa." *NPR Weekend Edition*, January 24, 2016.

78. "Leon de Winter Europe's Muslims Hate the West," *Politico*, March 29, 2016.

79. "Belgian Imams Refuse to Pray."

80. "Belgian Minister Says Many Muslims 'Danced' after Attacks," *AFP*, April 16, 2016.

81. "ISIS Celebrates Brussels Attacks, Belgian Members Vow to Drink Infidels' Blood, Paint White House Black," Clip 5414, MEMRI, March 26, 2016, http://www.memri.org/cliptranscript/en/5415.htm.

EPILOGUE:
"A TASTE OF VENGEANCE"

Introduction

Earlier chapters concentrated on the Caliphate's agenda, cadre, organization, structure, placement, and appeal. This epilogue will revisit some of the personalities and events of earlier chapters. At the time of writing, it has been over two years since Abu Bakr al-Baghdadi announced the birth of the Caliphate, and the fortunes of the Caliphate have waxed and waned since then.[1]

Vigils and Replacement

The Caliphate has spawned fear throughout the Western world. According to the Europol, 2015 had the highest number of terrorist attack in the European Union since records have been kept.[2] The close of 2016 could bring higher numbers still. In eight of the ten European nations surveyed, half or more believe incoming refugees increase the likelihood of terrorism in their country.[3] Many are convinced that Muslims do not want to become part of European society. In every country polled, the dominant view is that Muslims want to be distinct from the rest of society rather than adopt the nation's customs and ways of life. Six in ten or more hold this view in Greece, Hungary, Spain, Italy, and Germany.[4]

The "no-go zones," or *banlieues*, continue to fester, crippling business and leading to an unyielding social transformation. Pedestrians note that Muslim men pray in the street, even though there is ample space in local mosques. It is a declaration that these streets belong to Islam. Some call this the "Great Replacing," and it is occurring throughout Western Europe.

In Britain, Dewsbury's (Profile Three) Muslim population continues to grow. Dewsbury census figures show 14.5 percent of residents are Muslim. There is concern that Sharia is replacing British common law.[5] The roster of Islamic State suicide bombers from Dewsbury keeps growing. Baroness Warsi, who came from Dewsbury, found her name on a Caliphate kill list.[6]

Stories of Middle Eastern migrants attacking non-Muslim Europeans continue to proliferate on electronic and print media. There are weekly, sometimes daily, reports in European media. In July 2016, a woman vacationing at an Alpine resort in France along with her three daughters was stabbed and severely injured by a Moroccan-born man who reportedly shouted that they were too scantily dressed. The eight-year-old girl was rushed to the hospital with a punctured lung. The local mayor refused to "speculate about the motive of the attack."[7] The assailant's name was listed as "Mohammad B."[8] But, increasingly, if the attacks do not result in death, blinding, extremely brutal rape, or maiming, they do not command front-page news. This is the "new normal."

The Middle East

Palmyra (Profile One), has been wrested from the clasp of the Caliphate. Lovers of history, art, and Syria still mourn Palmyra's premier poet and scholar and they miss their ancient lion sculpture, now dust.[9] Most residents fled. Some will bring memories of Palmyra—its lion, poet and scholar, and its life—to their new homes in the West.[10]

Yazidis are still hunted, raped, and killed, and Yazidi men and women fight back, sometimes victoriously. Girls and women are still held as sex slaves, but others are freed or escape. According to one observer, Yazidi society is very traditional, and it has been traumatized by the mass sexual violations. In the current ordeal, values have changed, and girls who survive Caliphate torture are now, often, sought for marriage. Said a Yazidi elder, "It's no longer a shame for a woman to get raped."[11] Further, Yazidi leaders created a new ritual they call a "re-baptism," in which freed, former victims are brought into the embrace of their tribes once again and with love.[12]

Christians continue to suffer. Andrew White, the "Good Vicar of Baghdad" (Profile Twenty), begs the world to hear the pain of Christians in the Middle East.[13] Before he heard a higher calling, physician Dr. White was an anesthesiologist, but nothing dulls the emotional pain he feels for the suffering children of Iraq and Syria. Christians in Mesopotamia are "all petrified. They're all desperate. They all think they have

Yazidis in a Refugee Camp—"Devil Worshippers"

no future."[14] The United States continues to bring in Syrian refugees but allows very few Christians. In June 2016, the United States accepted 2,300 Syrians, only eight of whom were Christian.[15] In neighboring Iraq there were 1.4 million Christians in 2012. In summer 2016 there was less than one-fourth that number.[16] There are no Jewish communities and, perhaps, no Jews left in the Caliphate's realm.

Tunisian tourism is still smarting from the effects of the Jihadi beach killings (Profile Twenty-Six). At least seventy hotels have closed in Tunisia. Tourism contributes 10 percent of gross domestic product and employs 400,000 people, directly or indirectly.[17] Today, the Imperial Marhaba, the site of the slaughter, remains closed and deserted.[18] Istanbul, in summer 2016, has a similar lonely feel in the tourist districts. The shooting and suicide spree at the airport very quickly dried up the tourist industry. An eerie quiet replaced the previous year's sounds of bustling tourists. A guide grumbled, "I don't know if we [tourist guides] can go on. It's tragic."[19]

America's gay and straight communities struggle with the aftermath of the Orlando killings (Profile Twenty-Four). Central Floridians view Muslims more negatively after the attacks than they did before. Twenty-one percent of participants in a Mason-Dixon poll viewed Muslims in a more negative light, but the poll also reflects an increase in sympathy toward gays by the straight community.[20]

New York City held its annual LGBT Pride Parade soon after the slaying in Orlando. A widely circulated picture from the parade shows a group carrying a rainbow banner with the words "Republican Hate Kills," an apparent take on the Orlando shootings. But some countered that Omar Mateen was a registered Democrat and had tweeted his admiration for Hillary Clinton before his slaughter spree. Mateen had no known affiliation with the Republican Party.[21]

Celebrities are still conflicted about the Islamic element in the homeland killings. Hollywood searched for an artistic response, and forty-nine actors memorialized each of the dead. Artists including Jane Fonda, Cuba Gooding Jr., Rob Reiner, Caitlin Jenner, Sofia Vergara, and Angela Bassett read short eulogies and biographies for each victim.[22] But some viewers believe that tribute was tainted with politics. There was no mention of the killer's motive or his connection to the Islamic State. The tribute concluded with the words "love conquers hate." Nothing was spoken about Sharia.[23]

European journalists are still very careful about how they cover Islam. According to the French magazine Le Monde, some critics of Islam have been forced to flee France to avoid being arrested for violating hate-speech laws. French administrators monitor what some sarcastically call the "faschosphere," right-oriented blogs often critical of Islam.[24] A Paris-based publishing house was to publish a French version of the German best seller Der Islamische Faschismus (The Islamic Fascism), written by a German Egyptian, but stopped the press in late July after the slew of killings.[25]

First Amendment protections for free speech in the United States are still strong, but there is abiding concern of offending Muslims in the dominant media. In its official guidance, the American flagship Society of Professional Journalists (SPJ) urges journalists to avoid word combinations such as "Islamic terrorist" or "Muslim extremist" and "Jihad," unless they are quoting a source. The SPJ defines "Jihad" as self-betterment and not aggressive warfare.[26]

There are still concerns about European military men and women wearing their uniforms. Some are harassed and chased if they are alone.[27] RAF personnel have been warned to keep a low profile and told not to wear their uniforms in public after an attempted abduction and knife attack outside a military base.[28] Threats are not limited to the soldiers. Wives of British soldiers are fair game for Jihadi slaughter, as a military family discovered in summer 2015.[29]

Survivors of the Caliphate are physically and psychologically tormented. A woman who survived the State's attack in Tunisia recounted that she never adjusted. She sees a counselor to relieve anxiety and fear, but she cannot process loud noises because they trigger post-traumatic stress anxiety attacks. "I can't use London Underground, because I can't stand the noise or enclosed space. I panic."[30] When she eats out or stays at a hotel, she looks for exits. Panic attacks can come unexpectedly and anywhere. "The other night during a thunderstorm I woke up bolt upright shouting the word 'grenade.'"[31] Countless thousands live in similar gray zones between emotional composure and depression and panic. Some hate themselves for surviving when their friends and family perished.

WHERE ARE THEY NOW?

The world has changed many times in the few years of the Caliphate's existence. From junior varsity to the world's most-dangerous terrorist organization and one that has a global reach, the cruelty of the ever-creative Caliphate continues without pause. In July 2016, the Caliphate killed seven of their own by boiling them alive and videotaping it.[32] They have introduced the "flying carpet," which is a metal board with hinges in the middle onto which prisoners are strapped. It breaks ribs when it is closed.[33]

Europe's summer of 2016 was like none other in recent memory. On the sun-kissed beaches of St. Tropez, young women in bikinis strolled on the sand next to rifle-wielding French soldiers ready for another Caliphate-ordered mass shooting. But, for many Caliphate soldiers, the tide of war has changed; it is now they who are pursued, hunted down, and killed in the Middle East.

Politicians

Issues of the Caliphate and Islamism continue to rock the world of Western politics. Partly as a backlash against immigration, the European right is ascendant and some are emboldened. When asked to distance himself from antirefugee rhetoric and violence, Geert Wilders said that the politicians could "drop dead."[34] After the Nice killing, French president Hollande announced an expanded military deployment within France against the State.[35]

Former house speaker Newt Gingrich suggested a more aggressive approach to ferreting out radical Muslims, particularly those who serve in positions of trust in the United States. He looked to the House Un-American Activities Committee, or HUAC as it was commonly called, which investigated Communist infiltration in the government, unions, and positions of leadership during the Cold War.[36] Others point to HUAC as a warning of a "New McCarthyism," in the words of Todd Gitlin, a 1960s radical-turned-political commentator.[37]

Rosa Brooks (Profile Five), the former Obama official who recommended sending pictures of kissing homosexuals to humanize the Caliphate, still holds fast to her faith in compassion as a civilizing tool.[38] But the Caliphate is unpersuaded. One Iraqi homosexual explained the rigor with which State militants track down gays. They will examine a suspect's phone contacts and Facebook friends. "They are trying to track down every gay man. And it's like dominoes. If one goes, the others will be taken down, too."[39]

The new mayor of London continues to attack Donald Trump. He slammed British Conservatives, accusing them of using "Donald Trump's playbook" to divide the Muslim and non-Muslim communities in Britain.[40] The new prime minister of Britain is well experienced in dealing with Islamism and the Caliphate, having served as home secretary. In that capacity, in 2015, she announced to radical Muslims, "The game is up."[41] She continued, "We will no longer tolerate your behavior. Where you break the law, we will prosecute you. And together, we will defeat you."[42] As prime minister, she will have the opportunity to put muscle behind the promise.

The Foreign Fighters

By July 2016, French intelligence estimated that about a hundred foreign fighters were crossing Turkey into Syria each week.[43] If they are women, they can join the ranks of more seasoned foreign fighters. They could meet Aqsa Mahmood (Profile Ten), the Scottish Jihadi bride who became a top Caliphate propagandist and today rails against the refugees and migrants fleeing the State. They were, according to Aqsa, "rich" people "seeking to fulfill their whims."[44] Her parents have pleaded for her to return home. However, she would almost certainly face arrest in the United Kingdom. She has said she would rather die in Syria.

Sally Jones (Profile Twelve), whose husband was killed in a US air strike, tried to persuade an undercover reporter to kill the English queen on Victory over Japan Day in 2015.[45] The queen was unharmed, but Jones continues to recruit European, particularly British, girls and women.[46] There have been sightings of "Mrs. Terrorism" or "Granny Jones" in Britain. In August 2015, Special Branch officers went on full alert after Sally Jones was reportedly spotted in Birmingham,[47] but she was not to be found.[48]

Asghar Bukari (Profile Four), the ever-angry Briton who accused Mossad of stealing one of his shoes to torment him, has doubled down on his claim. He has stated that psychological warfare is standard Israeli tradecraft and that he was a victim of attempted gas-lighting. Some days after the alleged break-in, he said that his "Jewish neighbors" returned the shoe but that it had been chewed beyond repair by a fox.[49]

Anjem Choudary (Profile Twenty-Eight), now sentenced to jail, continues to be vocal about his Islamic convictions. In June 2016, he publicly reaffirmed his goal of killing homosexuals, as required under Islamic law. "They will face capital punishment. I mean, people differ about the way that that punishment would be implemented, but it would be the death penalty."[50]

Harry S. (Profile Thirty-One), the German who went to Syria and claimed to be overwhelmed with remorse, nonetheless received three years in a German prison for his membership in a terrorist organization abroad. He also acted in breach of the Weapons Control Act and the Weapons of War Control Act, said the court chairman.[51]

Intellectuals and the Common Culture

The controversial London play *Homegrown*, which was scrapped days before opening night, has fallen off of the London arts scene. Critics have noted the frequency with which events, speeches, and artistic enterprises are canceled in Britain if they involve commentary on Islam. U2's Bono, who recommended lampooning the Caliphate to deflate its image, thought twice about his suggestion. He snickered, "Beware the pithy quote out of context."[52] Islamist-driven terror certainly lost any humor to the aging rocker when police whisked him away from his vacation.

The bane of feminism and the gay darling of conservative America, Milo Yiannopoulos promises to organize a gay march in Sweden, claiming that "it's dangerous to be gay again."[53] Milo intends to defy both the Sharia of the Muslims and the bureaucrats of the Swedish government.[54] Undoubtedly, he will do so with panache, but he may have a hard time getting the word out. He, like many other Western critics of Islam, has had some social media accounts suspended indefinitely.

In July 2016, a French government committee took the testimony of the survivors of the Bataclan attack. With tears streaming down their cheeks, witnesses recalled how the Caliphate attackers disemboweled still-living victims, stabbed the genitals of women and men, and gouged the eyes out of their captives. Medics did not release the bodies of the dead to their families because of the anticipated shock.[55]

Parents Still Mourn

Westerners still fight against the Caliphate, and some fall in battle. The list of the American dead grows. One American, Levi Jonathan Shirley, fought with the Kurds. Shirley was born with very poor eyesight and, even after surgery, didn't make the standard for the US Marines. But the Kurds welcomed him to their ranks, where he served and died in July 2016.[56] He would have turned twenty-five the following month.[57]

The mother of the Dane Lukas Dam (chapter 4) is haunted by the last message she received from his cell phone in Syria. She tweeted to Lukas, "I love you so much my beloved son," but she received a response from someone else, who wrote, "Your son is in bits and pieces."[58] Ms. Dam does not know how he was killed or if he killed anybody. She is left with only anger and frustration. Denmark will not issue her a death certificate because she lacks forensic proof of her son's death. "I have his Facebook status. Nothing else," grieved Ms. Dam.[59]

Trying to make sense of her son's death, Ms. Dam has turned to other mothers who have lost children to the Caliphate. She is angry at the Danish government for, in her judgment, ignoring Islamist recruiting. "My son wasn't recruited online. I know who his recruiter is, and we are aware that he is still in touch with ISIS and trafficking money. Why the hell is he still walking the streets?"[60]

Christiane Boudreau, mother of the fallen Damian, battles her feelings of loss. Late nights and early mornings are often the worst times for Christiane. Her boy's war is over, but she battles with sleep. Sometimes, well past midnight, while others in the family are asleep, she will get into her car and scream at Damian's ghost for what he has done to the family. She will shout her anger and her envy at his being in perpetual peace while she is left in daily torment.[61]

Christiane has joined forces with Daniel Koehler, director of the German Institute on Radicalization and De-Radicalization Studies, to form Mothers for Life. The organization functions as a support group for mothers whose children have become radicalized. "If I knew back then what I know now, I may have seen it before my son left."[62]

Keith and Michele Harding, whose son "Surfie" Reece fell fighting with the Kurds, took up their son's cause. The Hardings have become very close to Kurdish leaders and fighters. Said Michele, "I've been a housewife for 24 years. . . . But when you see the suffering of others, how can you sit there and not try to make a difference?"[63]

The Islamic World

Ahmad, of chapter 6, was the Syrian pianist whose prized piano was set aflame by the Caliphate. He explained, "I am a storyteller—a pianist who tells stories with his music."[64] He journeyed to Germany, where there are thousands of Syrian refugees for whom he can play and with whom he can sing without any fear of the Caliphate. "When the war is over, I'll go home."[65]

The whereabouts of the Caliphate's "Bulldozer" are unknown to this author. The Bulldozer was the huge man who relished hacking off limbs and hands for offenses ranging from disloyalty to listening to pop music. The "dean of the Chopping Committee" was captured in June 2016. As of late summer 2016, he has a physical counterpart, though fighting for the opposing side. The 325-pound Iranian bodybuilder Sajad Gharibi, known as the Persian Hercules, announced his intention to fight for the Shia and defend their mosques in Syria.[66]

The Heroes

The Caliphate's battle with the West has brought out the most depraved, as well as the most valiant, human elements. On the blood-soaked beach in Tunisia, several Muslims risked their lives to protect European tourists they had never met. Several Tunisians yelled, "Come here! Come here!" to tourists, while shepherding and dragging them to safety. Locals joined a human shield to protect tourists, risking their own lives. One of the tourists said, "They [including the Muslims] used their bodies to stop him attacking a hotel next door and killing dozens more."[67]

This was not the only act of valor in the sordid tale of the Caliphate's killings. France's interior minister granted French citizenship to an Algerian-born, France-raised man who helped save dozens of people at the Bataclan concert hall. The middle-aged "Didi," a security guard, was standing outside when he heard gunfire; he rushed in to open a back door, allowing some to escape to safety. His "cool-headedness and courage saved lives," said a government official during a ceremony that granted Didi French citizenship.[68]

There were many heroes. One of the American students killed in the Dhaka restaurant attack chose death over deserting his friends. Emory student Faraaz Hossain was relaxing with his friends when attackers started killing with knives and guns. He was allowed to leave because he was Muslim, but he would not abandon his friends; he died with them.[69] He was lauded in death by the *Dhaka Tribune*. "He showed the world the best of Bangladesh and what it means to be a true Muslim."[70] There were many other heroes of all religions.

A Future—No Victory Parade

Though shaken, the Caliphate still stands. In late July 2016, Iraqi forces wrested control of the long-contested city of Falluja. The State has lost land, but it has dispersed its soldiers throughout the West. It inspires legions of admirers to kill for its sake. The Caliphate promises unrelenting killing until the West surrenders to its terms. These are based on Sharia, which mandates Islamic supremacy. The State declared after the restaurant killing in Bangladesh, "What happened in Dhaka was a glimpse, won't stop till there's Sharia around the world."[71] And the Caliphate's foreign fighters are returning to their homes in the West. Of the

Europeans who have left to fight with Jihadist groups in Syria and Iraq, at least 1,600—about one-third—are back in Europe.[72]

THIS AUTHOR'S MUSINGS

To all you liars, traitors, careerists, socialists. You hold the power now.
But in a decade WE will hold the power and We will hold you to account.
We will drag you before a Nuremberg-type court, you will be judged
for high treason. And for the first time, in a long while,
we will be your judges.

—Paul Weston, British politician, 2010[73]

Political language is designed to make lies
sound truthful and murder respectable.

—George Orwell[74]

The following commentary contains this author's views on some of the key issues and central points made in this book. They do not necessarily reflect the views of any agency of the United States government.

1. Is the Caliphate Islamic? Yes, it is.

The Islamic State is true to its name, though many practicing Muslims loathe it and are victimized by it. The Caliphate's leader has a PhD in Islam; its statement of principles is driven entirely by Islamic sacred texts; its legal system is Sharia; the cadre are all devout Muslims; it appeals to the Islamic world for recruits and funding; it defines its enemy in terms of those opposed to Islam; and its men behave as they believe Muhammad would have acted had he lived in contemporary times.

Islamic organizations regularly issue resolutions and fatwas declaring that the Caliphate is un-Islamic.[75] Some of these pronouncements are sincere, but others are not; they are evasive ploys sometimes called "phony fatwas." Many of these fatwas declare that the State is un-Islamic but do not explain how the State's philosophy contravenes the basic principles of the faith.[76]

Those who dismiss the Islamic element of the State often reason that Islam is a religion of peace. Therefore, people who commit violence in the name of Islam must be violating its fundamental philosophy. Under this logic, the perpetrators are either ignorant of Islam or they willfully "hijack" the religion for their own purposes.[77] If Caliphate leaders give Yazidi sex slaves to its men or if homosexuals are tossed from rooftops, or if the Caliphate crew commits mass murder, they must be violating Islam. After the killing in Nice, an imam there said, "This has nothing to do with Islam."[78] How, then, do these apologists reconcile the mandates of violence in the scared literature and Sharia? They usually avoid an in-depth exploration of Islamic texts and accept, as an article of faith, that Islam is peaceful and, therefore, that the Islamic State cannot be Islamic.

Caliphate leaders quote Koranic verses to justify their bloodletting. Nonetheless, after each killing, there is a chorus of blithe denials. Attacks are sniffed away as emotional aberrations or confused politics. Some claimed that Mohammad Lahouaiej-Bouhlel, the truck terrorist of Nice, was not a Muslim because he did not attend the mosque or pray five times each day. Similarly, Omar Mateen of the Florida nightclub carnage was a repressed homosexual in an antigay society. Nidal Hasan, who killed army personnel at Fort Hood, or the husband-and-wife murderers in San Bernardino, were perpetrators of "workplace violence" and were only nominally Muslim. In fact, all these persons quoted the sacred Islamic texts and explained that they were acting in the name of Islam for Islam. They also pledged solidarity with the Islamic State. The Islamic State is just that—Islamic.

2. If the West Negotiates with the State, Will It Relent in Its Hostility? Probably Not.

There is no evidence that the Caliphate is prepared to enter into meaningful negotiations. Even if it were so inclined, Western leaders would have to identify Caliphate leaders with whom they could negotiate. Would this require an end to targeted assassination? In the aftermath of the Bataclan theater massacre, in 2015, President Hollande declared France to be at war with the Caliphate. He reiterated this state of war after the carnage in Nice and again after the beheading of Father Jacques Hamel in Normandy later in summer 2016. Could any Western ally or friend negotiate with the Islamic State while France is fighting it in war? Further, many observers ask, what is there to negotiate? Unless the Caliphate is prepared to negotiate its own surrender, which is not likely, why would Western powers negotiate anything? Further, the Caliphate's demands are currently not subject to negotiation. They require that non-Muslims accept a subordinate, degraded status in all societies under Islam rule. Finally, the Caliphate has sworn to expand that rule across the globe, as required by Islamic mandates.

3. Can the West partner with non-Jihadi Muslims to defeat the State? Perhaps, but the goals would be very limited.

Many Muslims and Muslim states despise the Islamic State and would like to see it eliminated. Some Muslim states have deployed military resources to destroy the Caliphate. Western states have partnered with

Muslim allies to defeat common foes in the past. This happened in the nineteenth century when a charismatic Islamist leader known as the Mahdi built an Islamic state in Sudan and North Africa. He killed a famous British general and made an enemy of many Muslims whom he subjugated. But British general Horatio Kitchener led an expeditionary force of British, Egyptian, and Sudanese forces to obliterate the Mahdi's successor's armies at the battle of Omdurman in 1898.[79] Today, Islamic and Western states partner against the State on land and by air. So, it is possible that this alliance will vanquish the Caliphate.

But as the State's soldiers are dispersed from the Middle East, many are building new homes in the West. Of the several million Middle Eastern migrants who went to Europe and the United States, some are part of the Caliphate and many others are sympathetic to its agenda. For years, Western governments have tried to partner with moderate Islamic elements to defuse radicalism.[80] But sometimes activists use a mask of moderation, while their true goal is to replace Western liberalism with Sharia.[81]

4. Will the State's Violence Change the Way the West Views Islam? Yes and No.

In Europe and, to some extent, in the United States, common men and women have changed their views. The media is saturated with Jihadist attacks, many of which have been claimed by the Caliphate. There is increasing censorship in Europe, where there are no protections for free speech. There is pressure in the United States and Europe to curb criticism of Islam, and social media censors have done just that. However, there has been a gradual awakening. Earlier chapters of this book discussed the growth of anti-Islamist political parties in Europe.[82] When Donald Trump originally proposed a temporary ban on Muslims entering the country, polling showed that nearly six in ten Americans were opposed to the idea. But public opinion has gradually shifted.[83] By summer 2016, most Americans supported it.

What is not likely to change anytime soon is the view of intellectuals on Islam or Jihad. As discussed in chapter 3, there are a few gadflies, most notably Bill Maher, and the late Christopher Hitchens, but the view in Western universities is set. The pioneering generation of scholars who built Middle East Studies as an academic discipline is largely gone and has been replaced by scholars who combine advocacy with scholarship. They are often very open about this.[84]

It is a challenge to understand the silence of organized feminism. The National Organization for Women and the Women's Studies annual conference generally do not focus on the treatment of women in the context of Sharia.[85] For example, in North America, the National Women's Studies Association theme for the 2016 conference was "decoloniality . . . which is a worldview that denaturalizes settler colonial logics and structuring violences."[86] Much feminist scorn is reserved for the United States, Israel, and other Western states. The sex slavery, beatings, and honor killings in the Caliphate and elsewhere often get scant attention.

More difficult to understand still is the silence of the homosexual community, leaders of which are very vocal on religious issues. There are several prominent gays, such as Bruce Bawer and Milo Yiannopoulos, who loudly criticize the treatment of homosexuals,[87] but there are not many of them. Intellectuals are often well informed, particularly those who cover international relations or Middle Eastern studies, but many see the West as the source of much of the world's venom, and they see the Caliphate, odious though it might be, as a reaction to colonialism and white racism. There is a loose and unspoken code of *omertà* when it comes to Islamism.

5. Can the West undermine support for
the Caliphate through promoting sustainable development?
Probably not.

As discussed in earlier chapters, there is no proven direct causal link between poverty and terrorism. A spokesperson for the State Department remarked, "We can't kill our way out of this. . . . We need to address the root causes."[88] Perhaps. But, as of this writing, there is no corroborative evidence that the root cause of the birth or growth of the Islamic State was poverty.[89] Islamists are often highly educated and well fed.

6. Can the Islamic State Be Completely Defeated?
Not in the Near Term.

The Islamic State, as it exists in the Middle East, could be largely destroyed and its remnants scattered to the world. But this would be the problem—it would be scattered. This started to happen in mid-2016, as the land and, particularly, air power of opposing armies became overwhelming. The nucleus of the Islamic State will probably relocate from Raqqa, and its conventional military capabilities, largely paramilitary shooters with some artillery support, will be diminished. But it is flexible and can partner with other groups in North Africa and in Central Asia. In this sense, the Caliphate would be gone, but its agenda will still thrive. This is the agenda of Jihad.

But there is much the West can do, in this author's opinion. First, Islam would be reclassified for legal purposes as a hybrid religious-political system. Islam declares itself to be just that—a complete way of life to include political, religious, social, and economic mandates. Further, Islam demands the subordination of non-Muslims, as discussed earlier. For this reason, Sharia should be declared to be a hostile ideology as long as it advocates different legal standards for men and women; any punishment for converting out of Islam; punishing homosexuality; demanding payment by non-Muslims to Muslims through the jizya or a similar requirement; or any law or convention that gives Islam a status superior to other faiths.

America could set the standard for other Western countries. When Sharia becomes defined as a hostile ideology, those who advocate it can be subject to investigation by federal agencies. Those who encourage replacing the Constitution with Sharia could be monitored in ways similar to those who were active members of the Communist Party of the United States. Former speaker of the house Newt Gingrich suggested Congressional panels, similar to the HUAC. Opponents of HUAC claim that it trampled on the civil liberties of American citizens, but its supporters respond that the HUAC unmasked men and women who were Stalin loyalists and who committed crimes, namely espionage.

Investigative federal agencies, such as the FBI, and Congressional committees could then pursue linkages of individuals and front organizations to the Islamic Brotherhood. They could interrupt its financing, recruiting, and organizing. Further, national security agencies could overhaul and reinvigorate their training programs to give today's agents, analysts, and managers a solid understanding of Sharia and Jihad.

"A Taste of Vengeance"

An American Caliphate supporter praised Omar Mateen and urged more attacks on the United States: "Do you think you're at war with a small group of Mujahedeen in Iraq, Syria, Libya and other places? You are sadly mistaken. Then again, you have sadly made a great mistake," Al-Amriki says. "Oh America, indeed you are at war with all the true and sincere Muslims around the world."[90]

French prime minister Manuel Valls concedes, "Times have changed, and France is going to have to live with terrorism, and we must face this together and show our collective sangfroid."[91] He did not identify the source of terror in France. Religious terror in the West almost always comes from Muslims. In France there is no Jewish or Christian terrorism and, if trends continue, there will be fewer Christians and virtually no Jews left by the end of the first half of the twenty-first century. Prime Minister Valls's defeatism could have been spoken by François, the jaded old professor in Michel Houellebecq's *Submission* (Profile Two). François went further—he became, if only nominally, a Muslim himself because he saw the advance of Islam as an irresistible force. Like Prime Minster Valls, he recognized that "times have changed," which has become a common refrain in the West.

Similarly, American elites downplay or ignore the Islamic elements in the Caliphate's attacks. In reference to the Nice attacks, American commentator Rachel Maddow offered, "So, I mean, honestly we don't know much about the perpetrator. Maybe that's not important. I mean, maybe the most important thing is how many people lost their lives."[92] American professor Mia Bloom said, after the Nice attack, 'ISIS was not coming after us." She was more concerned the attack would promote "right-wing politics" and Islamophobia.[93]

The American Jihadi and Caliphate supporter Omar Mateen killed homosexuals to give the West, in his words, "a taste of vengeance." Even if Western political leaders and professors do not understand why he killed, the assailant knew exactly why he was killing. He murdered in the name of Islam and as an assassin for Caliphate. The forty-nine dead tasted the vengeance of the Caliphate's black heart. We, in the West, are certain to taste more.

"Die on My Feet"

It was Frenchman Charles "the Hammer" Martel who stopped the Muslim conquest of Europe in 732. This Christian took his inspiration and moniker from a Jew called Judah "Maccabee," "the Hammer." Martel knew that the West would be annihilated by Muslims if his ragtag line of Christian defenders faltered. But they held the line at Tours, and Europe did not fall to Islam. The Hammer is buried in the Basilica of Saint Denis and rests near the kings of France in a part of France that some would now call a Muslim "no-go zone."

Today, the Caliphate threatens the Middle East and the West. But, like the Hammer, some men and women of the West stand defiant, and more are sounding the alarm as the Islamic State continues its slaughter. They lock shields full force to defend Western and liberal values. Two men of France personify this resistance. One died as a Christian. In the last moments of his life, eighty-five-year-old French priest Father Jacques Hamel refused to kneel, as demanded by the two Islamists who came to kill him in his Norman church. One said to him, "You Christians, you kill us."[94] Father Jacques responded, perhaps with the last words of his life, by calling his assassin "Satan." He was then butchered. Today his body rests in Rouen Cathedral.

Another Frenchman died as part of Western civilization and in defiance of Islamism. Nearly two generations younger than Father Jacques, Stephane Charbonnier, "Charb," was the editor of the French satirical

Rouen Cathedral—Europe at Sunset

magazine *Charlie Hebdo.* Under police protection for years, he doodled cartoons of Muhammad, the Virgin Mary, and rabbis. He mocked left-wing and right-wing politics. He used his pen in the satirical tradition of European iconoclasts.

Charlie Hebdo's offices were firebombed in 2011, and the next day Charb named Islam's prophet Muhammad as editor-in-chief. Charb said, "Muhammad isn't sacred to me . . . I live under French law. I don't live under Koranic law."[95] He famously said, "I'd rather die standing than live on my knees."[96] And he did die standing.

In January 2015, during an editorial meeting, Islamist murderers shouting "Allahu Akbar" killed Charb and three others. At the same time, coconspirators went to one of the few remaining kosher restaurants in Paris to hunt down and kill Jews. At Charb's funeral, men quoted Voltaire: "I do not agree with what you have to say, but I'll defend to the death your right to say it."

Jacques and Charb were men of the West who died defiantly. One was a man of faith and the other a free spirit. They understood the risks of defending Western civilization, and they gave their last full measure of devotion to that tradition. They died on their feet. They did not kneel; they did not falter; they did not submit to Islam.

NOTES

1. "Iraq: Fallujah Freed," *Asia News Monitor*, June 21, 2016.

2. Kris Bayos, "'EU Marks Record-High Number of Terrorist Attacks in 2015,' Says Europol," *International Business Times*, July 21, 2016.

3. Hungarians, Poles, Greeks, Italians, and French identify this as their greatest concern. Sweden and Germany are the only countries where at least half say refugees make their nation stronger because of their work and talents. http://www.pewglobal.org/2016/07/11/europeans-fear-wave-of-refugees-will-mean-more-terrorism-fewer-jobs. Richard Wike, Bruce Stokes, and Katie Simmons, "Europeans Fear Wave of Refugees Will Mean More Terrorism, Fewer Jobs," *Pew Research Center*, July 11, 2016

4. Wike, Stokes, and Simmons, "Europeans Fear Wave of Refugees."

5. Tom Wells, "Cops Advise Abuse Caller: Try Sharia," *The Sun*, June 12, 2016.

6. Robert Sutcliffe, "'Anti Semite' School Under Investigation," *Huddersfield Daily Examiner*, April 2, 2016.

7. "Iraqi and Syrian Archaeology Experts: The Jews Responsible for Destruction of Palmyra, Looting of Iraqi Antiquities," The Middle East Media Research Institute, September 20, 2015, https://us-mg6.mail.yahoo.com/neo/launch?.rand=5bpnqgo8krtv3.

8. Tom Morgan, Camilla Turner, David Chazan, and Henry Samuel, "Man 'Knifes French Woman and Her Three Daughters' in Alps Resort," *Telegraph*, July 19, 2016.

9. "ISIS Beheads Elderly Chief of Antiquities in Ancient Syrian City, Official Says," *The Guardian* from *Reuters*, August 18, 2015.

10. The scholar's son, Walid Al-As'ad, director of Palmyra Museum, said that the Jews wanted "to destroy the city [of Palmyra] and wipe it off the face of the Earth," in order to erase the memory of their Babylonian exile. "Iraqi and Syrian Archaeology Experts."

11. Jacob Bojesson, "ISIS, It's a Privilege to Get Raped by Us," *The Daily Caller*, June 29, 2016.

12. "Yazidi Plan to Rebaptize Women Enslaved by ISIS Is Working . . . Sort Of," *PRI.org*, September 24, 2015.

13. Ben Lockhart, "'Vicar of Baghdad' Tells of Persecution by ISIS," *Desert News* (Salt Lake City, UT), June 23, 2015.

14. Ibid.

15. Stephen Dinan, "U.S. Accepts Record Number of Syrian Refugees in June Despite Terrorist Screening Worries," *Washington Times*, June 30, 2016.

16. Stoyan Zaimov, "Christian Iraqi Population Shrinking; Persecution 'Worse Than Under Saddam Hussein,'" *Christian Post*, June 5, 2016.

17. "70 Tunisia Hotels Closed Since Militant Attacks," *AFP* (Tunis), October 18, 2015.

18. Ibid.

19. "Istanbul Nearly a Ghost Town as Tourists Stay Away," *Two News*, July 4, 2016, http://zeenews.india.com/news/world/istanbul-nearly-a-ghost-town-as-tourists-stay-away_1903224.html.

Epilogue

20. Steven Lemongello, "Poll: Central Florida's Views of Muslims More Negative after Massacre," *Orlando Sentinel*, July 1, 2016.

21. Andrew Badinelli, "Gay Pride Celebrators Ignore Facts to Villainize Republicans," *National Review*, June 27, 2016.

22. "49 Top Stars Gather to Record Short Film to Honor Orlando Victims," *The Hollywood Reporter*, June 29, 2016.

23. The eighteen-minute film can be viewed at https://www.yahoo.com/celebrity/49-top-stars-gather-to-record-short-film-to-honor-193447383.html.

24. You can still see the video here, and here is the full transcript: "CENSORED: YouTube Uses Anti-ISIS Policy to Pull CounterJihad Video. Watch it here," *Counter Jihad*, July 6, 2016. https://counterjihadreport.com/category/prosecutions/.

25. Vijeta Uniyal, "Fearing Islamist Reprisal, French Publisher Revises Decision to Publish Book Critical of Islam," *Legal Insurrection*, July 28, 2016 (thanks to The Religion of Peace), http://legalinsurrection.com/2016/07/fearing-islamist-reprisal-french-publisher-revises-decision-to-publish-book-critical-of-islam/.

26. "Diversity Guidelines for Countering Racial, Ethnic and Religious Profiling, Society of Professional Journalists," accessed on January 16, 2016, https://www.youtube.com/watch?v=pe2aam4y52E.

27. "Ex-Soldier: 'I Was Targeted for Wearing Uniform,'" *LBC*, September 27, 2015 (thanks to The Religion of Peace), http://www.lbc.co.uk/ex-soldier-i-was-targeted-for-wearing-uniform-116927.

28. Stephanie Linning, "Police Hunt Two Arab Knifemen Who Tried to Kidnap Serviceman," *Daily Mail*, July 20, 2016.

29. Police in Lincolnshire, home to nine military bases, investigated a letter deposited in the home of serving soldiers. Chris Hughes, "Jihadis Threaten to Slaughter British Soldiers' Wives and Families as Police Issue Social Media Warning," *Mirror*, July 31, 2015.

30. James Fielding, "One Year on from Sousse ISIS Massacre 'When I go to a Restaurant I look for all the Exits,'" *Express (Online)*, June 26, 2016.

31. Ibid.

32. Gareth Davies, "Seven ISIS Fighters Who Fled the Battlefield Are Boiled Alive as Punishment in Iraq," *Daily News*, July 5, 2016.

33. Jennifer Newton, "Breaking Prisoners' Ribs on a 'Flying Carpet', Taunting Them with Severed Heads and Locking Women in Cages Filled with Skulls: Activists Reveal Horrific Torture Methods Used by ISIS," *Daily Mail*, July 13, 2016.

34. "Drop Dead Suckers, Geert Wilders Tells Politicians and the Press," *DutchNews*, December 21, 2015.

35. Angela Charlton, "Hollande Stung into Action as Nice Criticism Grows," *The Independent*, July 22, 2016.

36. "The New McCarthyism [incl. Steven Salaita and Norman Finkelstein, Ellen Schrecker]," *The Chronicle of Higher Education*, June 30, 2016.

37. Todd Gitlin, "Not the '60s: Apocalypse Then and Now," *New York Times*, July 23, 2016.

38. Samantha Power, "Making History: The First UN Security Council Meeting on LGBT Rights," *Medium.com*, August 24, 2015.

39. Jonah Hicap, "ISIS Out to Exterminate All Homosexuals in Mideast, Uses Facebook to Hunt Them Down," *Christian Today*, August 27, 2015.

40. Andre Walker, "Women Segregated at London Rally," *Townhall*, June 16, 2016.

41. Steven Swinford, "Theresa May Tells Islamist Extremists: 'The Game Is Up,'" *The Telegraph*, March 23, 2015.

42. Ibid.

43. "Syria/France: Nearly 100 Foreign Militants Enter Syria Via Turkish Border 'Each Week,'" *Asia News Monitor*, July 25, 2016.

44. David Leask, "Glasgow's Jihadi Bride Berates Syrian Refugees as 'Rich Following Their Whims,'" *Daily Mail*, September 22, 2015.

45. "U.S. Confirms Islamic State Computer Expert Killed in Air Strike," *Reuters*, August 29, 2015.

46. Stuart Ramsay, "UK Journalist Gives Detail on Undercover Sky TV Investigation of ISIL Recruiter," *London Sky News Online*, August 11, 2015.

47. Stephen Stewart, "ISIS Recruiters 'Prowling Britain' Warn Muslim Leaders as 'Mrs Terror' Slips Back into Country," *The Mirror*, August 15, 2015.

48. Peter Walker, "England—Boom, Brit Jihadi Bride 'Mrs. Terror' Threatens Summer Attacks in London," *Daily Star*, May 25, 2016.

49. Robert Spencer, "Video: Asghar Bukhari Triples Down: This Is Your Brain on Islamic Supremacism," *Jihad Watch*, June 19, 2015.

50. Aaron Klein, "Exclusive—Anjem Choudary: Put Practicing Gays to Death Wherever They Are," *Brietbart*, June 20, 2016.

51. "Germany: Court Sentences ISIL Returnee Harry Sarfo to Three Years' Imprisonment," *Radio Bremen*, July 5, 2016.

52. "U2 Rock Star Bono," *The Express on Sunday*, June 12, 2016.

53. "Conservative Gay Activist to Lead Pride March Through Swedish Muslim "Ghetto." CounterJihad, June 29, 2016, http://counterjihad.com/conservative-gay-activist-lead-pride-march-swedish-muslim-ghetto.

54. Shireen Qudosi, "ISIS Is a Footnote: The Real Threat Is Sharia and Islamic Supremacism," *Counterjihad.com*, June 29, 291.

55. Louise Mensch, "France 'Suppressed Reports of Gruesome Torture' at Bataclan Massacre," July 15, 2016.

56. Mohammed Tawfeeq and Susanna Capelouto, "American Volunteer Killed Fighting ISIS in Syria," *CNN Wire Service*, July 22, 2016.

57. Thomas Peipert, "Colorado Mother: Son Killed While Fighting ISIS in Syria," *AP Online*, 2016.

58. Julia Ioffe, "Mothers of ISIS: Their Children Abandoned Them to Join the Worst Terror Organization on Earth. Now All They Have Is Each Other," *Huffington Post*, accessed August 13, 2015.

59. Ibid.

60. Hollie McKay, "Lost Boys: Moms of Radicalized Western Jihadists Form Support Group," *FoxNews.com*, July 3, 2015.

61. Ioffe, "Mothers of ISIS."

62. McKay, "Lost Boys."

63. "Son Set That Proverb Does Sum It Up: Evil Prevails When Good People Do Nothing," *The Daily Post,* July 2, 2016.

64. "Syrian Pianist Tells Stories of War through Music," *Hindustan Times* (New Delhi, India), June 21, 2016.

65. Ibid.

66. "'Iranian Hulk' Monster ISIS Threat," *nzherald.co.nz,* July 6, 2016.

67. Simon Speakman and Trew Bel, "Year of Pain for Beach Massacre's Forgotten Heroes," *The Times,* June 27, 2016.

68. "France Grants Citizenship to Algerian Hero in Paris Attacks," *St. Louis Post-Dispatch,* June 17, 2016.

69. "Revealed: Heroic Emory Student Refused ISIS Terrorists' Offer to Leave Besieged Dhaka Cafe to Stay and Be Slaughtered with His Two Female Friends," *Daily Mail.com,* July 6, 2016.

70. "The World the Best of Bangladesh and What It Means to Be a True Muslim," *Scroll.in,* July 4, 2016.

71. Shaaddah Jandial, "ISIS Warning: What Happened in Dhaka Was a Glimpse," *Indiatoday.in,* July 6, 2016.

72. Jim Michaels, "Terrorism In Europe Poised to Expand; For ISIL, Region Is an Easier Target than U.S." *Dayton Daily News,* July 30, 2016.

73. Paul Weston, "'Paul Weston and Liberty GB' Age of Treason," March 3 2013, http://age-of-treason.com/tag/paul-weston/.

74. George Orwell, Quotes, Goodreads, Accessed September 18, 2016, http://www.goodreads.com/quotes/8215-political-language-is-designed-to-make-lies-sound-truthful-and.

75. As an example, in summer 2016, Near Eastern Muslim organizations passed a resolution, "The ISIS has nothing to do with Islam and its principles and tenets, and, in fact, all its activities and terror attacks are meant to strike at the very roots of Islam. The ISIS is not only unIslamic but acts as a tool in the hands of Western forces who are enemies of Islam. In the garb of Muslims, they are defaming Islam." "ISIS a Tool in the Hands of Anti-Islamic Forces, Say Muslim Groups," *IANS,* July 9, 2016.

76. "ISIS a Tool in the Hands of Anti-Islamic Forces, Say Muslim Groups," *New18-India,* July 9, 2016.

77. William Kilpatrick, "Good Islam vs. Bad Islam," *Crisis Magazine,* May 4, 2016.

78. Jamie Micklethwaite, "Nice Attack: 'This Has Nothing to Do with Islam,' Says Imam after Bastille Day Terror Atrocity," *Evening Standard,* July 15, 2016.

79. "The Enemy Within: What European and Arab Histories Tell Us about ISIS," *AlArabiya.Net,* May 14, 2016.

80. Ryan Bays, "Terror-Go-Round: Breaking the Cycle of Xenophobia," *The Humanist* 76, no. 1: January–February 2016.

81. "Islam Kills Women—Impact on Women's Rights in Europe Protest Central London, August 20th 2016 We Must Object to the Aim, Not Just the Method," *Sharia Watch* (UK), accessed August 16, 2016.

82. Daniel Pipes, "Jihad Awakens Europe," *Gatestone Institute,* July 15, 2016, http://www.danielpipes.org/16822/jihad-awakens-eur.

83. Alex Pfeiffer, "Americans Have Grown to Like the Idea of a Temporary Ban on Muslims," *Daily Caller*, June 22, 2016.

84. The reader is advised to look over the topics of conferences, panels, and lectures at the last several Middle East Studies Association annual meetings.

85. Phyllis Chesler, "As ISIS Brutalized Women, a Pathetic Feminist Silence," *New York Post*, June 7, 2015.

86. National Women's Studies Association Annual Conference, "Decoloniality," National Women's Studies Association, accessed August 2, 2016, http://www.nwsa.org/cfp.

87. Bruce Bawer, "No More: After Nice, Let's Stop the Nonsense," *City Journal*, July 16, 2016.

88. Steve Benen, "We Cannot Kill Our Way Out of This War," *MSNBC*, August 20, 2014.

89. Robert Gebelhoff, "How Do Domestic Terrorists Become Radicalized?" *Washington Post*, June 20, 2016.

90. "Alleged American ISIS Fighter Praises Orlando Gunman in New Video," *Fox News*, June 19, 2016.

91. Jack Moore, "Nice Attack: PM Manuel Valls Says France 'Faced with a War,'" *Newsweek*, July 15, 2016.

92. Jack Coleman, "Maddow Shrugs Off Motive of Terrorist in Nice: 'Maybe That's Not Important,'" *NewsBusters*, July 19, 2016.

93. "Georgia State Prof: 'ISIS Not Coming After Us,' France Attack 'Increases Right-Wing Politics,'" Mia Bloom, *The College Fix*, July 15, 2016.

94. Peter Allen and Julian Robinson, "'You Christians, You Kill Us': Nun Reveals Words of ISIS Knifemen Who Forced Elderly Priest, 84, to Kneel at Altar as They Slit His Throat on Camera after Invading Mass—Before Police Shot Them," Daily Mail, July 26, 2016, http://www.dailymail.co.uk/news/article-3708394/Two-men-armed-knives-people-hostage-French-church.html#ixzz4KcN5XRtq.

95. "Obituary: Defiant Charlie Hebdo Editor 'Charb,'" *BBC News*, January 7, 2015.

96. Meabh Ritchie, "'I'd Rather Die Standing than Live on My Knees': Charlie Hebdo, told in quotes," *The Telegraph*, January 8, 2015.

BIBLIOGRAPHY

Ali, Ayaan Hirsi. *Heretic—Why Islam Needs a Reformation Now*. New York: HarperCollins, 2015.

Alinsky, Saul. *Radicals*. New York: Vintage, 1971.

Bawer, Bruce. *While Europe Slept: How Radical Islam Is Destroying the West from Within*. New York: Broadway Books, 2006.

Byman, Daniel. *Al Qaeda, the Islamic State, and the Global Jihadist Movement: What Everyone Needs to Know*. Oxford, UK: Oxford University Press, 2015.

Caldwell, Christopher. *Reflections on the Revolutions in Europe; Immigration, Islam, and the West*. New York: First Anchor Books, 2009.

Cockburn, Patrick. *The Rise of the Islamic State: ISIS and the New Sunni Revolution*. London: Verso, 2014.

El Shamsy, Ahmed. *The Canonization of Islamic Law: A Social and Intellectual History*. New York: Cambridge University Press, 2015.

Gaffney, Frank. *The Muslim Brotherhood in the Obama Administration*. Sherman Oaks, CA: David Horowitz Freedom Center, 2012.

Gerges, Fawaz A. *A History of ISIS*. Princeton, NJ: Princeton University Press, 2016.

Goldberg, Jonah. *Liberal Fascism*. New York: Doubleday, 2007.

Gorka, Sebastian. *Defeating Jihad—The Winnable War*. Washington, DC: Regnery, 2016.

Flynn, Michael T. *The Field of Fight*. New York: St. Martin's Press, 2016.

Hallaq, Wael. *The Origins and Evolution of Islamic Law*. Cambridge, UK: Cambridge University Press, 2004.

Haney, Philip. *See Something Say Nothing*. Washington, DC: WND, 2016.

Harris, Sam. *Islam and the Future Tolerance: A Dialogue*. Cambridge, MA: Harvard University Press, 2015.

Hitchens, Christopher. *And Yet . . .* New York: Simon and Schuster Digital Sales, 2015.

Houellebecq, Michel. *Submission*. New York: Farrar, Straus, and Giroux, 2015.

Jasser, M. Zuhdi. *A Battle for the Soul of Islam*. New York: Threshold, 2012.

Lewis, Bernard. *The Crisis of Islam: Holy War and Unholy Terror*. New York: Random House, 2003.

Lewis, Bernard. *The Muslim Discovery of Europe*. New York: W. W. Norton, 2001.

———. *What Went Wrong: Western Impact and the Middle Eastern Response*. New York: Oxford University Response, 2002.

McCants, William. *The ISIS Apocalypse: The History, Strategy and Doomsday Vision of the Islamic State*. New York: St. Martins, 2015.

McCarthy, Andrew. *The Grand Jihad—How Islam and the Left Sabotage America*. New York: Encounter, 2010.

———. *How Obama Embraces Islam's Sharia Agenda*. New York: Encounter Broadside, no. 18, 2010.

Phillips, Melanie. *Londonistan*. New York: Encounter Books, 2016.

Poole, Patrick. *Shariah the Threat—Team B II Report*. Washington, DC: Center for Security Policy, 2010.

Ramadan, Tariq. *Islam and the Arab Awakening*. Oxford, UK: Oxford University Press, 2012.

Rapoport, Yossef, and Shahab Ahmed, *Ibn Taymiyya and His Times*. New York: Oxford University Press, 2015.

Reilly, Robert. *The Closing of the Muslim Mind: How Intellectual Suicide Created the Modern Islamist Crisis*. Willington, DE: ISI Books, 2014.

Said, Edward. *Orientalism*. New York: Vintage, 1979.

Scruton, Roger. *Fools, Frauds, and Firebrands: Thinkers of the New Left*. London: Bloomsbury, 2015.

Sekulow, Jay and Jordon Sekulow. *Rise of ISIS: A Threat We Can't Ignore*. New York: Howard/Simon and Schuster, 2014.

Shapiro, Ben. *How to Debate Leftists and Destroy Them: 11 Rules for Winning the Arguments*. Sherman Oaks, CA: David Horowitz Freedom Center, 2014.

Spencer, Robert. *Islamophobia: Thought Crime of the Totalitarian Future*. Sherman Oaks, CA: David Horowitz Freedom Center, 2011.

———. *Obama and Islam*. Sherman Oaks, CA: David Horowitz Freedom Center, 2011.

Warner, Bill. *Sharia Law for Non-Muslims. A Taste of Islam*. Washington, DC: USA CSPI Publishing, 2010.

Walsh, Michael. *The Devil's Pleasure Palace: The Cult of Critical Theory and the Subversion of the West*. New York: Encounter Books, 2015.

Weiss, Hassan Hassan. *ISIS: Inside the Army of Terror*. New York: Regan Arts, 2015.

Warrick, Joby. *Black Flags: The Rise of ISIS*. New York: Doubleday, 2015.

Ye'or Bat. *Decline of Eastern Christianity under Islam from Jihad to Dhimmitude*. Teaneck, NJ: Fairleigh Dickinson University Press, 1996.

Ye'or Bat. *Eurabia—The Euro-Arab Axis*. Teaneck, NJ: Fairleigh Dickinson University Press, 2005.

INDEX

MARK SILINSKY, PhD, is a thirty-three-year veteran analyst of the Department of Defense, an adjunct professor at the United States Army War College, and an affiliate professor at the University of Haifa. He has served in US Army intelligence; as an army civilian foreign area officer (FAO) for Eurasia, Russian language; as an Africa analyst for the Defense Intelligence Agency; as an action officer for the Joint Staff, J5; and as a research fellow as part of the Exceptional Analyst Program. He is the author of *The Taliban: Afghanistan's Most Lethal Insurgent Group* (Praeger, 2014).

CPSIA information can be obtained
at www.ICGtesting.com
Printed in the USA
BVOW06*1204161116

468047BV00009B/63/P